# Our Worthy Townsmen

The Forgotten Lives of
Mount Vernon Ohio's Jewish Families
1847 ~ 1920

Lois K. Hanson

*Lives Forgotten now Remembered*
*Lois Hanson*

EddSam Publishing
Mount Vernon, Ohio

*To Rachel - because she
asked the question.*

***Our Worthy Townsmen***

Lois K. Hanson



ISBN: 978-0-578-63075-5



The information printed herein was obtained from a variety of sources including: old books, newspapers, photographs and oral interviews. We have attempted to verify all information but, because of the historical nature of the subject matter, accuracy is not always certain. Due to the age of some of the photographs in the book, the name of the photographer is sometimes not known.

# Contents

Page

**Introduction ........ 5**

1 Henry Rosenthal and S. Oppenheim ........ 9
2 Adolf Wolff ........ 11
3 Ella Wolff Horkheimer ........ 32
4 A Tale of Three Widows ........ 36
5 Wolff Sons ........ 40
6 Epstein Brothers ........ 46
7 Leopold Munk ........ 51
8 Aaron Stadler ........ 56
9 Lonnie Huntsberry and Lena Oppenheimer ........ 74
10 Louis Goodfriend ........ 79
11 David Kahn ........ 86
12 Marx Leopold ........ 89
13 Samuel Weill ........ 97
14 Leopold Haymann ........ 137
15 Louis Hyman ........ 140
16 Marcus (Max) Hyman ........ 149
17 Isadore Hyman ........ 160
18 Samuel Hantman and Stella Hyman ........ 162
19 Max Meyers ........ 171
20 Marcus Rosenthall ........ 183
21 Isaac Rosenthall ........ 186
22 Aaron Rosenthall ........ 210
23 Schanfarber Brothers ........ 216
24 Dubinsky Family ........ 217
25 Isaac Dubinsky ........ 220
26 Ben Dubinsky ........ 223
27 Jacob Dubinsky ........ 235
28 Dora Dubinsky and Abraham Kurlander ........ 241

**Conclusion ........ 243**
**Acknowledgments ........ 246**
**The Minyan ........ 248**

**Left & Above**

Jewish German immigrants in Ohio often started as peddlers – first carrying everything on their backs, then riding horses, and finally carrying their goods in wagons.

***Left:*** *Illustration from The Autobiography of Charles Peters, La Grave Co. Publishers, 1915*

***Above:*** *Library of Congress*

# Introduction

As my daughter Rachel planned her wedding in 2007, she asked me when the last Jewish wedding had been in Mount Vernon. I didn't know and because Helen Zelkowitz, the Jewish grande dame of Mount Vernon, had died, I had no one to ask. I dithered and procrastinated about an answer. Then one day Lorle Porter, local historian and author of *Politics and Peril: Mount Vernon, Ohio in the Nineteenth Century*, was in Paragraphs Bookstore where I worked, and I casually asked if she had discovered any Jewish families in her research. She recalled reading about Adolph Wolff's daughter's wedding, the first Jewish wedding in town. Finding information about this 1865 wedding was easy because both local newspapers covered this social event. Now I had an answer, albeit not to the question my daughter had asked. She included some information about the Wolff family in her wedding program. Adolph Wolff had lived in Mount Vernon but was buried in Wheeling, West Virginia, because there was no Jewish cemetery here. I had grown up in Wheeling and now lived in Mount Vernon; I knew the Jewish cemetery where Wolff lay. When I drove to Wheeling to find his grave, there he was--just a few feet away from my paternal grandparents.

I now was really curious about Wolff. Who was he? As I searched for an answer, I decided to generate a list of all the Jewish families who had lived in Mount Vernon. I called this list a *minyan*, the name for a quorum of ten men needed for worship, and although I collected no names past the 1950s, my minyan included sixty names. But that is all I had--just a list of names. I wanted to know more. I decided to concentrate on the earliest families I could find; I knew they would be German Jews. I would stop with the first Russian Jews who came to Mount Vernon.

What were their lives like? What was it like to be Jewish in Mount Vernon in the nineteenth and early twentieth centuries? How had they practiced their Judaism? *Had* they even practiced their religion? What impact did they have on Mount Vernon and what impact did the town have on them? Why do the two iconic photographs of downtown Mount Vernon--taken about fifty years apart--show the businesses of two Jewish merchants? And what happened to all the families?

When Jews visit a cemetery, they place a stone atop the tombstone they have visited. Reasons for this range from the mystical (stones kept the soul in this world a little longer) to the historical (ancient graves were marked by stone cairns to protect the body from animals) to the Talmudic (during the days of the Temple, members of the Jewish priesthood became "ritually impure" if they came near a corpse; the stones told those men places to avoid) to my favorite: Someone has visited your grave. You are remembered.

The following narratives are metaphoric stones placed on the graves of Jewish families who chose to live in Mount Vernon. These are men and women who--except for their names on a family tree--may have been forgotten. Probably most of their stories are unknown. These chronicles are a way to remember them, to honor them, and to assure them a place in Mount Vernon's history.

There is nothing original about the immigration pattern of Jewish families into Ohio or Mount Vernon. Even stating that it's not original is not original. It follows the three waves of Jewish immigration into the United States, beginning in 1654 when twenty-three Jewish men, women, and children, fearing the introduction of the Inquisition in Brazil, sailed from there to New Amsterdam (now New York), where they were reluctantly accepted by Governor Peter Stuyvesant. These immigrants settled along the east coast and the Caribbean islands.

It was the second wave of Jewish immigrants from Germany who impacted Ohio. Starting in the 1840s, Jews poured out of Germany. After a series of liberal revolutions that had extended rights to minorities, a conservative backlash rescinding most of these advances convinced hundreds of thousands of German Jews to come to America. They came alone or with their families. They came speaking little or no English. They came with little money. They came with a dream.

Most landed in New York and many stayed there. For the young men their livelihood was the same: they became peddlers. They were loaned money by a kinsman or friend or established credit with a wholesaler and bought pins, buttons, needles, thread, combs, toothbrushes, toothpicks, ribbons, lace, bows, bolts of cloth, shoelaces, spices, and sundries. Carrying heavy packs, they walked out of the city and headed west to homes, farms, and villages. Knowing a few English phrases and gesturing, the peddler knocked on doors to show his wares. If the housewife was in a mood to welcome a peddler and had some extra money, she opened the door and invited him in. He spread his goods out on her floor to entice her and delight any children. So ubiquitous was the "Jew peddler" that he soon replaced the Yankee peddler in the American story.

Eventually the lone peddler repaid his creditors and saved his money. He bought a horse and then perhaps a wagon so he was no longer the beast of burden. He moved farther and farther west out of New York, into eastern Pennsylvania, then to Pittsburgh, and then down the Ohio River to Cincinnati. Always there were wholesalers to provide the peddler with more goods.

Joellyn Zollman wrote in "Jewish Immigration to America: Three Waves," "If German Jews had one city of their own invention, it was Cincinnati. German immigrants flocked to this area, which was considered a gateway to trade in the Midwest and West."

And not far away lay Knox County and Mount Vernon. Why did the first Jewish peddler decide to settle in Mount Vernon? The punchline is, "Because this is where the horse died." But the question should be, "Why *wouldn't* someone want to leave the road and settle here in the 1840s?" Mount Vernon had railroads and industries. The town boasted three newspapers, twenty dry goods stores, six groceries, two hardware stores, two bookstores, five sawmills, three grist mills, three apothecaries, eight churches, and, in 1846, over three thousand inhabitants. This was a place where a man could establish his own business, provide for his family, and be part of the American dream. Where he could become one of Mount Vernon's worthy townsmen.

**Above**
View looking south from the public square in Mount Vernon, Ohio, *ca*. late 1870s.
*Courtesy Knox County Ohio Historical Society*

# Henry Rosenthal and S. Oppenheim

## *The First German Jews*

One of the two iconic photographs of downtown Mount Vernon was taken in the 1870s from the Square facing south. On the southwest corner of Main Street, where Park National Bank is now, stood a three-story brick building that stretched from Main Street to Plum Alley behind. Rows of hooded arched windows stretched across the building on both the Square and Main Street sides. Below, the cornice corbels decorated the facade.

Plastered across the building is the name *A. Wolff's Clothing Store.* Adolph Wolff was undoubtedly the most important of the early Jewish entrepreneurs in Mount Vernon.

But during the early days of Wolff's business, there were two other Jewish merchants in town. They didn't stay long enough to be caught in a census or in a city directory. The only proof of their sojourn here comes from a few advertisements in the local papers. But Henry Rosenthal (with only one *l* at the end of his name) and S. Oppenheim deserve some recognition.

**Henry Rosenthal** was in Mount Vernon by 1851, when he began the two-year process towards naturalization. His store, the Eagle Clothing Manufactory, was in business on South Main Street around 1852.

Rosenthal advertised that he sold

Frock coats, dress coats, box coats (long loose overcoat), sack coats (loose fitting day coat), monkey coats (short, double breasted jacket)

Double breasted and single breasted vests

Pantaloons

Shirts, bosoms [Who knows what they are?], collars, undershirts, drawers, gloves, and socks

Cravats, ties, neck handkerchiefs, stocks, and suspenders

Hats, caps, and umbrellas

Carpet sacks, valises, and trunks.

He advertised that he would hire "only the best hands" of "pants and vest makers" for his store.

In 1852 Rosenthal became a United States citizen, and, even though they were competitors, Adolph Wolff vouched for his integrity.

Rosenthal's newspaper ads were original; each began with a bit of doggerel. An advertisement for E. S. S. Rouse's shoe shop which ran above Rosenthal's ad on September 7, 1852, also contained a poem, so probably someone at the newspaper crafted the poetry. (It may interest today's residents to know that Rouse advertised that his shop was opposite Kirk's between the TWO bookstores.)

*The season is changing--the fall has set in,*
*The cold is approaching--tis time to begin*
*To lay by your thin robes, coats, pants, vests & all,*
*And buy heavy clothing from H. Rosenthal.*

*Go visit his ware-house, and there you will find*
*Both style and economy, strictly combined,*
*A fit that can't fail for to satisfy all,*
*Who purchase their clothing from H. Rosenthal.*

*His new winter stock is selected with care,*
*Being purchased for Cash, with the public he'l [sic] share*
*This sterling advantage--so come one and all*
*And give a fair trial to H. Rosenthal.*

Another rhyming ad ran April 26, 1853, and stated that all his clothing was "manufactured on the premises, under the superintendence of a man of first rate ability" and that in "economy, style, workmanship, and quality" the Eagle Clothing Store had no equal.

After November 1853 there were no advertisements. Henry must have sold his business and left town.

**S. Oppenheim's** "New and Splendid Assortment of Ready-Made Clothing" could be purchased at the New City Clothing Store in the corner of the Banning Building on West High Street. An ad ran in the *Banner* on April 5, 1853, and then nothing more.

# Adolf Wolff

## *Mount Vernon's Premier Clothier*

**Adolph Wolff** was probably the first German Jew to arrive and settle in Mount Vernon. He left Hanover, Germany, around 1841 and disembarked in New York City. Having moved westward from there to Pittsburgh and then down the Ohio River to Cincinnati, Wolff and his wife Hannah were in the Queen City in 1841 when he began peddling. He later moved northeast to Mechanicsburg, Ohio, perhaps having found the Cincinnati area overcrowded. He peddled around this area for several years, visiting the countryside with his packs filled with dry goods and notions, before bringing his family to Knox County. By the time Hannah and he arrived in Mount Vernon in the winter of 1846-47 with baby daughter Sarah, Mount Vernon was a thriving city.

Railroads connected the city to Columbus, Cincinnati, Cleveland, Pittsburgh, and Chicago. The rails quickly brought goods to local merchants, allowing one grocer to advertise fresh oranges and lemons in April. Downtown Mount Vernon had dry goods stores, clothiers, millinery shops, book stores, druggists, cabinet makers, carpenters, and joiners. The Mount Vernon Woolen Factory had recently been established, and the Knox County Bank had reorganized under its new name, the Knox County National Bank. Taking advantage of inexpensive iron and coal markets and plenty of railroads, the Mount Vernon Iron Works advertised circular saw mills and stationary and portable engines, as did the Kokosing Iron Works. Kenyon College nested comfortably on a hill in nearby Gambier.

In Mount Vernon, Wolff's status changed; he would not be a peddler but a clothier with his own store. The Wolff family would live here for the next forty years.

In October 1848 an ad appeared in the *True Whig* proclaiming "The Beater Beat!! **A. Wolff and the Queen City Clothing Store**, No 4 Kremlin Building"[1] (on the southeast corner of the intersection of High

Street and the Public Square) was prepared to show citizens the "largest and best stock of Ready Made Clothing." Wolff knew he could sell clothing "cheaper and better" than anyone. He sold "elegant cloth," tweed coats, neck cloths, pocket handkerchiefs, and "cloaks of the latest Parissian [sic] style." Coats, pants,vests, drawers, undershirts, trunks, valises, and "gents' furnishing goods" could be found at Wolff's stand. Within two months, Wolff realized that a Cincinnati store name did not impress Knox County folk and now simply referred to his business as "A. Wolff, Clothier." It was important that Wolff's business prosper because his family had grown. Son Charles was born in 1846 and Simon two years later.

**Above**
The Kremlin Building in 2019.
*Photo by the Author*

A growing family and a growing business needed a U.S. citizen. In May 1848 Wolff declared his intention to become a citizen, and on Monday, November 25, 1850, he appeared in open court to renounce any allegiance to the King of Hanover in Germany and to declare his allegiance to the U.S. Constitution. Moses Liebenthal, a Mansfield merchant, swore that Wolff was a good man, and he became a naturalized citizen. Later that year Wolff gained a brother-in-law when Leopold Munk married his sister Sophia. The next year, Wolff became a member of Mt. Zion Masonic Lodge #9. His Americanization was complete. He was the head of a large family, a citizen, and a Mason.

The decade of the 1850s was one of personal and professional success for Adolph Wolff. Son Morris was born in 1850, Ella a year later, and Rudolph in 1857. To help with the large family, two servants, Fanny Earman and Mary Witham, lived with the Wolffs.

Wolff moved his store from the Kremlin Building to a site three doors south of the Kenyon House (today the home of Park National

Bank). And in the spring of 1852 he announced another move--this time "to the corner room in Woodward's New Brick Building" (the Woodward Opera House), directly under the office of the *Democratic Banner*. Wolff advertised ready-made clothing and also "clothing made to order." He had an agreement with W. O. Upfold, a tailor, to make clothing "warranted to fit well and not to rip." Wolff also became a wholesaler to "country merchants." He bought merchandise from "heavy dealers in Cincinnati and the East" who sold goods to Wolff at wholesale. Wolff then re-sold to smaller stores in Knox County, saving those merchants an expensive trip to large cities. However, Wolff warned them that he did not "warrant" (guarantee) those goods.

Wolff ran advertisements weekly in both the *Democratic Banner* and the *Mount Vernon Republican*. His ads often referenced topical events. He boasted that he would not be undersold by Know-Nothings or Locofocos (a faction of the Democratic party) or by "Jew or Gentile." His prices were the lowest in town. By now his brother-in-law Leopold Munk ran ads for his Lone Star Clothing Store right beside Wolff's. Was he the other Jewish merchant Wolff meant when he said he wouldn't be undersold?

J. W. F. Singer, a cutter (tailor), had left Mount Vernon in 1852 but returned two years later and worked for Wolff. Knowing that Singer's reputation would bring in customers, Wolff often mentioned him in his ads. Other merchants might purchase "miserable, dishonest, outlandish, rip-to-pieces slop shop work," but not Wolff, the city's premier dealer. Only the "industrious . . . goodly citizens" of Knox Country "cut his goods."

The *Democratic Banner* and Wolff's store were both in the Woodward building, and this might explain all the times Wolff was mentioned in the paper.

- May 25, 1858: John Pears rolled a barrel on the South Main pavement, and the sound spooked a horse attached to a buggy. The frightened steed ran south across two bridges and then three miles farther down Martinsburg Road. "Neighbor Wolff" suggested fining "them five dollars for going through the bridge at a faster gait than a walk." (Perhaps this was more humorous back in the day.)

- July 13, 1858: Colonel Joe Rush was in town and bought a satin vest at Wolff's. Rush rolled it up and then placed it in his wagon beside a tin bread pan he had purchased. The rays of the July sun reflected off the pan and set the vest on fire.
- And then there's the tantalizing tidbit that "a boy was snatched from the jaws of death by kind-hearted vigilant friend Adolph Wolff." Would that there had been more information about this. Perhaps a runaway horse had been involved?

In 1858, probably because of a national depression, Wolff stopped extending credit. It was cash only from now on. However, an examination of his estate at the time of his death showed that he was owed over $11,000. Evidently he still extended credit to some. Wolff traveled east on buying trips several times a year, and in 1858 along with "cords of goods" to be made into clothing, he purchased for 50 cents a section of Cyrus Field's transatlantic cable, which he displayed at his store. A local ad referred to Wolff as a "perfect Napoleon in the clothing business who defies all the world and the rest of mankind to enter into competition with him." This was probably a reference to Wolff's business acumen and not his height.

Article 1 Section 2 of the U.S. Constitution mandates that a census be taken every ten years. In June 1860 the Wolff family lived in the First Ward, and their neighbor was another Jewish merchant, Marx Leopold. In 1858 the family had lived on the west side of Gay between Gambier and Front Street, now Ohio Avenue. Now the census said that Wolff's real estate was valued at $3,000 (about $91,000 today). Given this valuation, Wolff might have already paid $5,000 for the big house at 105 East Gambier Street. Wolff's personal worth of $25,000 would equal about $760,000 today. His family included his six children and his older sister Caroline. Kate Smith, a servant, and Wallace Gott, who probably clerked for Wolff, completed the household. Wolff, indeed, was doing well.

The Civil War divided Mount Vernon just as it did the country. The *Democratic Banner* and the *Republican* represented their respective parties' platforms and passions. Tempers flared even before the declaration of war when Lecky Harper (D) and Dr. Robert Kirk (R) had a heated exchange on East High Street. Kirk grabbed Harper's cane and wrestled him to the ground; Adolph Wolff and Sam Israel separated the men.

Could Jews, who had been slaves in Egypt and who retold that story every year at the Passover Seder, support the slave South? It didn't appear so in Mount Vernon. Wolff ran very few ads in the *Banner* during the war years. Advertising revenue dropped enough that Lecky Harper wrote an editorial denouncing local businesses for their "foolish conduct" in withholding their "petty patronage" from

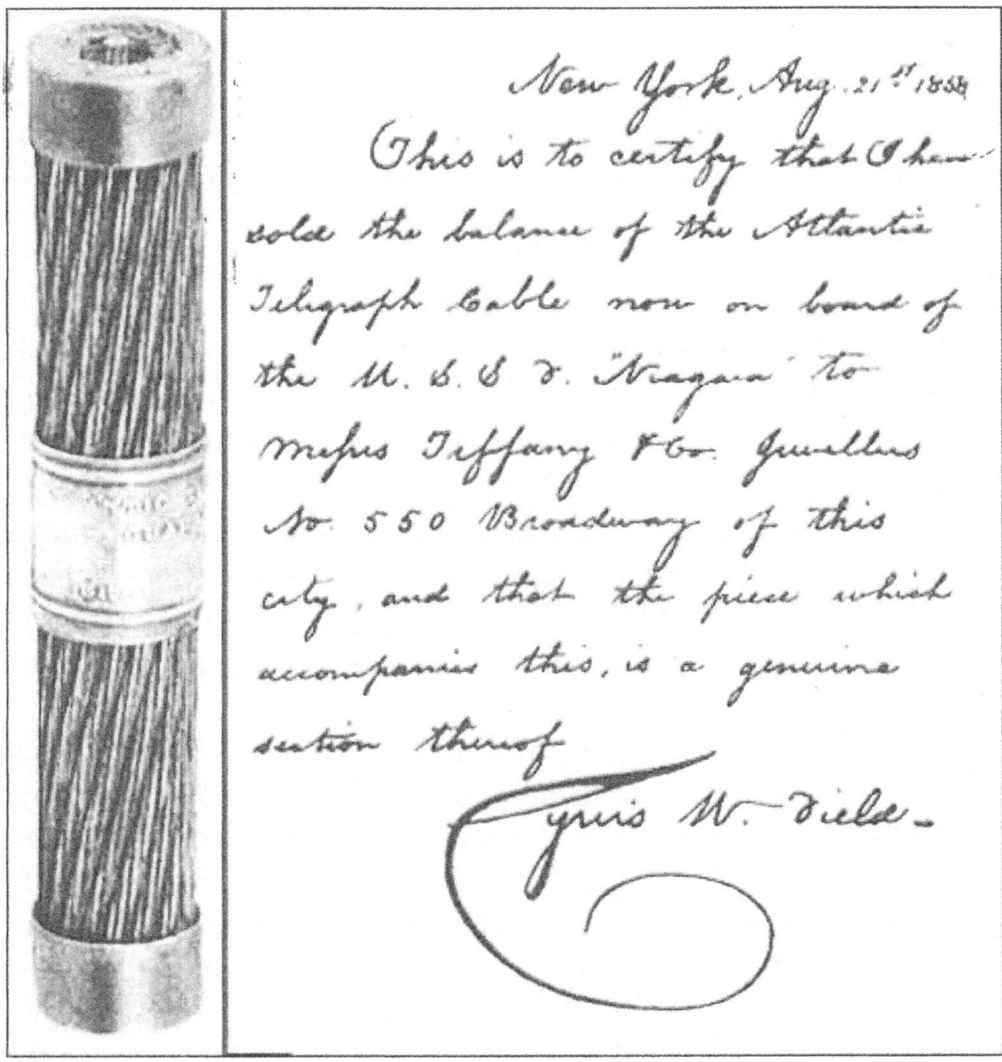

New York, Aug. 21st 1858

This is to certify that I have sold the balance of the Atlantic Telegraph Cable now on board of the U. S. S. F. "Niagara" to Messrs Tiffany & Co. Jewellers No. 550 Broadway of this city, and that the piece which accompanies this, is a genuine section thereof

Cyrus W. Field.

**Above**
An advertisement showing the kind of cable Wolff bought and displayed at his store.
*History of the Atlantic Cable & Undersea Communications*

his newspaper.

*The only sure way for a business to succeed is to mind his business and advertise…Those who advertise only in one paper or perhaps two of the same politics and do not advertise in a Democratic paper issue a proclamation to the world that they only desire the custom of men of their own way of thinking in politics and do not wish Democratic custom under any circumstance. We have several here in Mt. Vernon whose political prejudices are so deep rooted that rather than spend 10, 12, 14, or 15 dollars a year in advertising in the Banner, they would drive away their very best customers merely because they were Democrats.*

He insisted that the *Banner* was flourishing without their business and that withdrawing advertising would leave the boycotting businesses (none of which he named, "even those that had been the most active in trying to injure us during the past eighteen months") with "stacks of old [unused] goods."

Nevertheless several short mentions of Wolff made the *Banner*. Just a few days before Fort Sumter fell, Wolff's backyard apiary was vandalized. Since the same thing happened at C. Buckingham's house, the newspaper bemoaned this "meanness." The frames were broken open and because the young broods were forming, the hives were robbed of their winter supply. The next year thieves targeted East Gambier Street, and Wolff's home was burglarized. The robbers took twenty-five dollars after using a skeleton key to quietly open the front door.

In July 1862 a meeting was held at the courthouse to raise money for the war fund. Wolff donated $100; his neighbor Marx Leopold gave $23.00. And then silence about Wolff in the newspapers. Battles, strategies, and deaths occupied the broadsheets. When the war finally ended, Wolff purchased the Buckingham Emporium on the corner of Main and Gambier. He repainted the building and rented offices on the second floor of what the *Banner* called "one of the finest looking buildings in the city." Wolff, obviously, had not suffered during the war years. He was wealthy enough to also provide a grand wedding, the first Jewish wedding in Mount Vernon, for his daughter.

July 25, 1865, dawned clear and warm, a typical summer's day in Mount Vernon. The war had ended four months earlier, and this day promised the bounty of peace and the luxury of optimism. Trains arrived daily bringing Union soldiers home to warm welcomes. Local farmers looked at their fields and did not see "a single poor field of grain, wheat, or rye." Corn had filled in, and the oats looked better than farmers could ever remember. Clover and flax fields lay rich in the summer heat. Wheat sold at $1.20 a bushel, rye at 50 cents, and oats at 35 cents. Both local papers, no longer bordered in black to mourn President Lincoln's death, devoted newsprint to the week's most exciting event, the Wolff-Goldsmith nuptials.

Tuesday was a perfect day for a wedding, and not just any wedding. The *Banner* observed that Christian weddings were so common that they merited little attention, but this ceremony would be "conducted according to the ancient rules of the Hebrew church." The first Jewish wedding in Mount Vernon took place that evening at the bride's home on East Gambier Street. Sarah Wolff, twenty-one and the oldest of Adolph and Hannah's children, married Albert Goldsmith, a twenty-six-year-old German immigrant and traveling salesman for the clothing house of Mack and Brothers in Cincinnati.

Earlier that year Goldsmith had come to Mount Vernon and seen a busy town proud of its past and optimistic about its future. He would have stopped at all four clothiers in town--three of whom were Jewish. Wolff, his future father-in-law, occupied a prime site in the Woodward Building. Wolff's brother-in-law Leopold Munk operated under the sign of the Lone Star on the west side of Main Street, and Marx Leopold of Leopold & Co. rented space in the Kenyon House, a block north of Wolff's stand. Goldsmith would have been welcomed by this small enclave of German Jews and invited into their homes to meet their families and have meals. Thus he would have met the Wolff family and begun his courtship of Sarah.

Wolff's reputation as a man of "great liberality" shone on his daughter's wedding day and reflected his rise from immigrant peddler to successful merchant. The nuptials gave his Gentile friends and customers an opportunity to see this Jewish ritual. Everything had to be memorable. "A great event" and "one of the sensations of the week," the Wolff-Goldsmith wedding also reflected on the "reputation of our beautiful and hospitable city."

The guest list was large. Family members included Sarah's sister Ella, her four brothers, her aunt Caroline, and her Aunt Sophia and Uncle Leopold Munk who lived next door. Most of the town's prominent citizens received invitations. No guest list exists, and the local newspapers listed only a few attendees by name. Lecky Harper, the editor of the *Democratic Banner*, often referred to Wolff in his paper as a friend and neighbor; he most assuredly attended and wrote the report for the newspaper. The rival newspaper, *The Republican*, wrote about the wedding, and William Bascom, the editor, probably was a guest. Several Kenyon College professors rode down from Gambier for the seven o'clock ceremony. Out-of-town guests, including the rabbi, arrived from Cincinnati by train.

To prepare for the wedding, the family placed "fancy lanterns" around the yard, arranged tables and chairs under shade trees, and provided an abundance of food and drinks. The Mount Vernon Brass Band, reorganized and "in good healthy condition," played "popular airs." As darkness approached, a servant lit gas lights to illuminate the house and ensure that the "numerous, beautiful and costly" wedding gifts could be viewed. Anyone walking along Gambier Street that evening would have been impressed with the guests, music, and lights coming from 105 East Gambier Street. Undoubtedly the presence of the Cincinnati rabbi made the evening more impressive because he was Isaac M. Wise, the most prominent rabbi in America.

Although Wise's greatest accomplishments lay in the future, by 1865 he had created the *Minhag America*, a prayer book which reflected the changes he thought necessary to modernize Jewish liturgy and reflect the beliefs of Reform Judaism. Wise had been the rabbi at the premier Jewish Reform congregation in Cincinnati for eleven years. And on July 25, 1865, he was in Mount Vernon to perform a wedding.

Both local newspapers wrote about the event, but neither mentioned the actual ceremony. Rabbi Wise conducted portions of the wedding in English, and the *Banner* commented upon his "deeply affecting and eloquent" words. The rabbi probably stood in front of a small table that held wine and a goblet for *kiddush*, the blessing of the wine. Did the bride and groom stand beneath a *chuppa*, a canopy? Did the rabbi recite the traditional seven blessings? Did the bridegroom stomp on a wine glass at the end of the ceremony to remember the destruction of the Temple? There is no way of knowing what Jewish rituals were included.

We do know that the bride looked beautiful; the groom was happy. Sometime after the ceremony ended, the Union Brass Band entertained with "really first class music." Excellent food, drink, and conversation greeted the guests as they strolled outside to enjoy any breeze on that warm evening. The rabbi mingled with guests, and at one point the Methodist minister G. W. Bush, Dwight Hervey from the Presbyterian Church, Thomas E. Monroe from the Congregational

**Above**
Rabbi Isaac Wise, the most prominent nineteenth-century rabbi in the United States, performed the first Jewish wedding in Mount Vernon.
*Wikimedia Commons*

**Below**
Sarah Wolff and Albert Goldsmith's marriage license and certificate. Note Rabbi Wise's signature at the bottom right.
*Knox County Records Center, Mount Vernon, Ohio*

| PARTIES. | AFFIDAVIT. | RETURN. |
|---|---|---|
| Albert Goldsmith AND Sarah Wolff LICENSE Issued the 24 day of July A. D. 1865, to the above named parties, | THE STATE OF OHIO, KNOX COUNTY, SS. Albert Goldsmith having made application for a LICENSE, for and Sarah Wolff and being duly sworn says, that is of the age of 21 years, and has no wife living, and that is of the age of 18 years, a resident of said County, and has no husband living, and that said parties are not nearer kin than first cousins. Sworn to and subscribed before me, this day of A. D. 186 Probate Judge. | THE STATE OF OHIO, KNOX COUNTY, SS. I do hereby Certify, that Mr Albert Goldsmith AND Miss Sarah Wolff were joined in Marriage by me, on the 25 day of July A. D. 1865 Isaac M. Wise Rabbi |

Church, and two Episcopal ministers, James Muenscher and George Reece, engaged Wise in a lively discussion on "Biblical matters." Wise must have held his own because the *Republican* wrote, "We were very much pleased with Rabbi Wise." The *Banner* praised both the town's and the host's hospitality. Surely Wolff looked around and took pride in his accomplishments and largesse.

The *Banner* penned the perfect blessing for the wedding. Expressing the hope that the young couple would have a long, happy life, the writer asked that "heaven's richest blessing . . . ever be poured upon their heads." But this was not to be. A year after the wedding the following appeared in the *Banner*:

> *We are this week called upon to announce the death of Mrs. Sarah Goldsmith, wife of Albert Goldsmith, and daughter of our townsman Adolph Wolff, Esq., which took place at her residence in Cincinnati, on Monday last, in the 22d year of her age. Our readers will remember that we noticed the marriage of this worthy lady about one year ago, which took place in the presence of a large concourse of friends and invited guests. The husband and friends of the deceased have our heartfelt sympathies.*

A pregnant Sarah Wolff Goldsmith had died from eclampsia and was buried in a Jewish cemetery in Cincinnati.

It is impossible to capture the personal sorrows of the Wolff family at this time. Did they periodically go to Cincinnati, visit her grave, and put a small rock on her headstone? Did they keep in touch with her husband who re-married within a year? We don't know. All we can do is follow the public record.

In October 1865 Wolff advertised a large stock of mink and Siberian squirrel furs which were good for ladies' hoods. And Wolff's and Lecky Harper's friendship was back on track. Harper wrote, "Everybody in Knox county knows Adolph Wolff; and not to know him is to plead woful [sic] ignorance of mankind. Without disparagement to other dealers, it is no exaggeration to say that Wolff has the most extensive and well conducted clothing store in Central Ohio. He don't [sic] deal in slop-shop work, or the rejected trash of eastern manufacturers but buys his goods in the piece and has his clothing made here in Mt.

Vernon by the best workmen in the trade." Wolff couldn't have paid enough for that fulsome praise.

Looking ever forward, he sold the Buckingham property to George Potwin for $7,000, and three months after his daughter's death, Wolff bought the Kenyon House (where Park National Bank now stands) property from Dr. Kirk for $12,000 cash. Locals got a hint of Wolff's plans from a small item in the paper in January 1866. He would make improvements to the site, and the paper warned that "he might require the whole Woodward block including the Post Office and Upfold's saloon to accommodate his business."

The *Banner* knew that its readers wanted to be kept abreast of plans for the Kenyon House and followed events closely.

**January:** Wolff contemplated tearing down the building and erecting a large, more elegant structure on the site with offices on the second floor and a hall on the third.

**March:** Harper saw the drawings for the building and declared it would be "one of the finest buildings" in town.

**April:** Instead of being remodeled, the old Kenyon House was taken down to the foundation so that an entirely new building could "rise and surpass any edifice in our city."

**May:** The foundation was laid and the first "tier of joice [sic] placed on the wall."

**June:** The first story was up and looked "finely" in what Harper now called Wolff's new block. Because of rain, the brick supply ran low and progress slowed.

**October:** The first two floors of the building were completed. The post office moved from Vine Street to a room in "Wolff's splendid new building on the Public Square which has been fitted up in the most elegant and convenient manner." Dr. Kelsey, a dentist, and Dr. Stamp moved into their offices on the second floor.

**November 30, 1867:** A. Wolff's new Clothing Store on the corner of Main Street and Public Square opened.

Wolff placed huge ads in the papers. The headline shouted "The Great Clothing Store of Central Ohio" above a drawing of the new, impressive brick building. Wolff was grateful to the citizens of Knox

County and Mount Vernon for their patronage, and wanted them to know that he had moved all his goods to his "elegant new building." Not caring about the cost, Wolff "fitted" the space in "the most beautiful and attractive style." His "clothing and piece goods" were part of the largest stock anywhere in Ohio. His inventory included "cloths, cassimeres, vestings, ladies' cloakings, coats, pants, vests, drawers, undershirts, and gents' furnishing goods." If a customer wanted piece goods, he would be measured and in "short notice" have his clothing. Customers were exhorted to "examine my goods before purchasing elsewhere." "**Remember the place—New Stand, corner of Main Street and the Public Square**."

Six months later on a Thursday evening in May1868, Wolff's new hall on the third floor of his building opened in "grand style" to "an overflowing audience to witness Miss Caroline Hayes's Theatrical Troupe. The Hall, with its snowy white walls and high ceiling" was "bright and beautiful...and every person...felt proud and expressed great satisfaction...to have such a superb Hall in our city." It had easy access, was well ventilated, was "admirably adapted for public speaking or exhibitions," and, most importantly "its walls are so strong and secure that no fears can be entertained in regard to the security of the lives of patrons. Mr. Wolff deserves the thanks of the public for erecting a Hall that is both an honor and an ornament to our city." Now there were two halls a block away from each other--the Woodward and Wolff's Hall.

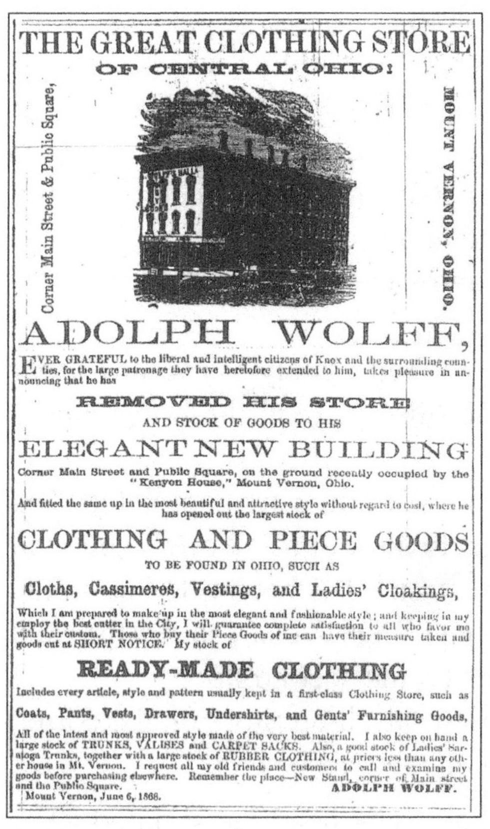
THE GREAT CLOTHING STORE
OF CENTRAL OHIO!
Corner Main Street & Public Square,
MOUNT VERNON, OHIO.
ADOLPH WOLFF,
EVER GRATEFUL to the liberal and intelligent citizens of Knox and the surrounding counties, for the large patronage they have heretofore extended to him, takes pleasure in announcing that he has
REMOVED HIS STORE
AND STOCK OF GOODS TO HIS
ELEGANT NEW BUILDING
Corner Main Street and Public Square, on the ground recently occupied by the "Kenyon House," Mount Vernon, Ohio.
And fitted the same up in the most beautiful and attractive style without regard to cost, where he has opened out the largest stock of
CLOTHING AND PIECE GOODS
TO BE FOUND IN OHIO, SUCH AS
Cloths, Cassimeres, Vestings, and Ladies' Cloakings,
Which I am prepared to make up in the most elegant and fashionable style; and keeping in my employ the best cutter in the City, I will guarantee complete satisfaction to all who favor me with their custom. Those who buy their Piece Goods of me can have their measure taken and goods cut at SHORT NOTICE. My stock of
READY-MADE CLOTHING
Includes every article, style and pattern usually kept in a first-class Clothing Store, such as
Coats, Pants, Vests, Drawers, Undershirts, and Gents' Furnishing Goods,
All of the latest and most approved style made of the very best material. I also keep on hand a large stock of TRUNKS, VALISES and CARPET SACKS. Also, a good stock of Ladies' Saratoga Trunks, together with a large stock of RUBBER CLOTHING, at prices less than any other house in Mt. Vernon. I request all my old friends and customers to call and examine my goods before purchasing elsewhere. Remember the place—New Stand, corner of Main street and the Public Square.
ADOLPH WOLFF.
Mount Vernon, June 6, 1868.

**Above**
Wolff's 1868 advertisement when he moved into his "elegant new building."
*Democratic Banner, June 6, 1868*

Scheduled events at Wolff's ranged from political, educational, and religious benefits to musical recitals and lectures. A sampling of events over a five-year period included the following:

- A theatrical company from Cincinnati
- St. Vincent de Paul's Sewing Society Fair, with all proceeds going to buy an organ
- A concert by local music teacher Professor Grebe
- Odd Fellows Grand Reunion and Oyster Supper
- A strawberry festival to benefit the Baptist Sabbath School
- Timon Knights of Pythias didn't want to anger either Woodward or Wolff, so a dinner was held at Wolff's Hall but the ball was scheduled for the Woodward.
- The Georgia Minstrels, "genuine colored gentlemen" as the *Banner* described them, played to an overflowing crowd in 1873. Later that evening the men serenaded guests at a party at William Harper's house. Harper invited the men in; they were fed and then performed for the guests.
- "Professor" Jackson performed with local musicians. Jackson never returned to this stage because the next month he was accused of improper conduct with a local, married woman. He claimed he was only making music arrangements for her children, but the couple was in a private room with the door locked. The Congregational Church investigated, found him guilty, and dismissed him from the church.
- A dinner and concert for the "plague stricken [yellow fever] victims of Memphis." Wolff donated the use of the Hall--including the gas for the lights--free. The Hall was so crowded that the music could scarcely be heard above the talking and rattling of dishes. Over $700 was raised.
- Mount Vernon Amateur Dramatic Association performed *The Poor Girl's Diary or All that Glitters is Not Good* to raise money for the poor.
- Temperance lectures
- The Methodist Episcopal Sunday School Festival to raise money for its library
- "A Night with Spirits" as "Professors" Baldwin and Cooke exposed and explained the tricks spiritualists used

- A Catholic Fair
- YMCA Raspberry Festival
- Morris Brothers' Minstrels starring Billy Emmett
- End-of-the-year public school exhibition of vocal and instrumental music, recitations, essays, tableaux, and charades
- Commencement exercises

General Admission was 25 cents and reserved seats cost 50 cents.

Wolff continued traveling to eastern cities to buy stock. In 1869 a rumor circulated that he was in Washington seeking an office in the Grant administration. Labeling this tale a "weak invention of the enemy" and "without a shadow of foundation," Wolff said his best job was "supplying the people of Knox County with the best stock of clothing to be found in the county."

Wolff was so successful he could help his son Charles start his own clothing store in the Masonic Hall Building. Charles was a "clever genial gentleman" whose store sold ready-made clothing and gentlemen's furnishings.

The 1870s started with success and happiness but did not end that way for Adolph Wolff. The census taker questioned Wolff on July 14, 1870. (On that same day, Marx Leopold, a retail clothing merchant, and William Sapp, a retail dry goods merchant, were enumerated one right after the other. The east side of town was where most merchants chose and could afford to live.) All of Wolff's children lived at home, and his sons all worked as clerks. Mary Page, an eighteen-year-old "mulatto" who had been born in Virginia, was a servant in the household. Wolff was a rich man. He had $35,000 (over $675,000 today) in real estate (his house and the Wolff Building) and $15,000 (about $289,000) personal worth. He traveled east twice a year to buy goods, and he boasted that his store was the first to have all the latest styles, the lowest prices, and "the best fits."

Later that year, on October 26, 1870, nineteen-year-old Ella Wolff, the sole surviving daughter, married Zanesville businessman Henry Horkheimer in Mount Vernon. Horkheimer was a wool merchant and was often in Mount Vernon because, as the *Banner* had noticed years earlier, local farmers were "gradually discarding the small, greasy-wooled sheep, which were introduced here a few years ago, by Vermont speculators at an enormous cost to our people. The good old 'Leicester,' which is much better for wool, and twenty times better for mutton, is now become a greater favorite with our farmers." In the coming years, Horkheimer's reputation and wealth would play an important part in his father-in-law's business.

Was the accident that Thomas Thompson, a Wolff employee, suffered in December 1874 an omen of a change in Wolff's fortunes? Thompson walked into the basement of the store to put more coal in the furnace. It was already "too heavily charged with coal," and when Thompson opened the vent, the accumulated "gas and smoke ignited and exploded in his face." He was flung backwards several feet and suffered severe burns on his face and singed whiskers and hair.

More shocking to the community was what it learned two months later. Although widely believed to be independently wealthy, Wolff went into assignment (bankruptcy). He could not pay his creditors. Two weeks later, an assignee's sale began which ran for three months. Both customers and other retail merchants benefitted from the sale. In fact, two local merchants bought Wolff's entire inventory for $20,000 and moved into Wolff's site in his own building.

Just in time for Christmas shopping, son Simon opened a new clothing emporium in the Woodbridge block. This allowed the family to earn money even though Wolff's debts had not yet cleared. It must have been a hard decision to make, but Wolff had to sell his real estate. The Wolff Building went on the block at a private assignee sale on December 3, 1875. Dr. Robert Kirk bought the property back for $27,000. Kirk quickly announced his plans to have the

**Above**
An ad after Wolff went into assignment emphasizing his son-in-law Harry Horkheimer.
*Democratic Banner, 1875*

Wolff Building repainted and repaired throughout. The interior walls were painted lavender with designs "representing various countries and the four seasons," the dressing rooms were carpeted, the "front bench seats" were replaced with "orchestra chairs," a "cozy" ticket office was cut into a room on the second floor near the Hall's entrance, and the venue was renamed Kirk's Hall.

With the infusion of cash, assignee Alex Cassil announced that he could pay the first dividend of 20 percent on all claims against Wolff and that the estate would pay 10 cents on the dollar. Impressively, even with his financial difficulties, Wolff's reputation was unsullied. He was lauded as an "enterprising citizen who had done much for Mt. Vernon."

About a year and a half later, all debts against Wolff were settled, and he could now receive payments from anyone who still owed him money. Wolff was ready to restart his business under his own name, but where? He no longer owned any buildings in town. For the last several years son Simon had run his business in the Woodbridge property, and now father and son moved to the Banning Block on West High Street. Even with a saloon under Wolff's clothing store (or perhaps because of it), he hoped to lure back old customers. Wolff stressed the country's hard financial times, said his business was doing better than expected, and reminded all that he was still "the clothing king."

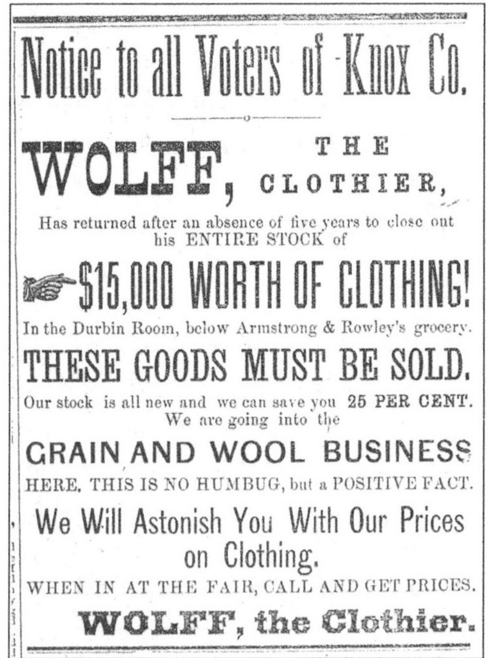
Notice to all Voters of Knox Co.

WOLFF, THE CLOTHIER,

Has returned after an absence of five years to close out his ENTIRE STOCK of

$15,000 WORTH OF CLOTHING!

In the Durbin Room, below Armstrong & Rowley's grocery.

THESE GOODS MUST BE SOLD.

Our stock is all new and we can save you 25 PER CENT. We are going into the

GRAIN AND WOOL BUSINESS

HERE. THIS IS NO HUMBUG, but a POSITIVE FACT.

We Will Astonish You With Our Prices on Clothing.

WHEN IN AT THE FAIR, CALL AND GET PRICES.

WOLFF, the Clothier.

**Above**
Wolff ad showing he was back in business.
*Democratic Banner*

In 1877 son Charles Wolff worked as a traveling salesman and was in Mount Vernon saying that trade had been "very satisfactory on the road during spring travels."

When Adolph Wolff traveled locally, Hannah or a servant packed a meal for him which he carried in his valise. Once, it was stolen as he waited at the Newark train station. The newspaper joked about the smell of the limburger cheese, but the gentle gibe showed that the Wolffs did not observe kosher. His sandwich of Cincinnati bologna and limburger cheese clearly mixed meat and dairy--forbidden in Jewish dietary laws.

The decline in Wolff fortunes continued with a robbery. The Wolffs walked from their grand house on East Gambier to their store daily. Simon entered the store on Monday, November 20, 1878. He glanced at the stock and thought the inventory looked messy. Perhaps he should talk to the clerks about making sure everything was in order before they closed. As he walked to the back of the store and the office where he hung his coat, he nearly stepped into a hole. Simon looked straight down to the basement. Thieves had forced open a basement window and used augers, bits, and chisels to bore a hole above them. They then climbed into the store and turned off the gas jet which stayed on all night to light the store's interior. Using lanterns, the thieves passed heaps of "overcoats, full matched suits, boys' suits, underwear, and furnishing goods" to the basement. The culprits left with over $1000 worth of "the finest stock." The exact time of the robbery was not known. Mrs. Jackson, the wife of a baker in the next block, said she heard "pounding and knocking" between 2 and 3 a.m., and her husband said he heard a wagon "drive rapidly away from the neighborhood." The neighborhood policemen on duty that night said that nothing attracted their attention. Wolff sent telegrams about the robbery "in all directions" and issued posters offering a $100 reward. The police claimed be be

**Above**
An ad that ran in the *Democratic Banner* in 1878 after Wolff's second assignment.

"shadowing" two or three people, but the theft was never solved.

That loss, equating to over $25,000 today, was the tipping point for what happened a month later; Wolff went into assignment again. "That old and well known clothing merchant, Mr. Adolph Wolff, made an assignment to Col. Alex Cassil for the benefit of his creditors," began the *Banner* article of December 6, 1878. Wolff's inventory was valued at $4,000, but his debts were at least four times that. Once again, everything had to be sold quickly, and son-in-law Henry Horkheimer took charge of the sale. (Horkheimer had been injured in a buggy accident in Sunbury when his horse shied and kicked his buggy to pieces. He suffered a broken leg, but by November had recovered enough to help his father-in-law.)

Advertisements for the sale said that Horkheimer was A. Wolff's successor. There would be a "Great Clothing Sale," and everything would be gone in sixty days. Now was the chance to buy "clothing, hats, caps and gents' furnishing goods" at low prices.

By May 1879, Wolff was back in business but with a few changes and a great deal of spin. Finances were such that Wolff's Mount Vernon store could not support the entire family. Unmarried sons needed to find work outside Knox County. Son Charles set out on his own. He was going on a buying trip back east before he opened his own store in Kenton, Ohio. That's what he told people, but in reality, Ike Rosenthall, another local clothier who had brothers and stores throughout the state, had offered Charles a job in his Kenton store. Money problems aside, one of the last things Wolff did in 1879 was hire painter Samuel Power to repaint his house and its veranda "in a very handsome style."

Wolff and his shop moved again--this time to "the store-room immediately South of Armstrong & Tilton's Grocery." Reminding his customers that he was reliable, Wolff also championed his reduced circumstances. Because he now had just one room and paid half as much rent as before, he advertised that he could sell many items 25 percent lower than anyone else in the county. Advertisements printed Henry Horkheimer's name in tiny letters above the bold, reliable name of Adolph Wolff. The two men were in business together; Horkheimer had the money and Wolff had the reputation. To cut costs, Wolff no longer paid for half-page or quarter-page ads in the *Banner*. Now ads were fewer and smaller than before. Wolff ran short blurbs like "Summer suits $10" or "finest dress suits" in the back of the papers.

Wolff might have lost money, but he hadn't lost his combativeness. On May 15, 1884, Peter Grief, a German, appeared before the mayor's court for assaulting Adolph Wolff--who was sixty-five at the time and just three months from his death. Peter testified that Wolff had insulted him by saying he was a "lineal descendent of a female canine." He said he wouldn't have minded if Wolff had insulted him in German because only he would have understood. But Wolff said it in English and everyone understood. Grief was fined $5.00 and court fees.

August 1884 was typical for Ohio--hot and humid. Surely an open window facing Gambier Street would allow some air into the second-floor bedroom where Adolph Wolff lay. He had been ill for some time with a "long continued disease" (cancer?) and hadn't worked for several months. Doctors prescribed narcotics to ease his suffering. Around 8:30 p.m. on a Tuesday night, "suffering from the effects of narcotic drugs and stimulants and while in a condition of high nervous excitement," Wolff climbed out his open bedroom window onto the roof of the verandah, and "in the darkness produced by the shade trees, stepped from the top" of the porch and fell fifteen feet to the "stone-flagging" below. Family and neighbors heard his cries, carried him inside, and summoned two physicians. Doctor Johnathan Burr (about eighty-four years old) and thirty-five-year-old Frank Larimore, one of the best-educated doctors in town, came to the house. Wolff had a "terrible scalp wound" and a long gash on his skull. He was very seriously injured, but his skull was not broken. He was unconscious, and one of the physicians said he was resting quietly and had about "an equal chance for life and death." Later the doctors expressed "grave doubts for his recovery." Wolff never regained consciousness and lingered until Sunday morning, August 12, at nine o'clock, when he died. An autopsy conducted the next day by doctors Larimore and John Russell determined cause of death as blood leakage in the left and right sides of the brain which led to a slight coma followed by a "profound coma" and then death.

Masonic services were held at the Wolff house, and then fellow

**Above**
The Wolff family home at 105 East Gambier Street where Sarah Wolff was married and where Adolph Wolff fell to his death.
*Photo by the Author*

**Above**
Adolph Wolff's tombstone in Mount Wood Cemetery in Wheeling, West Virginia.
*Photo by the Author*

Masons escorted the coffin to the B.&O. depot. Ella Horkheimer wanted her father buried in the Jewish cemetery in Wheeling, West Virginia, where she lived. The family accompanied the body there, and Wolff was buried in the Jewish section of Mount Wood cemetery. (This is where other Wolff family members would also be buried.)

Wolff was lauded as an active and energetic businessman and one of Mount Vernon's most prominent local merchants, who had built what was now known as the Kirk Block and whose influence continued to be felt in the community. He was survived by his wife Hannah, daughter Mrs. Ella Horkheimer, sons Simon, Morris, and Rudolph, and two brothers, Phillip of Fort Wayne, Indiana, and Abraham of New York.

## Hannah Wolff

It is difficult to illuminate Hannah Wolff's life so that she is seen as an individual and not just the typical nineteenth-century wife of Adolph Wolff. All we have are the bare facts available from the public record:

- She was born in Germany around 1819.

- Her maiden name was either Neibenthall or Riebenthall.
- She had six children in thirteen years--all born in Ohio.
- She outlived three of them.
- She was a housekeeper.
- Often her husband's clerks boarded in her house.
- She had servants to help.
- Niece Theresa Wolff lived with the family.
- Hannah had a pet parrot named Polly that her uncle had given her. The old bird, estimated to have been about seventy years old, met an ignominious death when she fell into a "vault" (a septic tank), caught cold, and died.
- As a widow she spent her winters with daughter Ella in Wheeling.
- Her sons and daughter visited her often in Mount Vernon.
- In 1891 her Gambier Street house was sold at a sheriff's sale. Daughter Ella bought the house for $3,667 and her mother continued to live there.
- Around 1901-1902 she sold the house to Grant and Minnie Smith and moved to Wheeling Island to live near Ella and her children.
- She died on July 30, 1904.

---

Footnote

**1**. The Kremlin Building was just three years old in 1848. On the eastern side of the Square, the Kremlin was made up of five sections, each costing about $5,000. The original occupants were David Potwin's dry goods store, Cooper & Co. general store, Curtis & McCormick hardware, Elias Cooper's stoves and tin shop, and A. Wolff, clothier.

Wolff and Potwin were in the same building but were not competitors. A dry goods store sold cloth, hardware, general notions, and even writing implements. A clothier was a men's and boys' clothing provider, selling everything a male needed–from suits to suitcases, and cloaks to combs.

# Ella Wolff Horkheimer

## *Adolph Wolff's Daughter*

**Ella Wolff Horkheimer** deserves a chapter to herself. Everything suggests she was a loving and generous daughter, wife, mother, and sister.

She was born in Mount Vernon on September 20, 1851--the fifth child and second daughter of Adolph and Hannah Wolff. She was fifteen when her older sister Sarah died.

On October 26, 1870, nineteen-year-old Ella married Henry Horkheimer, a German Jew five years her senior, at her home on East Gambier Street. Rabbi M. Greenblate traveled from Columbus to perform the ceremony. Horkheimer had come to the United States as a boy and worked in Wheeling, West Virginia, with his Uncle Simon; the family was well known in the Zanesville/Mount Vernon area. Because Henry and his business partner Henry Baer were the largest wool wholesalers in Ohio and West Virginia and paid the best prices,

PARTIES.

Henry Horkheimer

AND

Ella Wolff

LICENSE

Issued the 26 day of October A. D. 1870, to the above-named parties. C. E. Critchfield P. J.

AFFIDAVIT.

The State of Ohio, } ss. KNOX COUNTY,

Henry Horkheimer having made application for a LICENSE for himself and Ella Wolff, and being duly sworn, says that he is of the age of 21 years, and has no wife living, and that Ella Wolff is of the age of 18 years, a resident of said County, and has no husband living, and that said parties are not nearer kin than second cousins.

Henry Horkheimer

Sworn to and subscribed before me, this 26th day of October, A. D. 1870

C. E. Critchfield Probate Judge.

RETURN.

No. 609

The State of Ohio, } ss. KNOX COUNTY,

I do hereby Certify that on the 26" day of October 1870 I solemnized the MARRIAGE of Mr. Henry Horkheimer WITH Miss Ella Wolff.

M. Greenblate minister

**Above**
Ella Wolff and Henry Horkeimer's marriage license.
*Knox County Records Center, Mount Vernon, Ohio*

they were often in Knox County and Mount Vernon. The two men surely would have stopped at Wolff's business and then been invited to his home. Henry would have met and courted Ella there. This was a good match for her. The newlyweds moved to Zanesville, where son Benjamin was born in 1871; Sarah, named after Ella's dead sister as per Ashkenazi tradition, was born in 1874.

Henry traveled throughout Ohio buying wool. In the spring of 1877, Joseph Avery, another Zanesville businessman, and Horkheimer were in a buggy near Sunbury when the horse shied, kicked the buggy apart, and threw both men to the ground. Each suffered a broken leg, and two months later Henry had still not completely healed.

During Wolff's two bankruptcies son-in-law Horkheimer acted as assignee and provided necessary cash for the family and their business. Between 1880 and 1885, Ella and her children visited Mount Vernon frequently, often staying for the entire summer. Indeed in 1880 the Horkheimers were listed by the census enumerator as living in Mount Vernon. Henry visited for several days every few weeks, conducted business with local sheep farmers in Knox County, and then traveled to Guernsey, Delaware, or Morgan counties to look after "immense quantities of wool" he had already contracted. Then he headed home.

In 1880 the family moved to Wheeling, West Virginia, where Henry and his brothers Morris, Bernard, Julius, and Louis established and ran Horkheimer Brothers, purveyors of wool, pelts, and furs, and

**Above**
An advertisement in a Wheeling, West Virginia City Directory for Horkheimer Brothers' wool business. Note the logo – a copy of the insignia of the Knights of the Golden Fleece.

exporters of American ginseng. Henry was a Mason, an Odd Fellow, and a member of B'nai B'rith (a Jewish fraternal organization) and was on the Board of Directors of the Standard Fire Insurance Company.

When Ella's father died in Mount Vernon in 1884, his body was brought to Wheeling and buried in Mount Wood Cemetery.

On September 2, 1885, before the beginning of the school year, Ella and her children left Mount Vernon and returned to Wheeling. The family reunited, and a few weeks later Henry took the train to Pittsburgh on a business trip. After a few days, he probably complained of a severe headache, loss of appetite, and fatigue. He returned to Wheeling and his family. The physicians who came to his house and examined him diagnosed typhoid. Henry Horkheimer died on October 10 at the age of thirty-eight. He was "respected and esteemed by all" for his kindness and generosity, said the Wheeling *Intelligencer*, and his family had the sympathy of a "wide circle of friends." Board members on the Standard Fire Insurance Company said he was a "valued and respected member" and that they had lost the "most useful, valued, and trustworthy" friend. Hannah Wolff traveled to Wheeling for her son-in-law's funeral and burial in the same cemetery where her husband lay. Henry's will left everything to Ella; she inherited about $90,000 (over $2 million today).

Ella never remarried and had been left enough money that she had no need to. In 1893 she and "her charming daughter Sarah" visited the Chicago World's Fair just months before it closed. On their way home, they stopped in Mount Vernon to visit Hannah. Benjamin Horkheimer came up from Wheeling for this short family reunion. Ella and Sarah stayed for about ten days.

Ella's life in Wheeling was that of a wealthy widow. She lived at 33 Virginia Street on Wheeling Island. In its heyday, the Island, right in the middle of the Ohio River between West Virginia and Bridgeport, Ohio, was the most desirable part of the city for the wealthy. Grand, ornate Victorian houses lined the streets--many with large backyards which ran down to the river. (Unfortunately the Horkheimer home no longer exists.) She belonged to the Eoff Street Temple, the Reform Jewish congregation that all the German Jews joined. Ella played the piano and often performed at benefits for the Temple and small social meetings.

From the time of Henry's death until her own in 1921, Ella provided financial support to her family. Her mother Hannah had inherited the Gambier Street house in Mount Vernon when Adolph died in 1884. Perhaps she had trouble paying the taxes because in 1891 the house went on sale at a sheriff's auction. Ella bought it for $3,667 and gave it to her mother, who lived there until she moved to Wheeling.

**Above**
Henry Horkeimer's grave in Mount Wood Cemetery in Wheeling, West Virginia.
*Photo by the Author*

Every time Ella's brothers' businesses failed (and they always failed), they moved to Wheeling and lived with her either on Virginia Street on the Island or somewhere nearby. When they died, she made sure they were buried near their parents. Ella certainly made sure that daughter Sarah had an elegant wedding. (See the next chapter, *A Tale of Three Widows*.)

Ella died at age 70 from chronic inflammation of the kidneys leading to renal failure (Bright's Disease), arteriosclerosis, and endocarditis (inflammation of the heart lining). Ben S. Baer, her son-in-law, provided non-medical information for her death certificate, and it's not surprising that he had some facts wrong. He stated that her father was Simon Wolf [*sic*], who was her uncle. And for some unknown reason he said that she was the widow of Henry Baer, who was really her brother-in-law. She was buried in Mount Wood Cemetery near her parents, her brothers, and her beloved husband.

# A Tale of Three Widows

## *Three Generations of Wolff Women*

When **Hannah Wolff**, Adolph's widow, moved to Wheeling, West Virginia, in 1901, she lived with her widowed daughter, Ella, and widowed granddaughter Sarah on Wheeling Island.

**Ella Wolff Horkheimer** had married Henry Horkheimer in 1870. She had been a widow for sixteen years when her mother moved in with her.

Ten years after her father, Henry Horkheimer, died, **Sarah Rosetta Horkheimer** married Albert David Adler on February 13, 1895. The brilliant wedding caught the attention of the local newspaper in the same way her Aunt Sarah's wedding thirty years earlier had interested Mount Vernon. This marriage would end just as tragically.

The wedding at the Eoff Street Temple in Wheeling which had been dedicated just three years earlier and was part of the Moorish Revival movement in architecture and the reception that followed were deemed "the most stylish events ever seen in Wheeling." A canopy was erected from the temple's doorway across the sidewalk to protect guests from any wind or snow that might mar their arrival for the 7:30 p.m. ceremony. Carriages lined both

**Above**
Eoff Street Temple in Wheeling, West Virginia where Sarah Horkheimer married Albert Adler. The marriage lasted less than a year.
*Ohio County Library, Wheeling, West Virginia*

sides of the street as the well-dressed guests hurried into the temple. Inside, palms, potted plants, and cut flowers decorated the sanctuary. A large wedding bell made of flowers and entwined with the couple's initials impressed the guests.

At 7:40, trumpeters from the Wheeling Opera House orchestra sounded the beginning notes of Mendelssohn's Wedding March, and the groom's half-sister, Ida Rice, walked down the aisle. Then Albert Adler and his best man, Lou Stein, entered. Who was this man who had wooed and won "one of the most beautiful Jewish ladies of the city"?

The twenty-six-year-old groom was born in 1869. His father, D. A. Adler, had started a wholesale and retail business selling millinery and fancy goods (dress trimming, hosiery, furs). After his early death, his widow married A. L. Rice, who took over the business and changed its name to A. L. Rice Company. Albert Adler, a genial and popular young man, was a salesman for the company his father had started until 1894, when he became a partner. Perhaps he had already won Sarah's hand and knew he no longer wanted to travel throughout the state. As a partner, he had a career which promised the couple prosperity and happiness.

Sarah looked lovely as her brother Benjamin escorted her down the aisle. She wore a gown of brocaded satin, ornamented with diamonds, and a full veil. Rabbi Bonheim officiated, and then the couple exited to the strains of the *Lohengrin* wedding march. Carriages took the guests--who included the bride's grandmother, Hannah Wolff, and uncles Charles and Rudolph--uptown to the McLure House for a magnificent dinner. The newspaper exclaimed that the event was "lovely in all respects, elegant in its appointments, and auspicious of future happiness." The couple left on a month-long tour of eastern cities before returning to Wheeling to live with Sarah's mother on the Island.

Sometime that summer Albert became ill with a "liver ailment" and traveled to Baltimore (probably to Johns Hopkins) for treatment. Upon his return he said he felt better, but he was not cured and never fully recovered. He sold all his interests in the family business to his mother and made a will in August. He wrote that he knew "of the uncertainty of human life" and bequeathed his entire estate of $9,000 (about $270,000 today), his insurance premium, jewelry, and music to his "beloved wife." Lou Stein, his best man just months earlier, was named his executor. Seven months after his wedding, on September 25, 1895, Adler died at 4:00 a.m. at his mother-in-law's home. His death certificate listed cancer as the cause.

Albert's will gave his wife all his music. He was a gifted musician with both a "rare natural gift" and good training. He was a fine pianist and composer whose works had won favor with critics and audiences. At the age of twenty, Sarah was a widow.

Eventually three generations of widows lived on Virginia Street. But the house was not just draped in widow's weeds. Ella's son Benjamin and his wife of two years, May, were there, and Kate McDermott, a twenty-eight-year-old servant, lived in.

Hannah Wolff died in 1904 after falling and fracturing her femur. She never fully recovered from this injury. Her death certificate said cause of death was "senile exhaustion following fracture of the femur." She was eighty-five when she died and was "one of the best known women on the island." She was buried beside her husband in Mount Wood Cemetery in Wheeling.

Ella Wolff Horkheimer's death in 1921 was described in the previous chapter.

The saddest story was that of Sarah Horkheimer Adler Baer, whose first marriage lasted less than a year. In 1901 Rabbi Harry Levi officiated at Sara's (that's how she spelled her name on the marriage license) second marriage to Benjamin S. Baer, who had been a groomsman at her first wedding. The couple lived with her mother Ella on Virginia Street for many years. (In 1930 the house was valued at $25,000. In today's money, that would be about $350,000. Sadly the structure has been torn down.) In 1938 the Baers moved to Huntington, West Virginia, and lived in the Huntington Hotel. Ben died there of a stroke in the morning of October 8, 1940. Sarah continued to live in the hotel throughout the war years and on August 21, 1949, at the age of seventy-five, she committed suicide by drowning in her bathtub.

By now her brother Benjamin Horkheimer had been dead for thirty years. He died from a self-inflicted gunshot wound to the head in

1919 at the age of 48. He was buried in Mount Wood Cemetery in Wheeling.

This Wolff-Horkheimer-Adler-Baer family--which had once had great wealth and prestige--now came to a close in the Mount Vernon story.

**Above**
Ella Horkeimer's grave in Mount Wood Cemetery in Wheeling, West Virginia.
*Photo by the Author*

**Above**
Albert Adler's tomb in Mount Wood Cemetery in Wheeling, West Virginia.
*Photo by the Author*

**Above**
Another view of Adler's tomb.
*Photo by the Author*

# Wolff Sons

## *Adolf Wolff's Less-Than-Successful Sons*

All the Wolff sons were born in Mount Vernon. They grew up and worked here--perhaps under the shadow of their successful, strong-willed father. They clerked in the family business or managed their own businesses, which their father probably financed. (Wolff never changed his store's name to include "& Sons.") They lived in Mount Vernon as long as they could until finances pushed them out of the nest. But they seemed to lack their father's business acumen because their endeavors always failed and they would fall back on their sister Ella's largesse. They did know the retail trade and often ended their careers as salesmen. Only one brother married and it did not last.

**Charles Wolff** (1846–1900) spent his life as a salesman/merchant either in his father's store or one he started in Mount Vernon under his own name, Chas. Wolff & Co., or in Philadelphia or in Kenton, Ohio. He left Mount Vernon around 1877 to work in Philadelphia as a traveling salesman. Two years later, the *Banner* wrote that Charlie, "a clever, genial gentleman," was on an eastern buying trip because he was starting a store in Kenton. In reality brother Rudolph and he were living in a boarding house in Kenton and working there in a branch of Rosenthall Brothers. In April 1880 Charles showed up in Mount Vernon "happy as a big sunflower" because he was engaged. He married Harriet Kahn in September 1880 at Congregation Rodeph Shalom in

**Above**
Charles Wolff's headstone in Mount Wood Cemetery, Wheeling, West Virginia.
*Photo by the Author*

Philadelphia. Adolph Wolff and his daughter Ella Horkheimer attended the wedding. For the next several years Charles visited his parents in Mount Vernon either alone or with his wife and young daughter. I believe Harriet died in 1889, and several years later Charles moved to Pittsburgh. He returned to town for his cousin Theresa's wedding and visited his widowed mother yearly. He eventually moved to Wheeling, worked at a department store there, and lived with his sister Ella. He died from "lung trouble" in 1900.

Charles had a daughter, and I'm fairly sure that her name was **Evelyn S. Wolff** (her middle name might have been Sarah, after Charles's dead sister). Although she lived in Wheeling, she often visited her Grandmother Wolff in Mount Vernon. She attended Mount De Chantal Visitation Academy, a private girls' school in Wheeling, from 1897 to 1899. At the end-of-year ceremony in 1897, she won a prize for "fidelity to charges and stocking darning." (What *were* they teaching those girls?) Sadly, in her senior year her only award was for "fidelity." She stayed in Wheeling, and in 1900 she was a nurse at City

New Clothing Store.

CHAS. WOLFF & CO.

TAKE great pleasure in announcing to the citizens of Knox and the surrounding counties that they have opened an entirely new Clothing Store, in the room recently occupied by John Denny, in the

MASONIC HALL BUILDING,

On Main Street, Mt. Vernon, O.,

where they offer for sale a large and splendid stock of

READY-MADE

CLOTHING

—SUCH AS—

COATS, PANTS, VESTS, &c.,

And also a general assortment of

GENTLEMEN'S FURNISHING GOODS,

Including every article that is called for in a First-Class Clothing Store We have also on hand a magnificent stock of

HATS AND CAPS:

The Hats are from Beebe's renowned establishment in New York, and justly rank among the best, most beautiful and fashionable in America. We have likewise a fine assortment of rare and beautiful

LADIES' FURS!

Such as Mink, Fitch, Siberian Squirl, River Mink, Coney, &c., as well as a very pretty assortment of LADIES' HOODS, which cannot fail to give satisfaction, and which we will sell 20 per cent. lower than any other house in Mt. Vernon.

In addition to the above, we have in store and for sale, a superior stock of

Trunks, Carpet Sacks & Umbrellas,

Our Stock is all new, made of the best material, and will be warranted to turn out as represented in every instance.

☞ Please give us a call before purchasing elsewhere. Don't forget the place—Masonic Hall Building, Main street, Mt. Vernon.

Oct. 6 CHARLES WOLFF & CO.

**Above**

Charles Wolff started his own business in 1868.

*Democratic Banner*

Hospital. And then she disappeared. Perhaps she married or moved away.

**Simon Wolff** (1848–1918) followed his brother in all ways except for marrying. When his father declared bankruptcy in 1875, Simon

Mount Vernon's Latest Enterprise!

A NEW CLOTHING EMPORIUM.

SIMON WOLFF,

Late of A. WOLFF & CO., begs leave to announce to the citizens of Mount Vernon and Knox County has just purchased a select and complete stock of

READY-MADE CLOTHING,

PIECE GOODS,

—AND—

Gent's Furnishing Wear,

WITH A DIRECT VIEW OF ACCOMMODATING AND PLEASING ALL THE CUSTOMERS OF THE OLD FIRM.

THE MERCHANT TAILORING DEPARTMENT

IS UNDER THE SUPERVISION OF

MR. RICHARD WEST,

THE POPULAR AND RELIABLE CUTTER, WHO CANNOT FAIL TO GIVE ENTIRE SATISFACTION.

☞ Our place of business is in the new store-room in the WOODBRIDGE BLOCK, where we will be pleased to see all our old customers and as many new ones as will favor us with a call.

oct29tf SIMON WOLFF.

**Above**
An ad for Simon Wolff's store in the *Democratic Banner*, November 19, 1875.

started his own clothing emporium in the Woodbridge Block. He hired Mount Vernon's "most popular and reliable cutter," hoping this would bring more customers into his store. It didn't. In 1883 his business was in trouble, and the entire establishment was sold at public auction. Brother-in-law Henry Horkheimer came to the rescue, bought the entire inventory for $2,550, and transported the goods to Wheeling. Simon, eventually, moved to Wheeling, lived with his sister, and worked in a department store. He never married and died of "valvular heart disease" in 1918.

**Morris Wolff** (1850–1889) was an addict--alcohol, opium, and chloral hydrate. When he wasn't using, he had a good business sense and possessed a "wonderful talent for mimicry" which probably amused anyone who wasn't the target of his impersonations. Considered an "eccentric character," he was, however, well liked.

Morris's brief life seemed to both parallel his brothers' and then veer off on its own. Buggy riding on Gambier Road in 1870, Morris broke his left arm when the buggy lost a wheel, and he jumped off. A decade later Morris noticed a thief stealing an overcoat from Rosenthall's store, and he joined others to pursue the "tramp" and recover all the stolen property. Less than a half hour later, Morris saw the man again, now carrying a new pair of boots that he had stolen from James Sapp's store. The vagrant was detained once more.

By 1885 he lived in Kenton and visited his mother a week after the death of his brother-in-law Henry Horkheimer. The Kenton store, however, did not thrive. In 1887 the business was $700 in debt, and the establishment closed for the second time in eight months. That same year he visited his mother at least four times. Surely his addiction played a part in his business failures and accounted for his frequent trips back to Mount Vernon (for rest, sympathy, and money, perhaps). The Kenton store failed, and Morris returned to Mount Vernon after an absence of five years and started another clothing store which lasted only a few years.

Plans were afoot for Morris and Simon to go to Kendallville, Indiana, where their uncle Phillip lived. The brothers wanted to start their own business there, and Morris traveled to Chicago to buy goods. (Why did the family ever allow him to go there alone?) There was too much temptation in the metropolis. The *Banner* wrote, "It is supposed that he visited an opium joint and his system became impregnated with the deadly drug." Morris collapsed unconscious on a Chicago street. He carried identification and someone sent his mother a telegram. Simon took a train to bring his brother home. Morris never regained consciousness and died September 21, 1889, in his family home on East Gambier Street. He was buried in Wheeling, West Virginia.

**Rudolph Wolff** (1857–?). This youngest brother has been the hardest to track down. From 1879 through 1885, he lived in Kenton, Ohio, with brother Charles. Both were clerks and lived in a boarding house. Around 1895 he became a salesman for Wanamaker & Brown, a clothing and furnishing business in Philadelphia. He lived in Mount Vernon but would "push their [Wanamaker & Brown's] interests in this vicinity with his well-known hustling qualities." He lived with his

West Virginia, Wills and Probate Records, 1724-1...

Ohio › Executors Bonds Vol 10-12, 1920-1927

$45000 100 conditioned as the law directs. If, therefore, the above bound Theresa Kraft shall well and truly and faithfully perform and discharge all the duties of the office of Executrix as aforesaid, then the above obligation to be void, otherwise to remain in full force and virtue.

Signed, sealed and acknowledged before the Clerk of the County Court of Ohio County, in his office,

Theresa Kraft (SEAL)

(SEAL)

(SEAL)

(SEAL)

E F Brubaker
Clerk

**Above**
Theresa Kraft's signature on her husband's will.

mother on Gambier Street in 1898. I can find no further record of him after this date.

One final Wolff, a cousin, **Theresa Wolff**, lived in Mount Vernon around 1880. She was born in 1859 in Germany, and probably landed in New York around 1871. Until 1892 she helped her aunt Hannah run the Mount Vernon household, but, like single, well-off women of her time, she spent many months visiting relatives in Ohio and West Virginia:

1880: to Wheeling and Zanesville

1881: to Kenton to visit cousins Charles and Rudolph for months (and perhaps to be their housekeeper?)

1887: to Wheeling for the winter to stay with cousin Ella

1887: seven months later back to Wheeling

Sometime during the Wheeling sojourns, Theresa, now calling herself Tracey, met Aaron L. Kraft, a prosperous businessman and, according to the *Banner*, a "wealthy widower." "Wealthy widower" is fifty percent correct. Kraft was wealthy, but he wasn't a widower. He was divorced from Sarah Warnitz, but divorces were still considered an embarrassment, so Aaron became a widower with a daughter, Blanche.

The engagement was announced in September 1891 and four months later, a "swell wedding in Jewish circles" was held at the "commodious residence of her aunt" Hannah Wolff on East Gambier Street. Either Rabbi Levi (the name on the marriage certificate) or Rabbi Bonheim (the name in the *Banner*) traveled from Wheeling to perform the ceremony "joining a most charming young lady" with a prosperous merchant twenty years her senior. Cousins Charles and Simon arrived from Pittsburgh, and Ella and her children Ben and Sarah traveled from Wheeling for the event. After a two-week honeymoon, the couple settled in Wheeling. A daughter, Lena, was born in 1893, and Theresa would often take the girls to Mount Vernon to visit Aunt Hannah.

When her husband died from heart problems in 1925, Theresa inherited $45,000 (about $650,000 in 2018). Aaron left $150 (about $2,000) to his first wife. Theresa continued living in Wheeling until her death in 1933.

# Epstein Brothers

## *Wolff's Competitors*

Summers in central Ohio are hot and humid, and August 3, 1858, was especially sticky. Walking along any Mount Vernon street could make a person break out in a sweat. It was always refreshing to stop at the well on the 400 block of Gambier Street and ladle out some water. On this day, fourteen-year-old Henry Epstein stopped to get a drink as did John Durst, a twenty-one-year-old African American. For some reason, Durst threw a cup of water on Epstein, who retaliated and tossed back a larger amount of water. Durst grabbed the boy and punched him two or three times in the face. The two parted; Henry walked to his brothers' store, **J. Epstein & Brothers** on South Main Street. He grabbed the store's pistol and headed to Durst's shop. (I have not been able to discover what kind of shop Durst owned.) Walking in, Epstein fired at the man. Henry was a hothead, but, fortunately, he wasn't a good shot, and the pistol ball passed through the seat of the chair where Durst sat.

Two days later eyewitness Nathan Martin stood before Mayor and Justice of the Peace J. P. Thompson and swore that "with force and arms and malice" and "with intent to kill," Henry Epstein had assaulted John Durst. Thompson issued a warrant--the State of Ohio vs. Henry Epstein--and gave it to Constable Charles Bollinger Church, who charged the city 10 cents in mileage, 25 cents for his service, and 25 cents to arrest Epstein.

Epstein stood before the mayor with his young lawyer, Henry Banning, and asked for a continuance until August 7. Bail was set at $200, which Henry, his lawyer, and John Denny paid. The defense was still not ready for the trial on the 7th and asked for another continuance until August 9. Both Henry and his older brother Nathan agreed to pay $200 if Henry failed to appear at his trial.

The trial began at 8:00 a.m., and subpoenas were issued. (Church was paid $3.00 to deliver them.) Immediately Henry's lawyers, Messrs. Banning and Rich, "moved to have the prosecution quashed on the grounds of the insufficiency of the affidavit" which said "intent to kill." There was no Ohio statute against "intent to kill"; the state's language was "intent to murder." Judge George denied the motion on this technicality; a recess was taken until 6:00 p.m., when the witnesses arrived.

It's interesting to try to imagine what each witness knew and what he said. Joseph Jacobs was a chair maker, so perhaps he worked at Durst's shop. John Stevens was a clerk; did he work at Epstein's? Nathan Martin obviously had been in Durst's shop when Epstein charged in. He might have been a friend or an employee. Constable Church testified, as did John Denny, who had helped pay Henry's bail. All were paid 50 cents for their civic duty. (Other as-of-now untraceable witnesses were George Hildredth, Charles Jenning, B. Sacket, Robert Bolin, and G. Sturges.)

Thompson heard their testimony and found Henry guilty as charged in the complaint of "an assault with intent to murder." Henry and Nathan paid $300 to assure Henry's appearance before the Court of Common Pleas "on the first day of the next term."

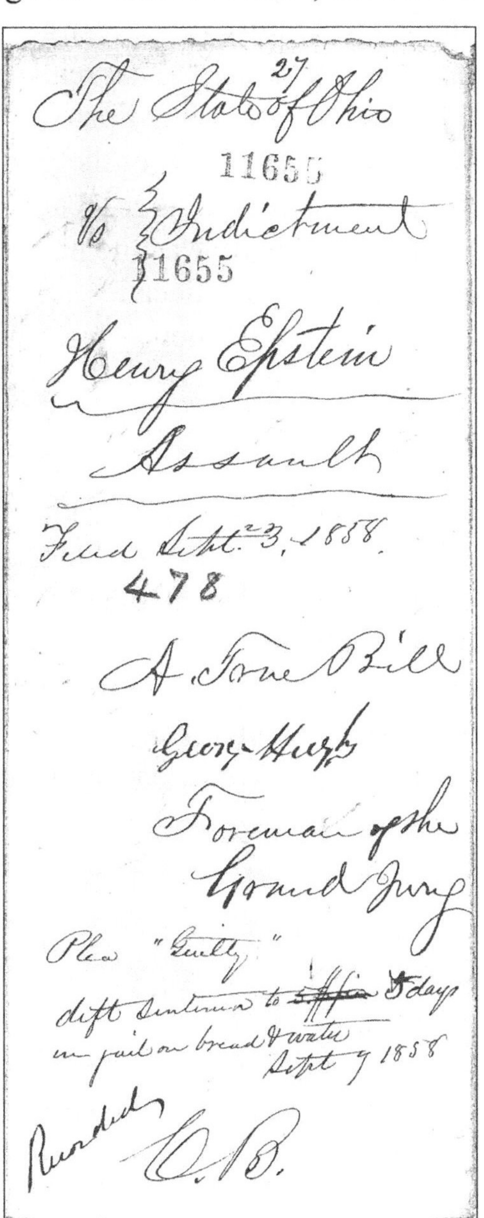
27
The State of Ohio
11655
vs Indictment
11655
Henry Epstein
Assault
Filed Sept. 3, 1858.
478
A True Bill
Foreman of the Grand Jury
Plea "Guilty"
in jail on bread & water
Sept 7 1858

**Above**
The sleeve for the court records of the State of Ohio vs. Henry Epstein. Note the guilty plea hand written on the bottom and Epstein's sentence of five days in jail with bread and water.

Henry appeared before a grand jury. The charge they heard was no longer intent to murder; Epstein was now charged with "assault in a menacing manner." The grand jury found enough evidence to indict Epstein, and he was brought in front of the Court of Common Pleas. Henry pled guilty to the charge and was sentenced to five days in jail on bread and water. (That really was the sentence.)

"The Case of Young Epstein," as the *Banner* headlined the incident, was hardly the publicity the Epstein brothers wanted after their very public feud with another local merchant, Adolph Wolff.

Wolff knew he was the premier clothier in Mount Vernon. He had arrived in town a decade earlier and had just moved his store to a larger room in the newly built Woodward Building. He could outfit a gentleman from hat to shoe with the best goods finished right in town by the "industrious poor" and not in the "slop shops" of New York City.

So when J. Epstein & Brothers of New York announced the opening of their new clothing store under the Lybrand House (on the northwest corner of South Main and Ohio Avenue where Paragraphs Bookstore now stands) in January 1857 and bragged that they "bought low and could sell low," Wolff *might* have referred to the brothers' merchandise as "the sweepings from bankrupt businesses," and to the Epsteins themselves as "transient merchants" who would "skim and swindle"

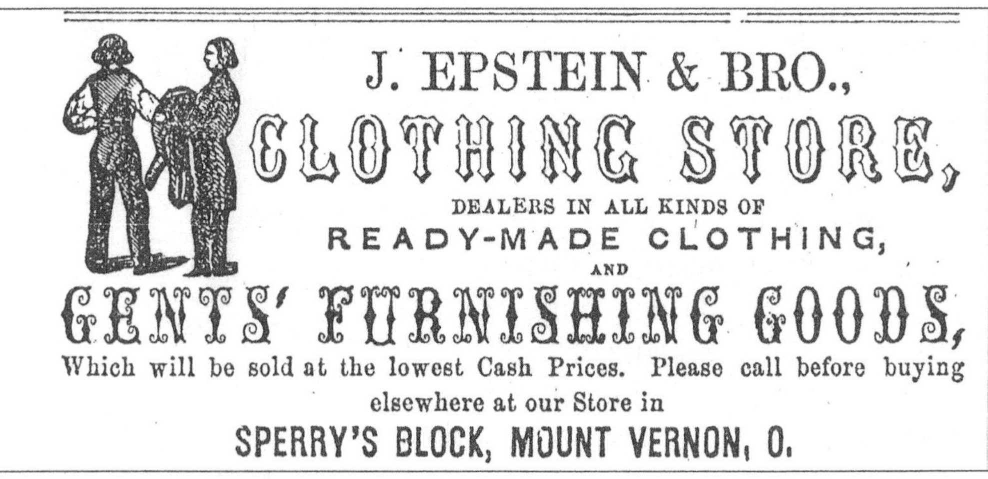


**Above**
The Epstein Brothers began running advertisements as soon as they arrived in Mount Vernon around 1857.

their customers. And that might have moved the brothers to tell the public that they had survived and captured A. Wolff (a wolf) and not to listen to the "inflammatory language" of their competitor because everyone knew that A. Wolff was "the meanest, most sneaking, sly and underhanded of animals." The predatory nature of A. Wolff was to "injure and mislead" the public, and this particular Wolff meant to "injure and drive" the Epsteins out of business.

The *Republican* archly mentioned an "active competition among clothing men" as Wolff replied that he was disposed to "devour somebody" and that he had come up against many "one horse establishments in the past," and that all had been "used up." The Epsteins took the high ground and said that they hadn't been the ones to issue insulting handbills with inflammatory language but would always denounce monopolies that allowed a merchant to take the "hard earnings of honest men [by] selling at exorbitant prices." The competitive salvos had been fired, demonstrating that Jacob, Nathan, and Henry Epstein, German Jewish immigrants like Adolph Wolff, were in town and meant to stay.

Jacob Epstein was obviously the senior brother of the firm and as such ran J. Epstein & Brothers from New York City. Brothers Nathan and Henry opened the Mount Vernon store. Henry was unmarried and lived in a boarding house at the corner of Front Street (now Ohio Avenue) and McKenzie. Nathan (age 27) was married, and he and his wife Rachel and daughter Hannah boarded on the south side of Front and Gay. Another daughter, Clara, was born in October 1859. From Front Street it was a short walk to J. Epstein & Brothers on South Main Street.

The store sold "splendid business coats, fine cloth dress and frock coats, plain and fancy cassimere [an archaic spelling of cashmere], pants, vests, and a full stock of gents' furnishing goods." The business prospered, and in May 1858 it moved to a "large and commodious store room" in Sperry's Block on the southwest corner of Public Square. The store sold everything a gentleman would ever need, and the brothers were proud to advertise their "cheap and fashionable clothing."

And then came the incident at the Gambier Street well. The store and its reputation might have suffered some financial repercussions, because by the next year Nathan Epstein was the business manager of another local clothier, M. Frois & Company. He not only worked on the floor of this store but made trips to New York to buy stock. Epstein & Brothers had probably declared bankruptcy, and Frois & Co. had purchased the inventory and changed the store's name. Nathan worked there until all creditors were paid, and he could re-open his store.

In March 1860 the firm of Epstein & Brothers reappeared on South Main Street with a large stock of ready-made goods on hand. The *Banner* wrote that "Mr. Epstein has been a resident of Mount Vernon for several years and has sustained the reputation of being an honest and honorable dealer." There was no mention of brother Henry.

Three months later in the 1860 census the only Epsteins in Mount Vernon were Nathan, age 27, a clothing merchant worth $1,000, his wife Rachel, age 29, and daughters Hannah and Clara.

Within a year, however, J. Epstein & Brothers closed again, and D. H. Arnold opened a new clothing store in the room "recently occupied by N. Epstein." By 1870 Nathan and his family lived in Chicago, where Nathan was a dealer in hides. It has been impossible to determine what happened to Henry.

And what about the competitor, A. Wolff? Called the "Napoleon of Clothiers" by his friend the editor of the *Banne*r, Wolff was still in business and would be until his death in 1884.

# Leopold Munk

## *Wolff's Brother-in-Law*

**Leopold Munk** lived in Mount Vernon for almost twenty-five years. He was never a big player and was overshadowed by his brother-in-law, Adolph Wolff. But his life exemplified that of a typical German immigrant and illuminates the difficulties facing a twenty-first-century researcher.

Born in Bavaria sometime either in 1824 or 1825, Munk was in Ohio by 1850. On November 5 of that year, Munk applied for a marriage license in Cuyahoga County to wed twenty-year-old Sophia Wolff, who had been born in Germany and was Adolph Wolff's sister. A copy of the marriage license confirms that date. The date that doesn't work is that of the birth of their first child Rosetta, who, according to census records, was born in Mount Vernon in 1850. Because no birth records were kept in Knox County at that time, the generous interpretation is that Rosetta was born sometime in 1851. But there definitely was a child within the first year of Leopold and Sophia's marriage.

Munk was the owner of the Lone Star Clothing Store on the west side of Main Street--two doors north of Gambier Street. Like all the other local clothiers, Munk's inventory included gentlemen's "latest-style of ready-made clothing--hats, umbrellas, trunks, and furnishing goods." Munk's family grew in 1856 with the birth of son Benjamin and the next year when daughter Clara was born. In 1857 Munk, now a naturalized citizen, was initiated at the first meeting of the Quindaro Lodge #316 of the Odd Fellows.

Business competition meant running advertisements in both local newspapers to draw customers to his store. Munk's ads often boasted that in addition to carrying the "best and latest styles," he also offered the cheapest goods. His clothing couldn't be "excelled for durability, style, quality and finish." The final reason to shop at the Lone Star Clothing Store? All his ready-made clothing was manufactured in

Mount Vernon, not in an "Eastern slop shop."

Munk took advantage of the store's name and the five-pointed star on his signs. One advertisement began "Twinkle, twinkle little star," then stated that his star never set and that no man should go "half-naked" or "look mean and feel miserable when he could dress himself for a song."

In 1860 the Munk family lived close enough to brother-in-law Adolph Wolff that a census worker visited Wolff's house first and then immediately showed up at Munk's. Leopold was thirty-five that year and worth about $4,000 (roughly $113,000 today). In addition to his wife and three children, Munk's household included Ohio-born Joseph Jacobs (age 21), who clerked for Munk. Leopold made sure that Sophia always had live-in help. Running a nineteenth-century household comprising husband, children, sister Caroline Wolff, and young clerks was the definition of work. Being able to afford a servant to help one's wife showed both love and financial success. At one time eighteen-year-old Lany Dall lived with the family, and later twenty-eight-year-old Jennie Conger was the servant.

**Above**
One of Leopold Munk's (Adolph Wolff's brother-in-law) typical advertisements.

Days before the outbreak of the Civil War, Munk ran an advertisement that today might be considered tone deaf but certainly showed his political leanings. On April 9, 1861, "No Civil War!" was the bold heading of an advertisement. A second headline read "One Star That Never Goes Down" and then lectured that "several stars illuminated in our glorious flag have paled in their hour of greatest prosperity." Munk pledged that his goods never went down and were still as cheap as always. Two years later Munk registered for the draft. A thirty-nine-year-old married man, he was classified as Class II and never called up.

Family took care of family. In 1860 Caroline Wolff, a sister of Adolph Wolff and Sophia Wolff Munk, lived in Mount Vernon at her brother's house. By 1868 she had moved next door and lived with the Munks. After a brief illness, she died on Christmas Day 1868 and was buried in Cleveland.

In February 1869 Rosetta (also known as Rosa) Munk married Marcus Cauffman of Rochester, New York, but, according to the marriage license, she was not yet eighteen, and her father applied for the document. How old was she? If she had been born in 1850, she would be eighteen. If born in 1851, it's possible that in February she wasn't yet eighteen.

Leopold certified that he was Rosetta's father and consented to the marriage. Cauffman was thirty years old--at least thirteen years Rosetta's senior. According to the *Democratic Banner*, the wedding was performed by the Rev. Dr. Meyer of Cleveland on February 24, 1869.

Or was it? A Knox County marriage license had three parts. The column on the left contained the names of the groom and bride, the date the license was issued, and the signature of a probate judge. The center section was labeled "Affidavit" and had the name of the applicant, the bride and groom's names, affirmation that the bride was of age, the date the license was issued, and the couple's signatures. The right-hand column was the "Return," and was where the wedding date of the two principals was certified by the officiant. But that part of Rosetta and Marcus' marriage license was blank!

The 1870 census added to the mystery and not just because Munk's worth was down a thousand dollars. That July all three of the Munk children still lived in his house. Twenty-year-old Rosa MUNK (not Cauffman) was enumerated as living in the household even though supposedly she had married a year before. Had the wedding taken place? I can't find another marriage license or any information about another wedding, but perhaps there had been a ceremony in another location.

Definitely, by June 1871 Rosa and Marcus were together in Rochester, New York, where their first child, David Marcus, was born. Over the next ten years, the couple had three more children, Benjamin, Harry, and Clementine. The marriage, however, did not last. On a rainy June day in 1881, so many couples' divorces became final that a local Rochester newspaper commented on the occurrence. The first couple listed was Marcus Cauffman and Rosa Munk Cauffman.

Munk's financial problems began in 1875. (This might have been part of the Long Depression that started with the panic of 1873. Eighteen thousand businesses failed between 1873 and 1875.) In January of that year, Leopold advertised "bottom prices" on his entire stock of clothing, which "will and MUST be sold." Ten days later Munk went into assignment (bankruptcy), and Benjamin Grant was appointed assignee. (The next month brother-in-law Adolph Wolff also went into assignment.) The entire Lone Star inventory was sold to pay Munk's creditors. The Lone Star Clothing Star was defunct.

In March, the local press noted that this "good Republican" was moving his family to Cleveland. In 1880 Leopold was an agent for a liquor store. Sometime within the next decade the family moved to Rochester, New York, where Leopold Munk, age 66, died and was buried. His widow, Sophia, lived with her married son Benjamin until her death in 1902.

One final anomaly--in the 1900 census Sophia stated that she immigrated in 1860! Since she was married in Ohio in 1850, that date is impossible. But it does highlight the challenge facing historians and genealogists today in trying to determine dates and ages.

**Above**
Leopold Munk's tomb in Mount Hope Cemetery, Rochester, New York.
*Findagrave*

# Aaron Stadler

## *The Second Generation of Jewish Clothiers*

Aaron Stadler

The horse and buggy stood on the grassy area between the Public Square and South Main Street. A bearded gentleman in striped trousers, suit coat, and beaver hat climbed out. He reached for his walking stick and then crossed the street to enter Stadler's One Price Clothing House. He stopped and looked at caps and hats, shirts, knee pants, suits, umbrellas, and "neckwear" in the display window on the west side of the store. Instead of entering there, he rounded the corner to see what was on display in the Main Street window. Only then did he enter the store. He knew what he wanted.

He walked down the long, narrow showroom. The overhead gas lights were lit even though three oval windows let in daylight. The wood floor creaked slightly as he walked down the main aisle. To his left were glass cases filled with shirts. One of the best clerks in town, Louis Goodfriend, was behind the counter, and turned to greet the customer by name. Piles of coats and trousers--two dozen in a pile and three piles across--lined tables from the front of the store to the back. But this man wanted a hat, and they were in hatboxes along a shelf.

This Mount Vernon John Doe liked buying at Stadler's. The clerk and **Aaron Stadler** himself knew who he was and were always courteous. What he most appreciated was that the prices of all the goods were marked in "plain figures." Price tags! There were still

**Above**
Stereoscopic photograph of Stadler's store.
*Postcard Collection of Winnifred Sturtevant*

clothing rooms in town that did not use these newfangled tags. There the clerks either knew you and your worth or took a look at you and made a decision about your wealth before they quoted a price. You could pay more or less for the same shirt than the next customer. But from the day Stadler opened for business, his motto was "strictly one price."

**"Rich and poor, high and low, smart and simple pay one and the same price."**

Aaron Stadler was a first-generation American. His parents, Moses and Cecelia, sailed from Germany and landed in New York about 1848. Instead of staying there with other Stadlers, they headed west and were settled in Urbana, Ohio, by 1852 when their first child, Aaron, was born. The family moved to Cincinnati, where Moses and two brothers started Stadler & Bros, a wholesale clothing and dry goods store. They were quite successful and by 1860 Moses's real estate holdings were worth $6,000 (about $180,000 today) and his personal wealth was $8,000 ($240,000). That was good because in addition to Aaron, there were three more children--Caroline, Gabriel, and Fannie. Two sons, Samuel and Nathan, had died as infants.

Cecelia Stadler was a thirty-year-old mother with four children--three of whom were under the age of five. Fortunately Moses could afford to pay two live-in servants. Another son, Max, was born in 1861 but only lived for a year. A final child, Henry, was born in 1864. Two years later Cecelia was dead at the age of thirty-five. She had been married for sixteen years and pregnant for twelve of them.

By 1870 Moses had a new wife, Lena, a German immigrant, and his personal worth totaled $25,000. Aaron graduated from high school and clerked in his father's store. Around 1872 Aaron left Ohio to work with a relative, Max Stadler, in his wholesale and retail clothing store in New York City. Over the next five years, he worked in every department in the store--holding positions from "trimmings" buyer to traveling salesman. By the time Aaron left, he knew every aspect of the retail business.

**Above**
Interior of Stadler's One Price Clothing Store.
*Republican Industrial Edition / Knox Co. Historical Society*

In 1877 the young bachelor and his friend Louis Goodfriend moved to Mount Vernon to open a "decidedly metropolitan emporium" where "strictly one price" was the rule. (Aaron's father had introduced "one price" in his stores in Cincinnati and Urbana.) The store opened on September 4 on the corner of Main and Public Square with an immense stock of "men's, youths', boys' and children's fine clothing."

Within a month Aaron penned a letter to the people of Knox County. "We have come among you and have come to stay. Our system of doing business has been approved . . . in every city in which we have located . . . We always do as we advertise." His business was immediately so successful that a competitor (Adolph Wolff perhaps?) gossiped that Stadler had opened his store for just a few months to "run off stock, take people's money, and leave." Stadler made sure that customers knew he was here to stay and that his business model of one price for all was what every "fair-minded person" understood.

Stadler established a personal/work pattern that lasted for decades. He visited his family in Urbana several times a year and traveled to New York or Cincinnati to buy goods twice a year. The large ads that he ran in the *Democratic Banner* repeated his business credo--his inventory was as good as custom work, his prices were cheap, and everyone paid the same price.

Aaron Stadler was a commercial success. He opened his business with one clerk, and nine months later he employed three. So in 1879 he concentrated on his personal life. A new year brought local customs to the forefront. Bachelors often hosted dinner parties at local hotels on New Year's Eve, and the next day eligible young ladies were "at home" to receive those same men (a tad weary, perhaps). Stadler and some of his gentlemen friends welcomed 1879 at the Curtis Hotel. The following day Louis Goodfriend and he visited many of Mount Vernon's unmarried women. Aaron's bachelor days, however, were numbered--forty-one to be exact.

Rodeph Shalom Synagogue in Philadelphia was part of the Moorish Revival in architecture and with its striped, Romanesque arches, it looked like the mosque at Cordoba Spain. On February 12, 1879, Aaron Stadler and Sarah Oppenheimer stood under a *chuppa* (canopy) as Marcus Jastrow, the synagogue's first rabbi, married them. After a wedding meal, the couple took a train to New York for their wedding trip before they returned to Mount Vernon.

Between visitors and trips, the next few months were busy for the newlyweds. All kinds of relatives showed up in Mount Vernon. Aaron's brother Gabe, his father Moses, his brother-in-law Isaac Henley, and Sarah's brother all visited the young couple in their Lamartine Square home. The Stadlers traveled to Cincinnati for an Exposition in September; this was one of their last out-of-town trips for a while because Sarah was pregnant. Her sister Lena arrived to help, and on Christmas Day, the Stadlers had a baby girl whom they named Celia, after Aaron's mother. At one time both Aaron's sister Fanny and Sarah's sister Lena were in Mount Vernon. Because Fanny Stadler was unmarried, she received the town's gentlemen callers at her brother's house on New Year's Day. She stayed for four months before leaving for Cincinnati to visit even more relatives.

Permission granted
to Mr. A M Stadler
and Miss Sarah Oppenheimer
to be married Febr 12 /79
Jastrow

**Above**
Aaron Stadler and Sarah Oppenheimer's marriage license 1879.
*Ancestry.com*

Aaron's business continued to flourish. His store was "synonymous with genteel appearance and square dealing." The public appreciated his one-price business model and custom-made clothing. When the fire department wanted "fancy ornamented flannel shirts" for the Fourth of July celebration (flannel in July?), Stadler won that contract. He upgraded his shop and bought large display cases. Aaron was twenty-eight years old with a lovely wife and a baby girl. He could afford two live-in servants to help his wife. Louis Goodfriend, who was worthy of his surname, boarded with the family. Life was good.

***(This is your choose your own adventure moment. You may either continue reading about the Stadlers or go to the next chapter about Lena Oppenheimer (Sarah Stadler's sister) and Lawrence Huntsberry and then return to the Stadlers. Your choice.)***

# IMPORTANT

--TO--

# PURCHASERS OF FINE CLOTHING!

IT IS A WELL KNOWN FACT that previous to our coming to Mt. Vernon, consumers of fine Clothing were obliged to leave their measure and pay exorbitant prices to Merchant Tailors. Our manner of doing business obviates the necessity of paying high prices. We make a specialty of FINE CUSTOM-MADE CLOTHING which we sell from 35 to 50 per cent. less than you can have them made to order. We are showing a large and elegant line of BUSINESS and DRESS SUITS, COATS and VESTS, FALL and WINTER OVERCOATS, ULSTERS and FINE CASSIMERE and WORSTED PANTS. These garments have been made by CUSTOM TAILORS and are equal to the best Custom Work.

**For $12 to $20 we will sell you a Suit that Merchant Tailors charge $25 to $35. For Suits that we sell from $20 to $25, Merchant Tailors charge from $38 to $50. We are selling good Overcoats well made and trimmed for $8, $9 and $10. Overcoats that we sell for $12 to $16, Merchant Tailors charge from $20 to $30. Our $15 and $20 Overcoats are the handsomest Garments to be found in the City.**

# STADLER, THE ONE-PRICE CLOTHIER!

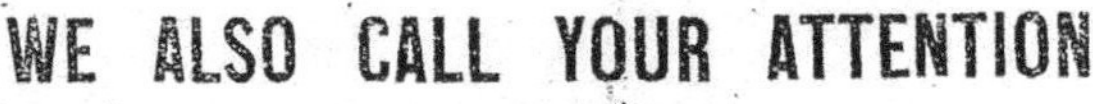

## WE ALSO CALL YOUR ATTENTION

TO OUR LARGE STOCK OF

## GENTS' FURNISHING GOODS!

Which we keep in connection with our Clothing. As we have no extra rent to pay, we can afford to sell them at a much lower price than exclusive Furnishing Good Houses. Our White Shirts and Collars we guarantee to be perfect fitting. We sell a good 4-ply Linen Collar for 10c. each, the same as others charge 20c. for. We are offering special inducements in Canton Flannel, Merino and all Wool Undershirts and Drawers. Our stock of Plain and Fancy Hosiery, Neckwear, Silk and Linen Handkerchief, Suspenders, Gloves, etc., will be found to be the most complete in the City.

**We carry a full line of medium and low-priced Suits, Pants and Overcoats. Also Boys' and Children's Clothing. Space will not admit to enumerate all articles. Call and examine our stock and prices and no fault will be found if you do not buy.**

**The price of each article is marked in plain figures, from which no deviation will be made.**

**STADLER, THE ONE-PRICE CLOTHIER,**

MAIN STREET, MT. VERNON, OHIO.

October 25, 1878.

**Above**

A typical Stadler advertisement from 1878.

*Democratic Banner*

Stadler believed a business had to spend money to make money. He believed in advertising and put the Stadler name and brand, OPCH (One Price Clothing House), wherever he could: horizontally across the facade of his store facing the square; in a large sign over the entrance on South Main Street; and the best place of all, on the gable of the wooden bridge that crossed the Kokosing River at the foot of Main Street. The bridge advertised "Stadlers One Price Clothing House" to all who crossed the river.

When most advertisements in the papers consisted of text, by 1881 Stadler's weekly advertisements contained drawings of men and boys. Customers often had chances to win gifts with their purchases at his store. Around the Fourth of July all boys left the store with the "latest

**Above**
Advertisement created by Max Stadler of New York showing a prize, a popgun, given to customers. Aaron Stadler ran the sale campaign with the same prize in Mount Vernon.
*Ancestry.com*

and best things out for boys, a perfectly harmless, attractive, amusing and durable" toy. What was this wonderful gift? It was a "Sure Pop Cane And Whip." What did it look like? What did it do? Max Stadler, the New York relative, ran the same promotional ad and even created a postcard to show the toy. (See the ad on the previous page.) In one year Aaron also gave away balls and bats, stem winding Waterbury watches, and nickel plate alarm clocks. During pumpkin season, Aaron advertised that whoever brought in the heaviest pumpkin would win a $20.00 suit. The pumpkin was then auctioned for charity and the proceeds went to the Widows and Orphans Fund of the Joe Hooker Post of the GAR.

A large crowd gathered at Stadler's on Tuesday evening of March 27, 1884, for a prize drawing. The Cooper Coronet Band played as all the tickets were placed in a box. Sam Peterman was master of ceremonies, and Harry Swetland turned the crank of the box to mix the tickets. A young boy was selected from the crowd and blindfolded, and he proceeded to pull out the winning numbers. Legrand Britton from Howard won the grand prize, a binder. H. K. Lauderbaugh of Gambier won a buggy. William Price from Sparta received a sewing machine, and H. E. Griffith from Mount Vernon won a gold watch. Two things were exceptional about this drawing. The size and cost of the prizes were significant. And Stadler's customer base was not limited to Mount Vernon but encompassed Howard (17 miles away) and Sparta (11 miles).

**Above**
Stadler's 1883 advertisement showing the prizes to be given away.
*Democratic Banner*

Aaron and Sarah's life was normal if having four children within a decade was normal--Celia (1881), Blanche (1883), Beatrice (1885), and Miles

(1891). To accommodate the growing family, they moved into a larger house at 607 North Main Street. Sarah didn't let her pregnancies stop her from traveling. After growing up in Philadelphia, she may not have enjoyed living in Mount Vernon. She took many opportunities to visit family and attend cultural events in Cincinnati and Philadelphia. Before Blanche's birth she was in Cincinnati for a "dramatic festival." She often accompanied her husband on his buying trips back East. She stayed with her family in Philadelphia for over a month as Aaron continued on to New York and then returned alone to Mount Vernon.

SELLING OUT
--AT AN--
ENORMOUS SACRIFICE
To reduce stock previous to moving into our New Room, Kirk Block, occupied by Ringwalt & Jennings.
The Greatest Bargains of the Age!
--IN--
Mens' Boys' and Children's
CLOTHING!
Preparatory to moving in February we intend to close out our entire stock within the next sixty days
At One-half of its Actual Value!
Heavy Gray Overcoats, worth \$4, now offered at \$2.
Chinchilla Overcoats, worth \$6, now offered at \$3.50.
Fur Beaver Overcoats, worth \$12, now offered at \$8.
Strong Working Suits, worth \$7, now offered at \$4.50.
Business Suits, Frock or Sack, worth \$11, now offered at \$8.
Working Pants, worth \$1.50 and \$2, now offered at \$1 and \$1.50.
Cassimere Pants, worth \$4 and \$5, now offered at \$2.50 and \$3.
Boys' and Children's Overcoats and Suits, from \$1.50 to \$6.
In Gloves, Knit Jackets. Underwear and Trunks, we allow no one to undersell us.
This IMMENSE SACRIFICE is made for the purpose of closing out the stock previous to moving, as also to open out, in our NEW ROOM, with a new and elegant stock for Spring Trade. Do not fail to attend the great sale and secure some of the best bargains ever offered to the Citizens of Knox County.
STADLER, THE ONE-PRICE CLOTHIER!
MOUNT VERNON, OHIO, January 10, 1879.

**Above**
A Stadler advertisement from 1879.
*Democratic Banner*

If necessary, Sarah would stay in town, and her family and in-laws came to her. A partial list of visitors from 1880 to 1882 includes Gabe Stadler, Clara Oppenheimer, Carrie Henley (née Stadler) and her husband Isaac, Harry Stadler, Edward Oppenheimer, Rosa Oppenheimer, Lena Stadler (Aaron's stepmother), and Fanny Oppenheimer. Not only did they visit, but several moved to town and worked with/for Aaron. In 1884 the Henleys arrived, and the next year, Clara Oppenheimer, Sarah's sister, married Louis Goodfriend. After their wedding Aaron opened a branch store in the Thrift Building in Fredericktown which his new brother-in-law managed. Business continued to come Stadler's way. He won the contract to provide one hundred "fatigue and dress uniforms" for the Kenyon Grammar School.

Aaron was ready to repay the community that welcomed his

business and his family. It was through his and John Levering's efforts that the Mount Vernon City Band performed for two days at the Ohio State Fair. But his largest civic effort was when he took responsibility for weather reports.

**Above**
Stadler's 1893 Knox County Fair advertisement.
*Democratic Banner*

Everyone understood how important it was for farmers, stockmen, shippers of perishable goods, and merchants to be forewarned about cold waves or sudden temperature drops. The Chief Signal Office in the War Department in Washington, DC, perfected a plan to telegraph such warnings to the public. All Mount Vernon City Council had to do was spend $50.00 to buy six banners. When the Council refused to spend the money, Stadler paid for the flags himself. A rope stretched from his store in the Kirk Block (where

**Above**
Stadler's advertisement on the cornice of the wooden bridge over the viaduct.
*Library of Mount Vernon and Knox County*

Park National Bank now stands) to the Curtis Hotel across the street. Stadler received daily telegrams from the War Department and then displayed the appropriate 6 x 6 foot bunting flag. At his own expense, Stadler designed and gave away a card that explained what each flag meant. Stadler also sent daily telegrams back to the US Signal Service to verify the accuracy of its predictions.

White flag with a large red sun--higher temperatures / warm
White flag with a large red crescent--lower temperatures / cold
White flag with a large red star--no change in temperatures
White flag with a large blue sun--general rain or snow
White flag with a large blue crescent--clear or fair
White flag with a large blue star--local rain or snow
White flag with black square--cold wave

Weather flags were also displayed in front of the *Banner* office, and there was often a discrepancy between the two forecasts. Stadler published a letter from the War Department that explained that he received weather reports specifically for Mount Vernon whereas the weather information the newspaper posted was taken from the Associated Press and applied to the entire Ohio Valley and Tennessee.

Everything was going well for Aaron. His sister-in-law Lena Huntsberry was safely back in Philadelphia. His family surrounded him at home and in business. He put a telephone in his business (#48) and one at his home. Aaron felt comfortable enough in town about his religion to take matzo to the *Republican* newspaper office and give them a sample of "unleavened bread used by the Hebrews in commemoration of the Feast of Passover." When an earthquake was felt in town on September 2, 1886, at 9:24 a.m., Mrs. Stadler and her children ran down from the second floor of their house into the street. Everyone was safe. The only failure Stadler had was the Fredericktown branch of his store. It closed within a year, and brother-in-law Louis Goodfriend and his wife returned to Mount Vernon.

And then this headline appeared in late July of 1887: "The Stadler Failure." At 7:30 a.m. on July 19, 1887, Stadler filed a deed of assignment to W. M. Koons. Aaron's debts of $22,848 exceeded his assets, and the business went into assignment. He owed money to everyone. The largest creditor was his sister Carrie Henley; he owed her $4,000. Ricka Hyman was owed $675, his brother-in-law Louis Goodfriend $275, his other brother-in-law Isaac Henley $235 (Could those have been for wages due?), his landlord R. C. Kirk $225 (rent due?). He owed Knox National Bank $600, William Turner $2,800, Frank Beam $50.00, J. S. Ringwalt $125.00, and Lecky Harper $35.00. All in all the list of creditors ran for two full pages. Stadler's assets were estimated to be $12,729 for the store's inventory and fixtures, $1,000 in uncollected debts, and real estate (I assume his house) of $3,734--for a total of $17,463.

Koons, the assignee, traveled to Urbana hoping to negotiate the sale of the store's inventory to Aaron's father. The visit was unsuccessful, and when the store reopened a week later, everything was on sale by order of the probate court. Stadler and his two brothers-in-law were the only clerks on the floor. The sale continued for several weeks and all money went to creditors. In September Sarah Stadler visited her father-in-law in Urbana. I believe she was sent to ask him for money because a few weeks later she had the funds to purchase all the remaining inventory from Koons. The paper announced that Stadler would be back in business and that everything would be conducted and managed as in the past and under the same name. Aaron publicly thanked his Mount Vernon friends for their "liberal patronage, good will, and confidence." Then he visited his family in Urbana. Did he

**Above**
Stadler's family home at 607 North Main Street then and now.

thank Moses for the loan? Did he sign papers about the loan? We don't know, but Stadler was back in business.

Aaron continued to

- Receive orders for uniforms for the cadets at the Military Academy in Gambier.
- Run weekly ads in the *Democratic Banner.*
- Travel East to buy new stock.
- Inform the community by putting both a telegraph and an operator in his storefront window in 1888 so citizens could have up-to-the-minute information about the Democratic and Republican National Conventions. Citizens lauded this "commendable enterprise."
- Take part in local business concerns when he was elected to the newly formed Board of Trade.
- Give away prizes--a bronze clock or a bicycle to whoever guessed the number of beans in a jar.
- Be a trend setter when he bought an automobile and actually "drove overland" to Urbana with his family.
- Travel to Cincinnati, Philadelphia, and, in 1893, to the Chicago World's Fair. Trains ran daily from Mount Vernon to Chicago on excursions set up by Colonel Leroy Hunt. The package included the train ticket, a room at the Hotel Kenyon on the corner of Michigan and 39$^{th}$ Street (which served as the headquarters for Knox County visitors), and entrance to the Exposition.

October in Ohio meant piles of leaves and children playing in those piles. In 1897 that's exactly what four-year-old Helen Critchfield and other neighborhood children did. One child lit a match and threw it on the leaf pile. The fire leapt onto Helen; the children screamed. Helen's mother ran outside when she heard the shouting and tried to help her daughter but was burned on her arms and hands. Neighbors Aaron Stadler and Melvin Beck also heard the shouts and ran to help. They grabbed a blanket from a clothesline and smothered the flames. Unfortunately the child did not survive.

What do we know about the Stadler women? When Sarah was at home, she took part in Mount Vernon's intellectual life. She belonged to the Shakespearean Society and the Monday Club where she once gave a presentation on "Conditions of Women in Germany and German Peasants." There were dinner parties, receptions, and club meetings. Daughter Celia hosted private parties and dinner/dance parties at her home. She attended Harcourt Place Seminary in Gambier although her two younger sisters attended Mount Vernon High School. After she graduated Celia lived in Philadelphia for a year before returning home in 1898 when her grandfather Moses died.

Moses Stadler was one of the best-known businessmen in Ohio. He and his two sons ran M. Stadler & Sons. Son Gabriel inherited two-thirds of the business, and Harry the remaining third. Household goods, real estate, and life insurance were divided between the two sons, daughter Fannie, and wife Lena. The rest of the estate went to grandchildren. **Aaron inherited nothing** because Moses stated in his will that during his lifetime he had given Aaron $4,600 for "services performed" and another $1,000 as an "advancement."

After ten years receiving daily telegraphic weather reports, Aaron was informed that the service would end in order to "reduce expenditures." Stadler not only posted the flags but sent out about fifty weather post cards to Knox Countians and kept daily, weekly, and monthly reports. He wrote to the War Department listing the advantages of the telegraphic service but to no avail. From then on Mount Vernon received a daily weather forecast by train, either on the 11:10 from Mansfield, the 12:32 from Millersburg, or the 1:30 from Columbus. In case of truly severe weather, Stadler would receive a telegram.

The turn of the century, 1900, meant Whist Club meetings, the Stadlers' twenty-second anniversary, Sarah's piano recitals for the Beethoven Club, Blanche's high school graduation in 1901, card parties, progressive euchre parties, thimble parties (whatever they were), and Beatrice's graduation.

Then, in 1902, a very small article taken from a Columbus newspaper appeared in the *Banner*. Aaron Stadler filed for bankruptcy. His debts were $12,600, and he had no assets. Three months later a judge in the U.S. Court in Columbus discharged A. M. Stadler from bankruptcy which meant that he was not liable for certain debts. There were some debts he had to pay, and in January 1903 an ad in the *Banner* said that $25,000 worth of goods went on sale to "satisfy the claims of creditors." The sale was successful and a month later, Stadler was back in business.

Stadler's setbacks never seemed to diminish his standing in the community. When Dan Emmett died in 1904, the funeral procession started at the Elks Club. The eight pallbearers were all Elks, and one of them was A. M. Stadler. He was named the local chairman of the

WE MUST VACATE

Our Present Premises

It is known to all that the Knox National Bank has leased the room we now occupy thus leaving us absolutely without a place in which to do business. Such are the conditions which confront us, and render imperative the quickest possible closing out

Entire New Fall And Winter Stock of Clothing For Men, Boys, Children,

Comprising all the latest styles and newest designs. This opportunity comes to you just at the proper season when you must supply your wants. The very hour when you need seasonable wearing apparel. This is a great sacrifice and loss to us, you will receive the benefit.

Greatest Harvest of Bargains Ever Offered

in the state. Overcoats, Suits, Underwear, Trousers, Mackintoshes, Gloves, Sweaters, Caps, Hats, Neckwear, Hosiery, Handkerchiefs, Suspenders, Trunks, Dress Suit Cases, Rain Coats

ALL ARE TO BE SOLD AT VACATE PRICES

Overcoats and Suits, $8 and $10 values, .......... Vacate prices $6 and $ 8
Suits and Overcoats, $12 and $15 values, .......... Vacate prices 10
Boys Overcoats, $5 and $6 values, .......... " " 3.50
Overcoats and Suits, hand-made garments, $18 and $20 values, .......... " " 15.00
Boys' Suits, $2 and $2.50 values, .......... " " 1.48
Knee Pants .......... 19c, 29c, .45
Heavy Winter Underwear, regular 25c and 35c Shirts and Drawers .......... " " 17c and .19
Heavy ribbed, fleeced 75c garments .......... " " .48
Suspenders 8c. Rubber Collars, best 19c, Handkerchiefs 3c

Pay us a visit and judge for yourself. We do as we advertise.

STADLER

CLOTHIER, HATTER & FURNISHER

Southwest corner Square and Main street. Red stamps, good as gold, for the asking.

**Above**
Stadler's announcement that his store was going out of business.
*Daily Banner, November 4, 1904*

Elks' fund to solicit money for a Dan Emmett monument, but this never came to fruition.

In November 1904 Stadler announced that he had to vacate his premises. Knox National Bank leased the room where Stadler's business was, and he had until the first of February to vacate. Aaron insisted that there were no suitable rooms on Main Street for him to rent. He ran huge sales and announced that after twenty-eight years, Stadler's was going out of business and the family would leave town. As the sale wound down, Smith Realty bought some of his stock, and the rest was sold at auction.

At first the town thought that Aaron had a job and lucrative salary as a managing partner in the True Fit Clothing Company in New Orleans. He left town in February 1905, but the rest of the family stayed until August. The New Orleans business either was a ruse or didn't work out, because when Aaron returned to town in July, he was living in New York. He now was a traveling salesman for a company that made "leather novelties" and had a territory as far west as Kansas City. Aaron was fifty-three years old. After years of owning a business bearing his name and of being the boss in the store, Aaron was now a traveling salesman with a huge territory. Surely a young man's job.

The rest of the family prepared to move to New York in August 1905. The final social event was a "handsome card party" hosted by Mrs. Ike Rosenthall to say goodbye to Sarah Stadler.

In Mount Vernon, the Stadler women never worked; they were part of the social scene. Now Sarah and all the children worked to help support the family. By 1910 Aaron was a traveling salesman for a knitting goods company, and Celia was a secretary at the same company. Blanche was the treasurer at a kindergarten, and

**Above**
Blanche Stadler's passport application in 1923.

Beatrice was a stenographer at a "fancy goods store." Miles was a clerk at a real estate agency.

Just to tie up loose ends--Beatrice died in 1912 after an operation "necessitated by an illness of short duration." Celia married in 1915 and named a daughter after her sister, Beatrice. Sarah died in 1916. By 1930 Aaron lived with his daughter Blanche, who was an elementary school teacher. Aaron died in 1934; he was eighty-one years old.

The *Democratic Banner* offered a final assessment of Aaron Stadler. He was an "aggressive citizen who always had the interests and welfare of the city at heart." He was always "ready to do his share in any movement calculated to building up the city and better the conditions of things generally." He made an impact on Mount Vernon; no such praise for him was found in any New York paper. He was sorely missed here.

*1st row* — Iva (Lewis) Deeley, Mary (Cassil) Reynard, Walter Sperry, (Cunningham) Anderson. *2nd row* — Esther (Condit) Murphy, Harry Moffitt Zadia (Moore) Hodell, Elizabeth Taft, Ida Westlake, Mona (Platt) Reese, Be land) McFeeley, Blanche Stadler. *3rd row* — Helen Anderson, Margaret (C Beck, Clellie (Brentlinger) Newton, Fred Hagaman, Harry Koons, Howard T — George Graham, Ada Graham, Harry Mitchell, Gail Freeman, Clay Parker, A field, Bertrum Rush, Norman Turner.

Blanche Stadler

**Above & Inset**
1901 senior class picture of Blanche Stadler – standing, second row, far right.
*Centennial 1958 Forum*

**Above**
Beatrice Stadler's senior class picture – standing at far left wearing glasses.
*Centennial 1958 Forum*

# Lonnie Huntsberry and Lena Oppenheimer

## *The Huntsberry Tragedy*

In the hot July days of 1880 **Lena Oppenheimer**, Sarah Stadler's "beautiful brunette" sister, came to town for a two-month visit. When their brother Abe arrived, she left and continued on to Cincinnati. She returned quickly in November to nurse Sarah, who was seriously ill. Within a month Sarah was well enough to celebrate her daughter's first birthday and accompany Aaron on a two-week trip to the Cincinnati Opera Festival. Lena stayed in Mount Vernon and was in town throughout the year as family members visited.

Perhaps a reason for some of the family's trips was to scrutinize **Lawrence** (aka Lonnie) **Huntsberry**, a well-known young man around town, who was courting Lena. Was he a suitable suitor? He was a bookkeeper for the Knox Mutual Insurance Company and lived with his elderly grandmother. (His mother had died at the age of twenty-six. There is no death record so we don't know the cause of death. Disease? Suicide? His father had died in 1873.) He was a Mason and a Knight of Pythias. Within months invitations for their wedding were sent, inviting friends to the ceremony on August 31, 1881, at 10:30 a.m. at the Stadler home on Lamartine Square. Although dubbed the "society event of the

— The society event of this week, was the marriage of our young friend Lawrence E. Huntsberry, book-keeper in the Knox Mutual Insurance office, to Miss Lena Oppenheimer, sister-in-law of Mr. Aaron M. Stadler, which occurred on Wednesday morning, at the home of Mr. Stadler, on Lamartine Square—the Rev. Dr. Bodine, of Gambier, officiating. Only the immediate relatives and a few personal friends were present to witness the ceremony. The bride was the recipient of many beautiful and useful presents. Mr. and Mrs. Huntsberry left on the 3 o'clock train, B. & O. road, for Put-in-Bay, where they will remain for two weeks.

**Above**
The Huntsberry/Oppenheimer wedding was "the society event of the week." Certainly there was no hint of the future tragedy.
*Democratic Banner*

week," this wedding presented a stark contrast to her sister's ceremony a few years earlier. This was a quiet, private affair--perhaps because the groom wasn't Jewish. A small group of friends attended, and the president of Kenyon College, William B. Bodine, officiated. After a "lavish wedding breakfast," the couple left for a two-week trip which included a stay at Put-in-Bay. They then returned to Lonnie's home on South Gay Street.

Four days after Christmas, Lena and Lonnie Huntsberry, who had been married a scant four months, woke around 7:00. The house was cold, and Lonnie said that he would get up to start the fire. Lena suggested that he stay in bed because he hadn't been feeling well; she left the bedroom to walk upstairs and get a dress from a trunk. Lonnie sat up and swung his feet to the floor. Thinking that he would shoot one of their backyard chickens for supper, he pulled out a five-barreled Smith & Wesson revolver that he kept under his pillow and examined it. Lena heard a bang but thought it was a trunk lid falling. When she walked back into the bedroom, she found Lonnie gasping on the bed and the smoking gun on the floor. "Why did I fool with that pistol?" he murmured.

Drs. Gordon and Russell arrived and examined the still-conscious

PARTIES.

Lawrence E. Huntsberry

AND

Lena Oppenheimer

LICENSE

Issued the 30 day of August A. D. 1881, to the above-named parties. C. E. Critchfield

AFFIDAVIT.

The State of Ohio, Knox County, ss.

Lawrence E. Huntsberry having made application for a LICENSE for himself and Lena Oppenheimer and being duly sworn, says that he is of the age of 21 years, and has no wife living, and that Lena Oppenheimer is of the age of 18 years, a resident of said County, and has no husband living, and that said parties are not nearer kin than second cousins.

Lawrence E. Huntsberry

Sworn to and subscribed before me, this 30th day of August A. D. 1881

C. E. Critchfield, Probate Judge.

RETURN.

No. 698

The State of Ohio, Knox County, ss.

I do hereby Certify that on the 31st day of August 1881 I solemnized the MARRIAGE of Mr. Lawrence E. Huntsberry WITH Miss Lena Oppenheimer

Wm. B. Bodine.

**Above**
Marriage license for Lawrence Huntsberry and Lena Oppenheimer.
*Knox County Records Center, Mount Vernon*

man. The 32-caliber ball had entered between Lonnie's sixth and seventh ribs and passed near the heart. The doctors believed that the bullet had "penetrated the stomach and passed in close proximity to the apex of the heart, and lodged near the spine. . . . the patient suffered a tingling and twitching sensation in the limbs and feet, similar to that complained of by President Garfield, shortly after he was shot." The doctors probed the wound but "the opening could not be penetrated over two or three inches," and the physicians said that the wound would prove fatal. They advised the distraught Lena to contact her husband's relatives. She asked one of the neighbors who had gathered in the house to send a telegram to Milo, Lonnie's younger brother in "Washington City," to come immediately. He arrived the next day.

Everything related above is exactly as the local newspapers reported under the headlines "ACCIDENTAL SHOOTING--With Probably Fatal Results" and "FATALLY SHOT--From the Careless Handling of a Revolver." Within days, however, another story circulated around town; the shooting was not an accident but a suicide attempt. And Lonnie's life from the day of the shooting onwards supported a melancholy/suicide theory. Because, to everyone's surprise, Lonnie Huntsberry didn't die.

His condition did not worsen, and Lonnie spent several fairly comfortable days before his temperature spiked at 104 degrees. The bullet had not been found, and the doctors feared blood poisoning. After an examination, they determined that an abscess had formed near his spine. When it was drained, Lonnie's condition improved, and the doctors talked to Lena about a possible recovery.

Two months after the "accident" Lonnie was allowed out of bed, and he walked the few blocks downtown from his Gay Street house and told well-wishers that he hoped to be back at work in a few weeks. Did he also tell people that Lena was pregnant?

The first of March arrived, and Lonnie returned to the Knox County Mutual Insurance Company. However, by July his behavior had become strangely erratic. He felt a "horrible inclination to commit self-destruction." Lena and their friends tried to keep him occupied so he wouldn't contemplate suicide. Finally he needed round-the-clock supervision, and he confirmed that the December shooting had been

Lawrence E. Huntsberry, of Mt. Vernon, who attempted suicide some time ago, has been adjudged insane.

**Above**
Huntsberry's insanity adjudgment was even mentioned in the Newark paper.
*Daily Advocate, July 6, 1882*

a "deliberate attempt at suicide while in a fit of melancholy." He stood before the Probate Court at an inquest of lunacy, was adjudged insane, and asked to be sent to the Columbus Mental Asylum where he hoped that "careful confinement and proper treatment" would be beneficial. One of the trustees at the asylum volunteered to accompany Huntsberry to Columbus and see him settled.

Lena had been "inconsolable" during the last few months of her pregnancy. Lonnie was sent to the Columbus Mental Asylum and was there in August 1882 when his daughter Hortense was born in Mount Vernon. After Christmas, a year after the suicide attempt, Lena took her child and returned to Philadelphia. For personal and societal reasons, she said she was a widow.

Two weeks later Lonnie returned to Mount Vernon but soon recognized he wasn't ready to be home and asked to return to the hospital. He boarded a train, but when it stopped in Newark, he disembarked and wandered around the depot. Dr. Bosley, who knew him, saw him at the station and put him back on the train to Columbus. He arrived safely at Union Depot, checked his valise, turned around, and walked out of town. He stopped in Galena and wrote his grandmother that he was coming home. Would she send him a ticket? But then he continued walking towards Centerburg. It was mid-January in Ohio. Freezing temperatures, snow, gray skies are the norm. A friend out driving his sleigh met Lonnie and drove him to Bangs, but Huntsberry refused his offer of a train ticket. Exhausted and cold, Lonnie lay down in the road until a farmer found him and took him in for the night.

Next day he asked directions to Mount Vernon and arrived--about five days after his wanderings began--"exhausted and in a most pitiable state," at his uncle's house. Two days later a friend accompanied him back to Columbus. The asylum allowed its patients considerable liberty, and in June 1883, Lonnie again walked away. He traveled through Utica, Fredericktown, Independence, and Bellville before friends found him and took him back to Columbus. He was still there a year later, but his mental health had improved enough for him to work as an assistant drug clerk.

Lena and Hortense now lived in Philadelphia. Lonnie was released from the Columbus hospital and by 1894 he, too, lived in Philadelphia. Perhaps this was to allow him to see his daughter. On a visit back to Mount Vernon, Huntsberry told locals that he worked in a department store. This was not true. From at least 1895 to 1911, Lonnie lived at the Pennsylvania Hospital (a psychiatric hospital) and worked as a clerk, then a waiter, and finally as an elevator operator there. Amazingly he outlived his wife. Lena died in 1907 "after many years of suffering," according to her obituary; she was fifty-three. Lawrence Huntsberry spent his final years in the Ohio Masonic Home in Springfield, Ohio, where he died in February 1927. His family plot is in Mound View Cemetery in Mount Vernon. All the family names are on one stone--father R. D. (1832–1873), mother Marion P. (1837–1863--look how young she was), Milo K. (1856–1909), and Lawrence. Even though his burial date is not on the family headstone, Lawrence's body was brought home, and he was interred on February 12, 1927.

**Above**
The Huntsberry family headstone in Mound View Cemetery, Mount Vernon, Ohio.
*Photo by the Author*

# Louis Goodfriend

## *Aaron Stadler's Really Good Friend*

How long did it take for a store to earn a reputation for fairness and service? To gain a community's trust that a clerk was honest and knowledgable? This didn't happen overnight, and in a small town in central Ohio those accolades had to be earned daily with every customer who entered Stadler's One Price Clothing House. Then word-of-mouth would do the rest.

Young, popular, and Jewish--those adjectives described **Louis Goodfriend**, who lived in Mount Vernon from 1877 until 1889. On August 9, 1878, the *Democratic Banner* noted that the twenty-five-

**Above**
As a child in New York, Louis saw the 1863 draft riot and the burning of the Colored Orphan Asylum on July 13, the first day of the riot.
*Mapping The African-American Past*

year-old Louis Goodfriend, "the popular clerk at Stadler's," left for two weeks to visit family and friends in New York. To have already earned the "popular" label, Goodfriend must have worked for some months in Stadler's clothing store at the southwest corner of Main and Public Square. And since Aaron Stadler had announced only a year earlier that his business had "come . . . to Mount Vernon . . . and had come to stay," Louis must have moved to Mount Vernon around 1877.

Both Stadler and Goodfriend were ready to make lives for themselves in Mount Vernon. On the first of January local unmarried ladies received bachelors at their homes. The men made their rounds, enjoying the ladies' attentions and paying them appropriate compliments. On January 3, 1879, two of those bachelors were A. M. Stadler and Louis Goodfriend. After Stadler married Sarah Oppenheimer in February, Louis became one of the few eligible Jewish bachelors in town. Later that year Goodfriend left on vacation to visit Urbana and other cities. This probably was not just a vacation because Aaron Stadler's father, a successful clothier, lived in Urbana. What business Goodfriend conducted there is unknown, but the trip indicated the level of trust Stadler had with his friend. Within a year, Louis was living with the Stadlers at 607 North Main Street.

A popular sales clerk, a trusted employee, and eventually a respected husband, Louis Goodfriend lived in Knox County for a dozen years. He was born in 1852 in New York City--the third of six children of Samuel and Zeporah (Deborah) Goodfriend. In the 1860 census Samuel was listed as a laborer, but ten years later the census listed him as a cattle dealer/drover. In 1863 the family lived only four blocks away from the Colored Orphan Asylum at Fifth Avenue and 43rd Street. The eleven-year-old Louis witnessed the New York draft riots that July and watched the orphanage burn down within twenty minutes. Sometime in the next decade he must have met Aaron Stadler, who was working in Max Stadler's New York store. The young men were co-workers who became friends, and when Aaron moved to Mount Vernon, Goodfriend came with him. Throughout their professional and personal lives, Louis was Aaron's good friend.

What would a typical work day have been like for Louis? He lived with his friend and employer. Meals were prepared by the cook, Julia

Gill, and his room was cleaned and his clothes were washed and ironed by the seventeen-year-old servant, Ellen Skelly. He walked downtown to the store, perhaps opened it, swept the sidewalks, straightened the inventory, and checked price tags. This "one-price" establishment made sure "that customers can not be imposed upon as all goods are marked in plain figures."

And for fun? One of the highlights of 1880 was the Leap Year (called *bessextile* in the local paper) Party held in April. Societal and gender roles were reversed for this dinner dance. The women, as always, prepared the meal, because even role reversal could neither imagine nor ask the men to cook. The ladies outdid themselves with cakes, sandwiches, bonbons, and ice cream. After the meal, the Columbus Cadet Band Orchestra played, and the gentlemen followed dance etiquette usually prescribed for women. The men were escorted by the women, who initiated all conversation and dance requests. The ladies were reminded to "show due sympathy for wall flowers" and to remember to "place the men under the care of a chaperone" if not dancing. Showing that they recognized the silliness of the rules, the distaff committee wrote that "gentlemen who do not dance are supposed to be radiantly grateful for any stray notice accorded them." Continuing the role reversal, the newspaper created fake descriptions of the men's attire. Louis Goodfriend was described as a "lovely brunette of pure spirituelle [*sic*] type" wearing a "short jacket with decollete with a gray merino vest stitched with turkey red cotton around the throat." From the other descriptions in the paper of what Goodfriend truly wore to the gala, we can assume this account had no validity whatsoever.

In the beginning of December, Louis's older brother, Jacob, a salesman who traveled in the South, stopped in Mount Vernon to visit. Louis took his brother to Stadler's "beautiful room" in the Kirk Building with its large show windows and ample inventory of "fancy linens and fine silk handkerchiefs, neckties, mufflers, fancy stock, and fine suspenders" and all kinds of ready-made clothing.

Over the next several years, Goodfriend's life was uneventful. He was included in a list of prominent Mount Vernon bachelors in 1882 and received a "handsome bunch of forget-me-nots" from a secret admirer in New York City at the first of the year. He left Mount Vernon for a two-week trip to the South in July 1883. He wanted to be in Louisville, Kentucky, for the opening of Louisville's Southern Exposition on August 1. He paid his 50 cents to enter the forty-five-acre venue devoted to art, industry, and agriculture. Perhaps he was one of the thousands who watched President Chester Arthur pull a silken cord which started some of the machinery. Hopefully he stayed into the evening and saw Edison's 4,600 incandescent light bulbs illuminate the night.

Still listed as one of Mount Vernon's eligible bachelors in 1884 (although not the foremost bachelor in town--that honor went to William Banning because of his "independent income"), Louis generously volunteered to work at the C.A.&C. shops on New Year's Day. He spent most of the day alone; his only customer was an employee of the railroad's boiler shop who wanted to purchase a trip pass to Akron. In February the Ohio River crested at seventy-one feet in Cincinnati, and Louis was among the hundreds of tourists who flocked to see the flooding. In April he took a train to Columbus specifically to see the elephants at the Sells Brothers Circus.

Two months later Goodfriend's life changed when Clara Oppenheimer traveled from Philadelphia to visit her sister, Mrs. Aaron Stadler. Louis no longer lived with the Stadlers, but he certainly met and was charmed by Clara.

In January of 1885 Aaron Stadler announced that he would open a branch store in Fredericktown in the Thrift Building and that Louis would be the manager. Louis moved to Fredericktown and worked six days a week but spent most Sundays in Mount Vernon. The *Banner* teased that Goodfriend "couldn't stand it over Sunday without visiting his Mt. Vernon girl." That girl was Clara Oppenheimer.

In March 1885 Louis traveled to Philadelphia and obtained a marriage license. He was thirty-two and Clara, who had been born in Germany, was twenty. They were married at Congregation Rodeph Shalom in Philadelphia on August 12, 1885. A week later the newlyweds were back in Mount Vernon and stayed with the Stadlers on North Main Street. It must have been a lively household because another sister, Rosa, had traveled from Philadelphia with the bride and groom.

Within a week the Goodfriends moved to Fredericktown to enjoy "all the connubial joy possible."

The couple was happy, but the branch store was not a financial success and in less than nine months, it closed. The Goodfriends returned to Mount Vernon and lived at 606 North Main Street directly across from the Stadlers. Clara Goodfriend was pregnant and probably appreciated having her sister across the street. Family members visited often. Aaron's younger brother Simon, a reporter for the Chicago Tribune, came before the baby, Morton, was born on June 28, 1886. Jacob Stadler, who lived in Alabama, visited afterwards. Louis and Clara's second and last child, Corine Rosa, was born in February 1889, and relatives showed up to help Clara and meet the baby.

Then something happened in the summer of that year. Simon Goodfriend, now a reporter for the *New York Sun*, had just been on a world trip with major-league, all-star baseball players to promote this truly American game. Sponsored by Albert G. Spalding, who also wanted to promote his new sporting goods stores, the tour started in Chicago

**Above**
Klara (Clara) Goodfriend, a dignified matron.
*From a Private Collection*

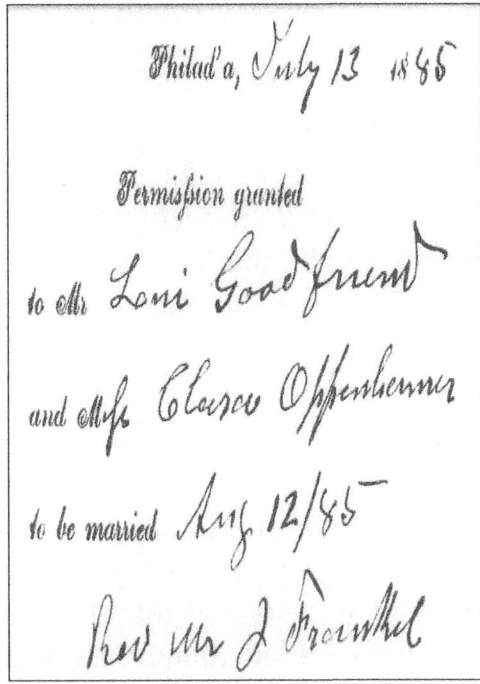

Philad'a, July 13 1885

Permission granted

to Mr Loui Goodfriend

and Miss Clara Oppenheimer

to be married Aug 12/85

Rev Mr J Frankel

**Above**
Marriage license of Louis Goodfriend and Clara Oppenheimer.
*Ancestry.com*

**Above**
One of the last photographs of Louis Goodfriend. Note his thin face and dark, sunken eyes showing the ravages of tuberculosis.
*Ancestry.com*

and headed west to Hawaii, Australia, Egypt, and then on to Naples, Rome, Paris, London, Glasgow, Belfast, and Dublin. Before Simon returned to New York in July, he stopped in Mount Vernon to see his brother. He noticed Louis's appearance and perhaps asked about his health. He must have said something to Louis because within a month Louis announced that he was moving back to New York City. He gave no reason for his decision, but his family still lived in New York, and, perhaps, there were fears about Louis's health. The first mention of this decision was noted in the *Republican* on July 27. The newspaper wished him success and noted that he would probably engage in business, although "he has not fully decided as to his future movements." Without a job in hand, the Goodfriend family left Mount Vernon on August 8.

There was nothing in any paper about Louis Goodfriend until three years later, in November 1892, when his brother-in-law Aaron Stadler announced that he had received word that Louis was seriously ill and would not recover.

Three months later the news arrived of Louis's death from consumption on February 17, 1893, at the age of forty-two. He was survived by his wife and four-year-old daughter. Son Morton had died in 1890 at the age of four. In accordance with Jewish tradition, Louis was buried immediately. He left his wife a $1,000 insurance policy (worth about $25,000 today)

The papers mentioned that Louis had had a long illness, and probably the ravages of consumption were evident when Simon was in Mount Vernon a few years earlier. Perhaps the brothers agreed that Louis needed to be near his family for his remaining years and that Clara would eventually need their support too.

The Goodfriend family took care of the widow and her daughter. In 1900 Clara and Cora lived with two of Louis's brothers, Myer and Joseph, on East 125th Street in Manhattan. Myer, a diamond merchant, made yearly trips to Europe, and when Cora was 17, he took her with him on a buying trip abroad. In the following decade, mother and daughter lived in Newark, New Jersey, with brothers-in-law Myer and Simon. By 1920 Cora had married Lou Kohn, and Clara lived with them and her granddaughter Judith.

# David Kahn

## *The First Absentee Clothier*

**David Kahn** was exactly the kind of businessman whom the local clothiers disliked. Kahn lived in Cincinnati, where he was a partner in the wholesale business of Kahn, Nathan & Company. He opened a retail business in Mount Vernon in 1879 but never moved here with his wife Hannah and their children.

The *Democratic Banner* announced in May 1879 that Kahn would open a store in a corner room of the Ward Block on the corner of Main and Vine Street. He hired Dennis Quaid (yes, his real name), a "popular and attentive salesman," as manager. The store's name, *The Star Square Dealing Clothing House*, was a branding disaster. Within two years it was renamed the *Lucky Clothing Store*--complete with a new logo, a golden horseshoe.

According to his passport application in 1912, David Kahn was born in Germany on October 29, 1839, and came to America when he was fifteen. In 1865 he lived and worked in Sidney, Ohio and became a naturalized citizen there. By 1869 he was in Cincinnati and married to Ohio-born Hannah Ranschoff. In 1870 Kahn ran a clothing store while his wife was a homemaker, taking care of their first child, Solomon. David's personal estate was valued at $1,000 (about $18,500 today) and, interestingly, his wife's personal estate was also listed as $1,000 and her real estate wealth totaled another thousand dollars. Either the census enumerator placed the real estate value on the wrong line (hers instead of her husband's), or she had her own wealth--which might have been useful because the family ultimately included seven children.

Kahn certainly was an absentee businessman but often took the train to Mount Vernon to check his store. He boasted that his prices were "below any one's West of the Allegheny Mountains" and that his store sold the "nobbiest [superior] neckwear." Kahn's advertisements assured the public that his manufactured, ready-made clothing was equal to "custom work."

Even though Kahn did not live in Mount Vernon, he insisted that his store close on the Jewish High Holy Days. The following notice appeared in the *Banner* on September 21, 1882.

> *We the undersigned will close our places of business from 6 p.m. Friday until 6-30 p.m on Saturday on account of holiday.*
>
> *A. M. Stadler*      *D. Kahn & Co.*
> *M. Hyman*      *S. Weill*
> *I & D Rosenthall*

All the signees were Jewish merchants in town; they were closing for *Yom Kippur*, the Day of Atonement. The stores had also closed ten days earlier for *Rosh Hashanah*, the Jewish New Year. For several years Jewish merchants always placed announcements informing their customers about their stores' closings. The businesses reopened after sundown when the Holy Day ended.

In addition to announcing store hours, local newspapers often ran informative articles explaining Rosh Hashanah and Yom Kippur to their readers. The papers had problems deciding how to refer to Mount Vernon Jews. They were "our Hebrew fellow citizens," "Israelites," "people of that faith," "Jewish fellow citizens," "the faithful," "fellow citizens of that religious faith," "Jewish citizens," "Hebrews of this city" and my favorite, "Israelitish friends." Trying to decide how to spell the holidays' names was a phonetic nightmare. Rosh-a-Shone, Rosh Hashona (pretty close), and Yung Kepper for Yom Kippur were all tried until the papers decided to simply refer to the holidays as the Jewish New Year and Day of Atonement.

The *Banner* wrote, "Last Monday being Atonement Day in the Jewish calendar, and observed by the Israelites to this day, the more strict of this sect closed their places of business until six o'clock in the evening that they might more devoutly observe the day of fasting." Did that mean some less-strict Jews didn't close their stores? Adolph Wolff never announced that his store closed.

Even though most of the clothiers in town were Jewish, that did not stop them from advertising against other Jewish-owned

TELEGRAM!

Announcing the Largest Arrival of

Fine, Ready-Made

CLOTHING

HATS, CAPS,

And Gent's Furnising Goods. in the City. Your attention is called to the same, and a visit solicited.

No trouble to show Goods at the

Lucky Clothing House

—OF—

D. KAHN & CO.,

SIGN OF THE

GOLDEN

HORSE-SHOE.

**Above**
A typical Kahn ad in 1880.
*Democratic Banner*

businesses they considered fly-by-night operations--ones that opened quickly, undersold their competition, were not committed enough to live in Mount Vernon, and soon disappeared.

That is what happened to the Lucky Clothing Store. In November 1883 the "People of Knox County" read that Kahn's store would hold a closeout sale and that this was a chance for customers to save money. Within a few weeks, the store shut down in Mount Vernon.

Kahn continued working in Cincinnati, and by 1900 he had retired with enough money that he could state that he had his own income. When he applied for a passport in 1912, he was seventy-two years old, stood 5'8", and had gray hair and mustache. From his arrival in Ohio until his death in 1920, his life centered around Cincinnati. Mount Vernon was just a side show.

# Marx Leopold

## *Immigrant, Soldier, Clothier*

He was born **Marx Leopold** (pronounced *Lay-pold*) in Worrstardt, Bavaria, in May 1837. He died Max Leopold (pronounced *Leo-pold*) in Mount Vernon on June 28, 1877. His journey was not unique for a nineteenth-century German Jew, but the glimpses of his Ohio sojourn offer some interesting variations in the usual narrative.

There were two Marx Leopolds in Ohio at the same time. One was in Sandusky, Ohio, and the other one in Mount Vernon. One arrived around 1856 and the other around 1860. One declared his intention to become an American citizen in Van Wert, Ohio in 1857. And one lived in Fremont, Ohio, in 1860. Unable to definitively sort out immigration and naturalization dates, I believe the Fremont Marx Leopold is Mount Vernon's Marx Leopold.

In 1860 Leopold was a twenty-two-year-old merchant living in Fremont. With a net worth of $200 (roughly $5,500 in today's currency), Marx was ready to start out on his own. A bachelor with no family in Ohio, he could settle wherever he wanted. He was definitely in Mount Vernon on July 28, 1862, when a meeting was held at the courthouse to raise money for the Union war effort. Leopold donated $23.00 (about $530) to the cause.

Why did Marx choose to settle here? Perhaps he had heard that F. Buschman, who owned a clothing store in the Kenyon House (on the southwest corner of South Main and the Public Square--where Park National Bank now stands), was ready to sell because on September 30, 1862, the Kenyon Clothing Store "passed into the hands of M. Leopold," who was "determined to keep up the former . . . reputation selling the lowest living prices." Over the next year Leopold devoted his time to his "first-class establishment" and advertised in both local papers to announce his stock of "superior goods."

Then in February 1864, Max (as he was now called) Leopold

enlisted in the Union Army. More specifically he joined the 142nd Ohio Volunteer Infantry under the command of local lawyer William C. Cooper. The enlistees served for one hundred days and like today's National Guard were tasked with protecting supply lines, allowing regular soldiers to fight with General Grant as he pushed to capture Richmond, Virginia. According to the *Banner*, "most of the young men of Mt. Vernon, married and single, are members of the Guard," and Max was one of them.

He traveled to Columbus on May 13 to report for duty with the rest of K Company. The next day the regiment moved out to Martinsburg, West Virginia. Four days later they were in Washington, D.C., and then continued on to Fort Lyon near Alexandria, Virginia. The men guarded rail lines in that state and then marched to Petersburg, Virginia, where they came under heavy fire defending supply trains. Then they moved on to Point of Rocks, Virginia, and worked at an observation post. Their one hundred days were up in August; the regiment returned to Columbus and mustered out on September 2, 1864. Forty-two

**Above**
Civil War draft registration showing Marx Leopld's name in row 10.
*Ohio Civil War Roster / Ohio Genealogical Society*

**Above**
Leopold was in the Kenyon House in 1865.
*Democratic Banner*

enlisted men had died--all from disease--but Max Leopold returned to Mount Vernon healthy and having shown his patriotism for his adopted country not only with a donation but also in service.

Perhaps the fighting and dying he had seen convinced Max it was time to start a family. How he met his future wife, the daughter of a Cleveland grocer, remains a mystery. (Perhaps a Jewish family here knew a Jewish family there, and someone invited Max to Cleveland…) Celia (sometimes spelled Zelia) Tuch was born in Ohio around 1845 and was the second child of Max and Etta Tuch, German immigrants. In 1860, she lived in Cleveland's First Ward with her parents and siblings Simeon, Fanny, Esther, and Moses. In October 1866 she and Max were married in Cuyahoga County by Rabbi G. M. Cohen. Max brought his bride back to Mount Vernon to a changed life. His bachelor days were over; he never anticipated business reversals.

Leopold & Co. had been housed at the Kenyon House since 1862. Selling the standard inventory of all clothiers and with a motto of not being "undersold here or elsewhere," Max provided healthy competition to the other merchants in town. And in November 1865 one of them, Adolph Wolff, bought the Kenyon House. There was no way Leopold could stay in that building. He would have to find a new

THE STATE OF OHIO, } *SS.*
CUYAHOGA COUNTY,

*Marx Leopold having made application for a* **Marriage License** *for himself and Celia Fuch of said County, and being duly sworn, on his oath, says that he is of the age of twenty-one years, that he has no wife living, that said C is of the age of eighteen years, that she has no husband living, and that the parties are not nearer of kin than first cousins, as he verily believes.*

*Subscribed and sworn to, the* 15 *day of* Oct, 1866, *before me,*

PROBATE JUDGE.

D Tarr DEPUTY CLERK.

M. Leopold

**Above**
Marx Leopold and Celia Fuch's marriage license in Cleveland.
*Ancestry.com*

"stand" downtown for business.

For the next few months Leopold awaited the birth of his first child and tried to find a new site for his store. In March, he held a huge sale to reduce inventory before his first move. The next month his stand was in a "new establishment next door to George's grocery" (on the southeast corner of Main and Gambier where La Paloma is now). In June, he moved again to rooms "formerly occupied by Sapp & Company, one door south of J. E. Woodbridge's dry goods store." He stayed there until the end of the year, when he moved for the third and final time into the "new and elegant room" in the Woodward Block--perhaps to the very space formerly occupied by Adolph Wolff.

**Above**

A typical Leopold advertisement from 1868.

*Democratic Banner*

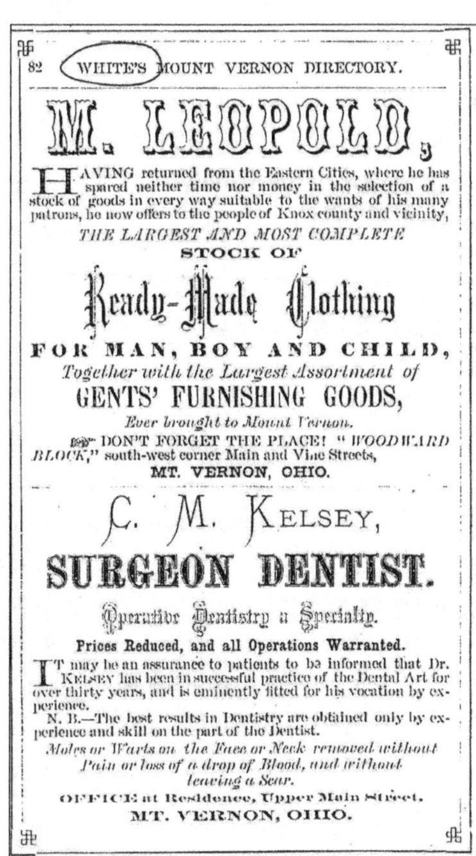
82 WHITE'S MOUNT VERNON DIRECTORY.

M. LEOPOLD,

HAVING returned from the Eastern Cities, where he has spared neither time nor money in the selection of a stock of goods in every way suitable to the wants of his many patrons, he now offers to the people of Knox county and vicinity,

*THE LARGEST AND MOST COMPLETE*
STOCK OF
Ready-Made Clothing
FOR MAN, BOY AND CHILD,
*Together with the Largest Assortment of*
GENTS' FURNISHING GOODS,
*Ever brought to Mount Vernon.*

DON'T FORGET THE PLACE! "*WOODWARD BLOCK*," south-west corner Main and Vine Streets,
MT. VERNON, OHIO.

C. M. KELSEY,
SURGEON DENTIST.
Operative Dentistry a Specialty.
Prices Reduced, and all Operations Warranted.

IT may be an assurance to patients to be informed that Dr. KELSEY has been in successful practice of the Dental Art for over thirty years, and is eminently fitted for his vocation by experience.

N. B.—The best results in Dentistry are obtained only by experience and skill on the part of the Dentist.

*Moles or Warts on the Face or Neck removed without Pain or loss of a drop of Blood, and without leaving a Scar.*

OFFICE at Residence, Upper Main Street.
MT. VERNON, OHIO.

**Above**

Leopold's advertisement in White's 1876 Mount Vernon Directory.

Business was good once Leopold found a permanent site. And life was good at home on the corner of Gay and Vine Streets with the birth of his second son, Albert. The 1870 census presented a clear picture of the Leopold household. He lived in the First Ward--just a few houses north from Adolph Wolff. At thirty-three Leopold had a net worth of $5,000 (over $95,000) which supported his wife and their two sons, Lawrence and Albert, and Celia's younger siblings who lived with them. Seventeen-year-old Esther, younger brother Moses, and their twenty-four-year-old sister Fanny with her husband Louis Strauss all lived with Mr. and Mrs. Leopold. Two years younger than Max, Louis worked in a retail notion store. Since Leopold & Co. was always listed as a clothier store, Louis probably did not work for his brother-in-law but at a different establishment in town. Remember his name; Louis would play an important role seven years later when Max died.

Knowing the end of the story--that Max died in 1877--gave the remaining years a certain poignancy as I searched for clues about his life. But, of course, there was nothing unusual to be found.

Max was one of the advertisers listed at the bottom of the 1871 Mount Vernon map. Listed as "M. Lapold," he stated that "all orders will be promptly filled when ordered." In newspaper advertisements, he was listed as a merchant/tailor who had "cutting done to order on short notice." He traveled east and purchased $20,000 worth of "ready-made clothing" for his store. To counter Adolph Wolff's moniker of "clothing king," Leopold styled himself the "Boss Clothier" and the "People's Clothier." He announced that he sold men's, boys', and children's ready-made clothing cheap, and he gained a reputation as a fair and honorable businessman. In November 1872, one of his young sons fell fifteen feet from a second-story window but wasn't hurt. Life for the Leopold family was good.

The last two weeks of June 1877 were typical for central Ohio. Temperatures were in the high, humid 80s, and thunderstorms rolled through the county, uprooting trees, tearing down fences, and breaking some windows in the Banning Building. A derrick stood on the Square to slowly raise the soldiers' monument which would be completed on June 28--the soldier's face veiled until the Fourth of July celebration.

And sometime on Tuesday, June 19, Max Leopold had a stroke, an "attack of paralysis" which left him unconscious and paralyzed on his left side. He lingered for ten days but died on June 29. The *Banner* wrote that death resulted "from the drying up of a chronic abscess in his head; the same breaking inwardly causing paralysis." Probably neither Max nor Celia knew that she was pregnant with their third child.

Because there was no Jewish cemetery in Mount Vernon, the body of one of Mount Vernon's "most popular and prominent businessmen" was accompanied to the C.Mt.V.&C. depot (south of the viaduct) by his family and fellow I.O.O.F. Lodge members. Taken to Cleveland, he was buried in the Willet Street Cemetery, Cleveland's first Jewish cemetery. The widow then returned to Mount Vernon to close the store and prepare to move to Cleveland. Celia was appointed "administratix" by the Probate Court to settle the business's accounts.

To appreciate what happened next, one must understand something about nineteenth-century retail practices. If you walked into any clothier in 1877 and picked up an item--perhaps a suit, hat, traveling trunk, or vest--you would ask a clerk the cost because there were no price tags. And the sales clerk quoted a price. Would it be the same price for everyone? Probably not. Clerks knew the cost of the goods, and they knew their customers. They knew who could afford to pay a little more than others and would adjust prices higher or lower to make a sale. Not until three months after Leopold's death--when Aaron Stadler came to town, put price tags on his merchandise, and boasted about being the "One Price Clothier"--would there be price uniformity in the stores.

At Max Leopold's death, the inventory had to be appraised. Louis Strauss, Celia's brother-in-law who had once lived in the Leopold household but now lived in Cleveland, and a Philadelphia cousin, Simon Leopold, arrived to console the widow. Max owed Simon $2,300, and because Simon was eager to return to Philadelphia as soon as possible, he volunteered to help Louis and the three men who had been appointed by the court to appraise the goods. Two of the men, J. J. Fultz and Dennis Quaid, had worked for Leopold & Co., and the third, John Denny (sometimes spelled Denney), worked as a salesman for a dry goods establishment.

**Above**
Celia Leopold's application for her husband's Civil War pension.
*Ancestry.com*

Inventory began immediately

as the three men touched all the goods, gave a count, and then told the price of the goods, which Strauss recorded. At some point, the clerks felt that Strauss wasn't recording the prices accurately. Nothing was said, but the next day Fultz kept a second ledger where he surreptitiously recorded prices on a slip of paper. After about thirty items had been priced, and immediately after Denny had called out "thirty-eight coats at $3.50 each," he approached Strauss's desk and asked to see the last entry. Strauss replied that everything was fine, turned the pages of the book, and began looking for something. Denny grabbed the log and saw that the thirty-eight coats had been listed at $2.75--75 cents less than the appraised value. Strauss explained that he simply recorded what he heard, but when Fultz's second copy was revealed, all thirty entries for that day were at least 25 to 30 percent below the appraiser's valuations. Strauss and Leopold said that Fultz and Quaid's prices were too high, that the lower prices were more accurate, and that they were simply acting in Mrs. Leopold's interests.

The *Democratic Banner* minced no words in labeling Strauss's and Leopold's action as "infamous and dishonest." Their actions would "swindle a distressed, heart-broken woman who had just buried her husband . . . and wrong other creditors." The appraisement stopped immediately, and Mrs. Leopold was replaced as the executor by Judge C. E. Critchfield, who assured all that the business would be settled in a "fair and honorable manner." What happened to Strauss and Leopold? Perhaps they wisely left town.

I've read the account dozens of times to see if there was any hint of anti-Semitism in the newspaper. But from the ironic headline, "A New Way to Mark Goods," to the end of the article, the attitude is more that Mount Vernon's small-town boys weren't taken in by the big-city slickers.

Critchfield ran an administrator's sale for the next three months, pricing all goods below cost, and then sold the remaining inventory to one of Adolph Wolff's sons who worked in Indiana. In November 1877, accompanied by her younger brother Moses (called Mosey by the local papers), the thirty-four-year-old widow and her children moved to Cleveland to a house beside her parents' home. It is here that Etta M. (perhaps her middle name was in memory of her father

**Above**
Marx's headstone in Cleveland. You can just make out "at Mount Vernon" at the bottom.
*Ancestry.com*

Marx) Leopold was born in April 1876. Moses returned to Mount Vernon for a while to work for J. H. Milless and Company, which moved into Leopold's old stand in the Woodward Block.

Other than a visit nine years later by Lawrence Leopold to "renew old acquaintances," Leopold & Company disappeared from the history of Mount Vernon.

**Above**
Celia Leopold's headstone in Cleveland.
*Ancestry.com*

# Samuel Weill

## *The Head of the Weill / Hyman Clan*

When **Samuel Weill** died at the age of seventy in 1901, his widow Fannie provided information for his obituary. According to Fannie, Samuel was born May 5, 1830, in Kipenheim, Baden, Germany, and immigrated in 1848. He settled in New Orleans and spent the early years of the Civil War there, where he was in charge of Confederate mail contracts for New Orleans and surrounding areas. In 1866 he moved to St. Louis, where he lived for several years, and later moved on to Dayton. He arrived in Mount Vernon in 1872 and opened a grocery business. In 1876 he married Fannie Wechler of Columbus and the couple eventually had four children, only one of whom, Julius, was still alive when his father died.

My first thought when I read the obituary was that there was no mention of Samuel's first wife, Caroline. Understandable. They had been childless; Caroline had committed suicide and Samuel's second marriage to Fannie lasted twenty-five years. Why bring Caroline's name up at all?

Then I found one error. Fannie thought Samuel had arrived in Mount Vernon in 1872, but Caroline and he must have been living here two years earlier because they are listed in the 1870 census in Knox County. This was certainly a minor error, and it's plausible that second-wife Fannie would not have known or remembered the exact date. But could there be other errors in the obituary?

Caroline Weill's obituary appeared in the *Democratic Banner* on June 4, 1875. I assume that Samuel provided the information. Caroline Weill, née Brodenheimer, was born in Germany and immigrated to the United States in 1851 when she was twenty-two. She married Samuel in 1853 in New Orleans. They were only there for about eighteen months and then moved to Memphis until 1863. Then on to Dayton, until the couple arrived in Mount Vernon in 1869. That date is corroborated by the national census of 1870. So Fannie was wrong there. Were there other discrepancies?

| **Caroline's Obituary (1875)** | **Samuel's Obituary (1901)** |
|---|---|
| | immigrated in 1848 |
| married in New Orleans 1853 | lived in New Orleans |
| | handled Confederate mail |
| lived in Memphis 1855–1863 | lived in St. Louis 1866–1868 |
| lived in Dayton | lived in Dayton 1868–1872 |
| moved to Mount Vernon 1869 | moved to Mount Vernon 1872 |

Did Samuel and Caroline ever live in St. Louis as Fannie thought? I found no information to support that they had. However, there was a childless couple, Sam and Caroline Wile [*sic*], who lived in Memphis, Tennessee, in 1860. Both of those respondents were born in Germany and were the correct age. Those facts supported the details Samuel, who certainly knew where he had lived, provided for his first wife's obituary.

Caroline's obituary said she had lived in Dayton. There was a Samuel Weill who lived in Dayton, was a shoemaker, and joined the Union Army. Nothing about those details squares with Mount Vernon's Samuel except living in Dayton. Was this a different Samuel Weill? Was this a relative with the same name? Or was it our Samuel Weil, who said he and his wife had lived in Dayton?

Could Samuel and Caroline have been in Memphis until 1863 and then moved to New Orleans, where Samuel was in charge of mail for the Confederacy in that area? It's certainly possible. There was a large number of Weills in New Orleans, and Samuel was probably related to most of them. There was a Private Samuel Weill in the French Brigade Militia in Louisiana, but that hardly corresponds with being in charge of Confederate mail. When Caroline died in 1875, the Civil War had been over for less than a decade. Perhaps it was the better part of valor not to mention a Confederate connection then, but there were no such qualms when Samuel died in 1901. Although some of the early facts are murky, details do exist that illuminate Samuel Weill's life in Mount Vernon--a mundane nineteenth-century existence punctuated by great happiness and tragic sadness.

When the childless Weills arrived in Mount Vernon, Caroline was in her early forties and had suffered for years from some kind of spinal disease. Despite constant pain, this generous, kind-hearted woman was always ready to help others. The couple lived above Andrew's Store on Main Street, seven doors south of Gambier Street. Jennie

In the Name of the Benevolent
Father of All –

I Carmina Weill of the City of
Mount Vernon, Knox County and State
of Ohio, do make and publish, this my
last Will and Testament:–

First, It is my will that my
just debts and charges be paid out
of my Estate

Item, I give and devise all the residue
of my Estate, both real and personal
to Samuel Weill my beloved husband
to be to him, his heirs and assigns
forever.

Item I hereby appoint and make
the said Samuel Weill Executor of this
my last will and testament and desire
that he administer upon my Estate
without an appraisement and without
giving bond therefor

**Above**
Caroline Weill's will – note her altered or misspelled name in the second paragraph.
*Knox County Records Center, Mount Vernon*

Weill, Samuel's younger sister, lived with the couple--perhaps to help Caroline with the household duties.

In 1870 Samuel was a peddler with property valued at $1,800. That might have been the value of his "peddling wagon" and its contents, or he might have already opened his wholesale/retail grocery store. For at least five years, the Weills' lives seemed uneventful except for Caroline's constant pain. In the summer of 1874 she made a will leaving her estate to her "beloved husband." (Charles Wolff, one of the witnesses who signed the document, was Adolph Wolff's son and another Jewish merchant in town.) There is no record that Samuel made a will at the same time. Had Caroline's pain increased and made her suffering unbearable?

Eleven months later on a Sunday afternoon Caroline Weill slit her throat with a large carving knife. She cut a six-inch gash that partially severed her windpipe but missed the jugular. She lost a great deal of blood before a doctor arrived who sewed up her throat and told her husband that she would recover. But within a few days, Caroline grew weaker, and, unable to cough or spit, she suffocated from the mucus in her throat. Her body was taken to Columbus the next day for burial in a Jewish cemetery. Her obituary mentioned her sympathies toward others who were sick and suffering and explained her suicide by saying that her physical pain had "greatly affected her mind."

Samuel's unhappy life continued for the next few months. He was badly injured in an accident at Mount Holly, Warren County (What was he doing there?), and was brought home two days later to recuperate. His sister lived with him and helped him convalesce and ran the household. Four months after Caroline's death, on a Saturday night, thieves tried to break into his peddler's wagon, which stood near his barn at the back of the George Building (on the corner of Gambier Street and Main) in Blackberry Alley. Frightened by police whistles, the burglars ran off mid-crime and left their tools behind.

Within a year Samuel remarried--a Columbus girl about seventeen years his junior. Fannie Wechler (or Wechsler, or Wexner--all variations of how her maiden name was spelled in various records) was born in Bavaria around 1847. By 1870 she lived with her sister Caroline Goodman and her brother-in-law Jacob, a furniture salesman.

In January 1876 she became Mrs. Samuel Weill of South Main Street, Mount Vernon. Her new husband listed himself as a dealer in furs and peltries; obviously he was still peddling.

**Above**
Samuel Weill's 1877 advertisement selling groceries and liquor.
*Democratic Banner*

In March 1877 Samuel sold a like-new "one top buggy," two harness sets, a three-spring wagon (a wagon often used in rural areas to haul merchandise), and one horse, suitable for farm work. Perhaps the fact that Fannie was pregnant and Samuel about to become a father for the first time at forty-seven convinced him that he shouldn't be on the road peddling and away from his wife and child. Perhaps this is when he started his grocery store at 89 Main Street, because in 1880, he described himself as a grocer.

Two days after the "for sale" ad ran in the paper, Louis Weill, son of Samuel and Fannie, was born. Samuel was overjoyed! Even the *Banner* noted that "this being his first child and a male one at that, Mr. Weill [was] elated." Or as Weill would have said, "What *naches*! [happiness]." Weill wanted to share his joy with his friends. He invited Lecky Harper, editor of the *Democratic Banner*, W. M. King from the *Republican* newspaper, two representatives from the *Columbus Dispatch*, Fannie's family from Columbus, friends, and all the local Jewish families to Louis's *bris* (circumcision) eight days later. Adolph and Hannah Wolff, Max and Celia Leopold, Max and Ricka Hyman, and Michael and Rachel Galena, all families in the Jewish community, attended. Other guests included the shoemaker James Hutchinson and his wife Sarah, and a farmer, Ezra Hook, and his wife Honor.

The *mohel* (described in the local papers as the "circumcisionist"), I. M. Schlesinger, came from Columbus, but just to ensure the baby's safety Weill also invited two local physicians, Drs. Russell and McMillan.

Fannie carried the baby into a formal room where the guests stood. The *mohel* picked up the sharp, double-edged knife, recited the traditional blessing in Hebrew, and performed the procedure quickly and skillfully. Both physicians examined the baby and complimented the mohel, who then completed the ritual in Hebrew by naming the child and giving him his Hebrew name.

Then all retired to a dining room and a "sumptuous and inviting" meal. Before eating, Schlesinger recited *kiddush*, the blessing of the wine. And there certainly was wine; each guest had his own bottle of Rhine wine to drink along with a "bountiful supply of sweet-meats." After the meal, the men retired to the parlor for an hour of cigars and conversation. Did the women stay in the dining room? Or was there another parlor for the distaff side?

For the next several years the Weill family grew--all boys. If they were being circumcised (as we must assume they were) the event was no longer newsworthy, because there is little mention of the events. Julius was born in 1879, Harry in 1886, and Morton, who lived for only two months, in 1889. To make sure the young family understood Jewish practices or because other Jewish merchants were doing so or because Fannie insisted, Weill now closed his grocery store for Rosh Hashanah and then again ten days later for Yom Kippur. Weill put announcements in the *Banner* giving the days and times of the closings (from sundown to sundown) and asked his customers to "please bear this fact in mind."

In addition to his wife and children, Weill's life revolved around sisters, nieces, and nephews. In July 1878, Sophia Weill, Samuel's niece, married Louis Hyman of Newark in Samuel's house above his store on South Main Street. Although both were Jewish, a justice of the peace, not a rabbi, performed the ceremony. Hyman established the County Dry Goods House on the east side of Main Street (near Weill's business?) in the Rogers Arcade. He must not have been a very good businessman because in April 1879, Weill announced that he was the successor to Louis Hyman's dry goods store. Louis continued to work in that store and sell chenille and Shetland shawls, linen and calico suits, wrappers and dusters for women, and thousands of yards of Hamburg embroidering. Weill still advertised and ran his wholesale and retail grocery and liquor store.

The 1880s saw a growth in Ohio's temperance movement and because Weill's grocery sold alcohol, he ran afoul of the reformers. When Ohio Republicans took control of the General Assembly in 1883, the state legislature passed the Pond Law, which required both a fee to receive a liquor license and a $1,000 bond to guarantee payment of that fee. Because of its population, Knox County liquor dealers had to pay $200 for a license.

Who sold liquor in Mount Vernon at this time? Two "saloonists," Jacob Styres and Jeff Irvine, druggist Thomas Taylor, grocers Fred Gehret and Samuel Weill (now at 212 S. Main Street), merchant William Philo, brewer Dennis Corcoran, brothers Charles and James Tivenan, and Messers Hunt and Patterson from the Curtis House. All paid the $200 fee, and many, like Corcoran, Weill, and Irvine, stood surety for the other liquor men. (Other prominent citizens who agreed to pay the bond were Sheriff John Gay, and attorneys Henry Curtis and Joseph Deven.) Within two months the Ohio

**Above**

Weill took over his niece's husband's dry goods store in 1879.

*Democratic Banner*

**Above**

Temperance women outside a local business that sold liquor. Surely they would have also stood outside Weill's store.

*Ohiomemory.org*

Supreme Court declared the law unconstitutional. When Mount Vernon received telegrams about the decision on Tuesday morning, May 30, the news spread quickly throughout town; the Pond Law was out. Gentlemen gathered on the street and jubilant saloonists, grocers, and other "liquor dealers" welcomed the news with free, unlimited beer. There surely were some happy men that day.

Samuel Weill's Notice to Customers.

The grocery store of Mr. Samuel Weill will be closed from Faiday evening Sept. 23d at 6 o'clock, until Saturday evening, Sept. 24th at 6 o'clock, to observe the Jewish New Year. Also October 3d, the feast of the Atonement, until 6 o'clock in the evening. My customers will please bear this fact in mind.

sept23-2t SAMUEL WEILL.

**Above**
An example of the notices that Jewish businessmen ran in the local newspapers to alert and educate their customers about closing their stores for the Jewish holidays of Rosh Hashanah and Yom Kippur.
*Democratic Banner*

In November 1883 Weill announced that he wanted to sell his grocery and provision store. He cited failing health and assured prospective buyers that they could take immediate possession. The business was centrally located and a good investment. The advertisement ran in the *Banner* for over two months, but there was no buyer. Perhaps Weill wasn't really ill but was having a cash flow problem. That December he won a judgment against another niece's husband, M. Hyman, for a promissory note of $1,873. It is not known if it was paid; however, the ads to sell the business stopped.

Sometime in 1884 Samuel hired his nephew David Weill. David's two sisters had married the two Hyman brothers from Zanesville and all were living in Mount Vernon. This was just one more example of Samuel's helping his extended family. This time, however, national politics burst into local life, and things did not turn out well. The presidential election of 1884 involved an impropriety which played out in national and local papers. Grover Cleveland, the Democratic nominee, was involved in a sex scandal.

The *Buffalo* (New York) *Evening Telegraph* publicized that ten years earlier Cleveland had had an illegitimate child with a widow, Maria Halpin. This information became public in July, and a month later, David Weill visited the local Republican newspaper to say that he had just been in Buffalo and had seen Cleveland's "bastard son." (This part of the story is probably untrue because the baby was quickly taken away from his mother.) Weill asserted that he had talked with many people familiar with the "disgusting scandal" and that their sympathy lay with Mrs. Halpin, a respectable and virtuous woman who had been dishonored by the presidential candidate. Weill stressed that he had always been a Democrat and it was that assertion which convinced the *Republican* that Weill's tale was true. The *Republican* was only too happy to print Weill's account.

The *Democratic Banner* struck back, calling Weill a "flannel-mouthed, unnaturalized Hebrew" and accusing him of circulating lies which the *Republican* was foolish enough to print. (For the record, Cleveland's PR team admitted the existence of the child, said that the sex had been consensual, and that several of Cleveland's friends had also been her lovers. Since Cleveland was the only bachelor among the men, he had agreed to accept the paternity. This information had not yet reached Mount Vernon.)

David's uncle Samuel, a "respected and intelligent" merchant according to the *Banner*, visited the newspaper office and told Lecky Harper that his nephew was a "dishonest rogue" whom he had fired months earlier for stealing, and that he wouldn't even trust his nephew's words under oath. Several days later Samuel returned to the newspaper office, saying that "certain parties" had warned him he could get in trouble by accusing his nephew of dishonesty. Weill retracted his statement about the theft but stood firm on David's untruthfulness. The newspaper now took the high road, said that it cared nothing about the business, and simply announced to the public that David Weill was a notorious liar. Cleveland won the election, and Samuel Weill's personal life disappeared from the local newspapers for some time.

Both newspapers reported burglaries in town and regularly recounted the "consternation" and "alarm" of discovering a thief in a house, and of single women deploring the "absence of a strong-armed male for protection." Four policemen walked the night beat in town, and in April 1885 they heard Samuel Weill shouting for help, yelling that his store was being burglarized. He knew that he had closed his shop and locked his watchdog inside. He lived above the store and was awakened by a dog--his dog, he realized--barking in the street. Weill and an officer entered the store and found that a panel in the back door had been sawed out, enabling thieves to unlock the door and remove the wood bar. The cash drawer had been rifled and $3.00 taken along with some cigars, liquor, and watch chains. But the burglars' real aim was the safe. A brace and bit, a long screwdriver, a drill, and a sledgehammer lay near it. Two holes had been drilled near the lock, but the dog's barking had scared the thieves away. The police discovered that the tools had been purchased locally at Graff's carriage works and that "the police are at work on a clew [*sic*] that may lead to arrests." There were no arrests.

In 1886, the Weill family was again in the news, under the headline "Horrible Affair--A Boy Throws a Cupful of Burning Coal Oil upon a Companion."

It was a Wednesday in early September--typical Ohio weather, still summer-like and warm enough for children to play outside. A circus had recently been in town, and some boys were playing circus in Blackberry Alley behind Samuel Weill's store. Nine-year-old Harry Weaver was the oldest in the group, which included both Harry and Julius Weill and other boys from the age of four to nine. The children were "performing antics" in a shed in the alley. Inside the shed were two old lamp tops, and one was placed on a tea cup and filled with coal oil to light the building. The wick was lit and illuminated the boys as they turned cartwheels and performed handstands.

The lamp suddenly shot up several feet, and young Weaver realized that the shed could catch on fire. He grabbed the cup and burned his hands as he threw the blazing liquid down. When he tossed the lamp, he did not see four-year-old Harry Weill standing nearby. Harry was engulfed in flames as his clothing was saturated with the coal oil. The boys shouted, and several men ran to help. They extinguished the flames, but Harry had been severely burned. Doctors Gordon, Fulton, and Robinson did what they could to ease the child's suffering. Five hours later Harry died. He was buried the next day in Greenlawn Cemetery in Columbus.

The first report of the tragedy mistakenly stated that Harry Weaver had "without provocation thrown the burning oil on Harry Weill." But two days later, "the Weill parents were convinced that Harry's death was purely accidental." We can only imagine the family's grief. The town offered the sad family its sympathies and condolences.

Samuel Weil continued to help his extended family. In the fall of 1888, a Mrs. Weill from Germany visited her brother-in-law Samuel in Mount Vernon. She was accompanied by her three sons, Harry, Louis, and Ely (or Eli). Six weeks later the two older boys, Harry and Louis, started the process of becoming citizens under the auspices of their Uncle Samuel. Ely was only seventeen at the time--too young to apply for citizenship. It wasn't until 1897, when he was twenty-six, that he became a citizen.

Samuel's life continued to be a mixture of the mundane and the tragic. The year 1889 saw the birth of another son, Morton. But the April 24, 1889, Republican paper said everything with the headline "Double Tragedy: Samuel Weill Assigns on the Day His Child Dies." Samuel Weill, grocer and liquor merchant, closed the door to his store at 9:00 A.M. on Monday, April 22. He turned over all his property and assets (estimated at real estate $3,000, assets $5,500, and personal worth $2,500) to David Ewing. Weill's liabilities were not listed but must have exceeded his $11,000 worth of assets. That same evening, three-month-old Morton died in his family's apartment over the store. The infant's body was taken to Columbus, where he was interred near his brother Harry.

When Weill declared bankruptcy, the family was allowed to keep the following according to bankruptcy laws:

Their clothes
Bed and bedding
One cooking stove and pipe
Enough fuel for sixty days
One cow or household furniture worth no more than $35.00
Two swine or household furniture worth no more than $15.00
Six sheep and wool or household furniture worth no more than $15.00
Bibles, hymn books, psalm books, testaments, school books and family pictures
Food not exceeding $50.00 in value
Any personal natural history or science articles, specimens, or

cabinets

J. C. Armstrong, who was a grocer, W. J. Hormer, and farmer J. M. Blocher appraised everything in Weill's store, starting in one section and then moving on to the next. The list of goods ran to thirty-seven pages and provides us with a clearer view of Weill's store than just calling it a grocery store.

Because *everything* had to be sold, a picture of the store's interior is available from the inventory. Shelves stocked with goods stood against the walls. Six glass showcases (probably three on each side) held products. Perhaps the twenty-one candy jars filled with chewing gum, rock candy, mixed candy, and chocolate drops were on the counters or in showcases. A coffee mill was needed because Weill stocked over three hundred pounds of coffee. Clerks weighed goods on three counter scales and reached top shelves with a step ladder. Sixteen food scoops, two cheese safes, and a large scale were in the store. (I didn't find a cash register listed in the inventory.) Samuel's office was in the back where his desk, desk light, chair, and iron safe (burglar-proof) were.

Of course there were groceries, everything a nineteenth-century housewife needed:

Honey / alspice [*sic*] / alum / maple sugar / corn starch / mustard / catsup / horseradish / pepper sauce / cloves / pickles / olive oil / vanilla / lemon extract / salt peter

Cans of: peaches / salmon / whitefish / corn / pumpkin / apples / lima beans / oysters /

sardines / sugar cane

Coffee / teas / jelly

Pickled pork--the only meat product I could find

Fresh Pine Apple [*sic*]

Candies: mixed candies / stick candy / chewing gum

For the household--turpentine / castor oil / carpet tacks / toothpicks / spools of thread / ammonia / buckets

Odds and Ends: fish hooks / marbles

Tobacco--lots and lots of different brands: Mail Pouch products / Hiawatha tobacco / Star tobacco / Sweet Russet / A.B.C. / J.T. / and at least seven more varieties of tobacco

The store sold liquor not only by the bottle but also at a bar, which was for sale along with whiskey, beer glasses, and a beer cooler. Alcohol on hand included the following:

2 cases of beer
11 gallons of whiskey @ $1.00 a gallon
5 gallons of blackberry wine @ 60c
10 gallons of Rock & Rye @ $1.15
40 gallons of No. 2 / 90 Proof @ $1.50 per
25 gallons of No. 1 / 90 Proof @ $1.50 per
22 gallons of gin @ $1.00 per
9 dozen 1 pint bottles of whiskey @ 24c per bottle
18 dozen half-pint bottles @ 20c per
2 bottles of brandy @ 50c per
2 bottles of Catawba wine
6 bottles of brandy @ $4.00 per
4 bottles of Snap (could this be schnapps?) @ 20 c
6 bottles of ginger ale @ 10c per
7 gallons of rum @ $1.00 per
32 gallons of 90 Proof @ $1.05 per
13 gallons of white whiskey @ $1.25 per
15 gallons of Proof
8 gallons of port @ $1.00 per
29 gallons of 90 proof whiskey @ $1.00
8 gallons of brandy @ $1.25

*(See a complete inventory list at the end of this chapter.)*

The sale of goods in the store was not enough to clear all Weill's debts. He had to sell his only real estate--his building at 212 S. Main Street. There were six outstanding liens against the mortgage of the building. Fred Eichberg had the largest claim of $1,500 and, according to court records, would be the third person to be paid. It is unclear how long it took Ewing to pay off Weill's debts, but Samuel still had to earn a living for his family. He advertised that he had "a complete set of air tight barrels and (was) prepared to clean vaults" quickly and satisfactorily. Modern translation--Weill and son Louis cleaned septic tanks and outhouses. By 1892 only Louis's name was on the business that cleaned day or night and took noxious substances away in airtight barrels.

At some time, Fannie Weill moved from being a housekeeper to helping run the now-back-in-business grocery store. Both she and Samuel were defendants in a suit brought by Emma Elliot, who claimed that the Weill establishment had sold liquor to her husband after being asked not to. The Weills denied the charge. In 1891 Samuel was arrested for having his saloon open on a Sunday. Whether he was running a saloon or just selling liquor in his grocery store is unknown.

Everyone in the family worked. Fannie and Samuel ran the store. Louis was in the night soil business. What about thirteen-year-old Julius Weill? He was running away from home to join the Ogarita Acting Company headed by Ogarita Booth, who claimed to be the daughter of John Wilkes Booth. Young Julius made it all the way to Newark, where he was arrested and jailed. A local policeman brought him home, but he promptly ran away again. He was found in Wheeling and returned to Mount Vernon. There was not a hint of gossip in the papers as to why he ran. But around the same time Julius entered the Kenyon Military Academy. Perhaps the family hoped that some military discipline would curb the boy's wanderlust.

Researching Julius's life was complicated. He was born around 1879, making him about thirteen when he ran away in 1892. So how was he listed as a law student the next year in the Mount Vernon City Directory? Curious!

The Chicago World's Fair of 1893 set the country and Knox County agog with curiosity. Tourists filled the railroad cars that traveled from Mount Vernon to Chicago daily. They stayed at the Hotel Kenyon, saw the sights, and returned home. One of those August tourists was Louis Weill. By now Samuel's widowed sister-in-law and her son Henry lived at 100 East Front Street, and Henry clerked at the grocery store with his cousin Louis. Fannie also worked at the store, and Samuel was listed as the manager. But it was Fannie whose name was listed as paying the Dow liquor tax, an annual tax on the selling of liquor.

In 1896 the Dow tax increased by $100. Rather than pay the extra $100, two barkeeps quit the business, leaving *only* twenty saloons in Mount Vernon. Fannie and her niece by marriage, R. Hyman, wanted to pay the tax under protest, but the treasurer refused to accept the money that way. So both women paid to prevent their inventory from being seized.

The grocery store prepared for the Fourth of July with fireworks. Unfortunately there was a small fire in the store and $30.00 worth of fireworks exploded and burned.

The year was almost over; 1897 was just days away. Before Christmas, a group of young men headed for Coshocton County to hunt ducks. The hunters included Louis Weill, Harry Bunn, William Lease (remember that surname; it will come up again), Phil Allen, and Clem Shrimplin, both of whom were Lease's relatives. The group headquartered at Newcastle, and the hunters bagged several ducks the first day. Around noon the following day, they watched a brace of fowls land on the Walhonding. Shrimplin and seventeen-year-old Allen walked in front toward the river with Weill about four feet behind. Bunn and Lease brought up the back about two hundred yards.

It was no surprise that Weill and Allen were in the same group. Although they had just met on this hunting trip, the two boys quickly became friends and were inseparable--hunting together while the other three formed another party.

The ducks startled and rose from the river. Weill carried his gun about halfway up his shoulder and began to cock it as he raised it. His fingers, however, were cold and perhaps numb, and they slipped from the hammer. The cartridge exploded and hit Allen in the left hip. The boy staggered and partially sank to the ground before getting back up, apparently unaware that he'd been shot. The others saw a fist-sized hole in his left hip and immediately put tobacco on the wound and bound it with Weill's undershirt.

The hunters were two and a half miles from any house, but fortunately a farmer drove by with an empty hay wagon and took the boys to his home. Allen's wound was cleaned and the tobacco wad, the shot, and bits of trouser were removed. Because Allen had been so close to the muzzle of the gun, the shot hadn't shattered or penetrated his bowels. One shot went cleanly through the boy's groin. Doctors later said that had Allen been farther ahead, the heavily loaded shot would have scattered and probably killed him instantly. The boy recovered and did not blame Weill; all agreed it was an accident.

Louis Weill liked his guns. Two weeks later on January 2, the East End Gun Club held a shoot; Louis Weill shot six birds.

Of all this family, Louis Weill's life was the saddest. As the oldest son, his birth had been celebrated with a lavish, and perhaps the first, *bris* in Mount Vernon. He was hunter. He was a carpenter and lived with his parents and brother above their store. His friends said that he liked the girls and was "easily infatuated." And he was dead at twenty-three.

Louis had been seeing/wooing/courting/walking out with a young woman named Maude Lease. She may or may not have returned his affections. Unkind reports about her stated that she took Louis's money and affections until "the former was nearly gone," and that she saw other men. On February 16, 1897, Louis escorted Maude to a dance somewhere south of town. It might just have been across the viaduct because after the dance, the couple walked to Gambier Street, where they had a fight about Maude's flirting (or was she just smiling?) at another man. They separated and each walked home--Louis to South Main Street and Maude to East Front Street, now Ohio Avenue.

Louis entered his home, borrowed his mother's writing desk, retired to his room, and wrote two letters--one to his parents and sole surviving brother Julius and one to Maude. He wrote:

*Dear Maude:*
*It is for you that I do this act. I have never kept a secret from you as you have from me. I have loved you only as one can love to the bottom of my heart, but I think you treat me most cruel. I wish that you only will view my remains and gaze on me only as one who loved you with all his soul. I will pen my folks to allow you to come and see me and bring Mandy or any friend you may desire. I will now bid you a loving farewell and hope you will not show this missive to any one or tell any one its contents. As ever your lover,*
*Louis H. Weill*

And to his parents and brother, Louis penned:

*Mt. Vernon, O., Feb'y 16, 1897.*
*Dear Parents and Brother:*
*I only ask forgiveness for what I have ever done and ask you only to admit any one to see me after I am dead, no matter who they may be, and if Maude comes treat her as kindly as you can, as it is my last desire, and I know you can't help but grant it. Wishing you all success and a long life of happiness, I now bid you a sweet farewell, mother, father and brother.*
*Your affectionate son and brother,*
*Louis*

Then he found a bottle of laudanum, swallowed about an ounce, and prepared to die. The drug, however, had lost most of its potency because of age, and Louis slept soundly through the night.

At breakfast the next morning he said nothing about his failed suicide attempt but crossed the street to Baker's Drug and bought arsenic "to kill some rats," he said. Then he visited Maude. He accused her of keeping secrets from him and said that his parents did not approve of their being together.

He walked back into town, stopped at Stamp's barber shop, and told his friend Charlie Harris that he intended to kill himself. Charlie had heard Louis make similar threats before and did not pay much attention. Going home, Louis entered his bedroom, undressed, swallowed half an ounce of arsenic and lay on his bed to die. By now Louis's parents had become concerned about his behavior. One report said they had seen him purchase the arsenic, but how could that have been? Yes, Baker's Drug was across the street, but surely the transaction had occurred inside the shop. (Had they seen him carrying the bottle?) Samuel and Fannie sent for Charlie and asked him to check on Louis. (Why didn't they check on their son?)

Harris found Weill conscious but with an empty arsenic bottle nearby. Dr. George Bunn arrived and forced a stomach pump down the boy's throat. Louis fought against being saved and was forcefully restrained while Bunn inserted the pump. The physician totally emptied Weill's stomach but feared that the poison had spread. By noon Louis was having seizures and lost consciousness. Despite the doctor's efforts, Louis Weill died.

Once the news spread, Maude Lease was promptly interviewed by both local newspapers. She denied any quarrel and said she had told Louis that people thought he was too good for her and that they should quit going together. He had insisted that she divulge the names of the people; she refused. She reported that Louis was worried and threatened suicide, but she would not share the letter Weill had written her.

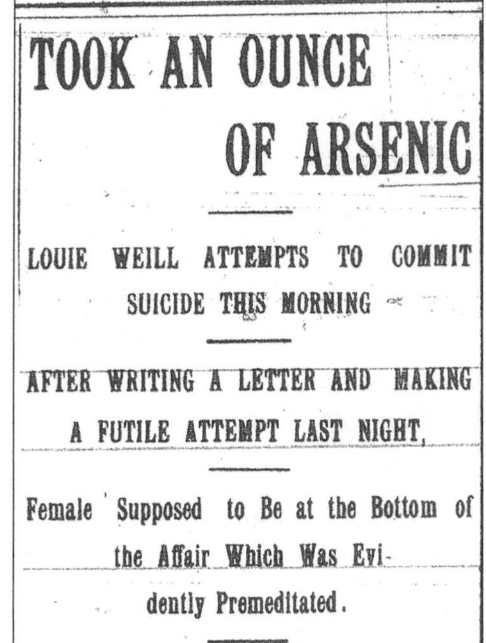

TOOK AN OUNCE OF ARSENIC

LOUIE WEILL ATTEMPTS TO COMMIT SUICIDE THIS MORNING

AFTER WRITING A LETTER AND MAKING A FUTILE ATTEMPT LAST NIGHT,

Female Supposed to Be at the Bottom of the Affair Which Was Evidently Premeditated.

**Above**
Louis Weill's suicide was well documented by the local newspapers.
*Democratic Banner*

By the next week, after Louis's burial at a Jewish cemetery in Columbus, Maude shared her side of the story. She released Louis's letter and said she had tried to see him as he lay dying but that his family hadn't let her. She tried to send him a farewell letter that promised to meet him "in a better land" and threatened vengeance upon his family. Once again we have no idea how the family handled their grief and the publicity that accompanied this suicide.

**Above**
Louis Weill's grave in Greenlawn Cemetery in Columbus, Ohio.
*Photo by the Author*

The Weill family was now sadly reduced to three--Samuel, Fannie, and Julius. A member of the Ohio National Guard, Julius was part of the hospital corps. He accompanied a Private Burke of the 14th Regiment to Centerburg after Burke was bayoneted through his right thigh. By the 1900 census Julius was listed as head of the household and ran the grocery store.

Samuel had been ill for some time, but Fannie and he celebrated their twenty-fifth anniversary in January 1901. Two months later, at 8:20 a.m. on Monday, March 4, Samuel died from pneumonia and an enlarged liver. Two obituaries--one in the *Democratic Banner* and one in the *Republican*--offered different and incorrect information about the death of this "prominent businessman." The most glaring error was that he was survived by three daughters. (This was probably a reference to his three sisters.) Samuel was buried in Green Lawn cemetery in Columbus near sons Morton, Harry, and Louis.

Two months later Fannie sold the store, and she and Julius moved to Columbus. Another Jewish family cut its ties with Mount Vernon.

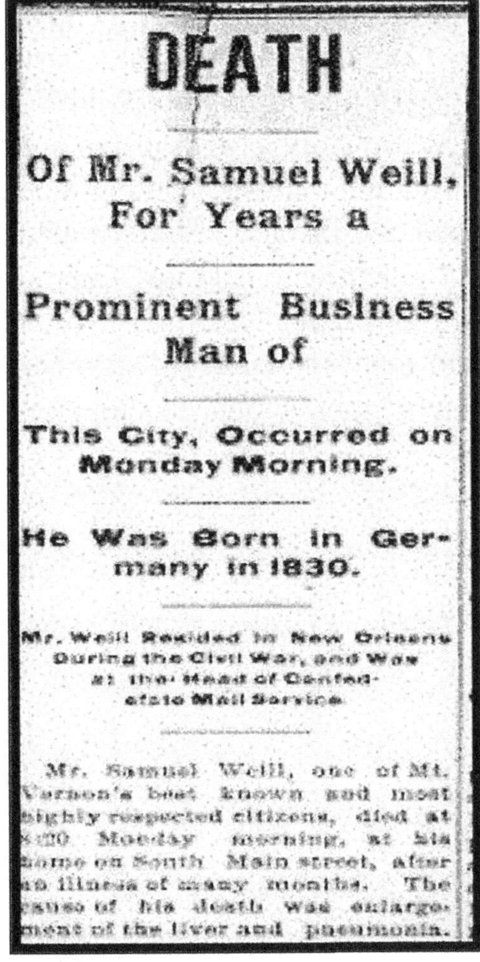

DEATH

Of Mr. Samuel Weill, For Years a

Prominent Business Man of

This City, Occurred on Monday Morning.

He Was Born in Germany in 1830.

Mr. Weill Resided in New Orleans During the Civil War, and Was at the Head of Confederate Mail Service.

Mr. Samuel Weill, one of Mt. Vernon's best known and most highly respected citizens, died at 8:20 Monday morning, at his home on South Main street, after an illness of many months. The cause of his death was enlargement of the liver and pneumonia.

**Above**
Samuel Weill's obituary.
*Democratic Banner*

**Above**
Samuel Weill's grave near his son's in Greenlawn Cemetery in Columbus, Ohio.
*Photo by the Author*

**Samuel Weill Inventory Pages**

Copying, cutting, and pasting pages of handwritten inventory items found in Samuel Weill's grocery store at the time of his death was probably as tedious as actually taking the inventory. The thrill of finding the lists, reading them, and marveling at the availability of food and the abundance of alcohol and tobacco products proved too enlightening to pass up. A perusal of the items showcase the diversity of foods that a local housewife could purchase for her family's meals and that Samuel Weill's grocery store was also a hardware store, a liquor store, a tobacco shop, and a toy store.

# INVENTORY AND APPRAISEMENT.

*Assignment of* Samuel Weill

## SCHEDULE E.

### PERSONAL GOODS AND CHATTELS.

| | | | |
|---|---|---|---|
| 1½ | " Leader " 20¢ | | 30 |
| 2 | Doz No. 1. Chimneys 25¢ | | 50 |
| 2 | " Hoiy " 10¢ | | 20 |
| 35 | Cane poles 2¢ | | 70 |
| 680 | Gal stone ware 5¢ | 34 | 00 |
| 3 | Clothes Racks 10¢ | | 30 |
| 2 | Cheese Safes × | 2 | 00 |
| 1 | Desk (Writing) | 5 | 00 |
| 1 | Molasses bbl | | 50 |
| 3 | Whisky " 50¢ | 1 | 50 |
| 4 | 10 Gal " Kegs 25¢ | 2 | 50 |
| 10 | Scoops 10¢ | 1 | 00 |
| 100 | Fire Kindler | 2 | 60 |
| 4 | Sacks Graham Flour 20¢ | | 50 |
| 4 | Buckets Herring 35¢ | | 80 |
| 3 | Doz Cans Salmon $1.50 per doz. | 4 | 50 |
| 2½ | lbs. hops 15¢ per lb. | | 38 |
| 2 | doz measure 60¢ per doz | 1 | 20 |
| ¾ | Doz pumpkins 75¢ per doz | | 57 |
| 11 | Packages Wheat — | | 00 |

| Qty | Item | | $ | ¢ |
|---|---|---|---|---|
| 2 | Doz. cans 75¢ per doz. | | 1 | 50 |
| | Shott - Case | | 1 | 50 |
| 8 | Slates 3¢ | | | 24 |
| 8 | Boxes tooth-picks 2½¢ box | | | 20 |
| 2½ | Lb Cream tartar 20¢ per lb. | | | 50 |
| 3 | Lb. Nutmeg 60¢ per lb | | 1 | 80 |
| 1 | Doz can peaches 75¢ per doz. | | | 75 |
| 8½ | Lb. Raisins 2¢ | | | 17 |
| 16 | Cans Corn 4¢ per can | | | .64 |
| 12 | Lb. Layer raisins 10¢ per lb. | | 1 | 20 |
| 21 | Cans Df. smoked-beef 12½¢ per c | | 2 | 62 |
| 25 | Cans Cocoa 15¢ per box | | 3 | 75 |
| 8 | Lb lead 5¢ | | | 40 |
| 4 | lb. ground-allspice 10¢ per lb. | | | 40 |
| 3 | " " cinnamon 20¢ per lb | | | 60 |
| 6 | Lb. pearl-barley | | | 00 |
| 4½ | " Caraway seed 6¢ per lb. | | | 27 |
| 4 | " ginger 10¢ per lb | | | 40 |
| 4 | lbs ground-cloves 20¢ per lb. | | | 80 |
| 18 | Cans Cherrys | | | 00 |
| 2 | lbs caraway seed 4¢ per lb | | | 08 |
| 11 | " Bartlett pears 16⅔¢ per c | | 1 | 83 |
| 6 | " Pie peaches 4¢ | " | | 24 |
| | | 2493 | | |

| Qty | Item | $ | ¢ |
|---|---|---|---|
| 10 | Cans Pine Apples 6¼¢ per can | | 62 |
| 31 | Packages Carpet-tacks 2¢ per pa | | 62 |
| 4 | Sacks shot 100¢ per sack. | 4 | 00 |
| 3 | Lbs. powder 20¢ per lb. | | 60 |
| 22 | Boxes common cap 2¢ | | 44 |
| 17 | Boxes Waterproof Caps. 5¢ | | 85 |
| 8 | Cans -pears 16⅔¢ per-can | 1 | 33 |
| 18 | " String-beans 5¢ per-can- | | 90 |
| 13 | " Sugar corn 5¢ " " | | 65 |
| 9 | Cans Peas 8¢ per can. | | 72 |
| 3½ | Doz Table Knives or 6 sett 18¢ per se | 1 | 05 |
| — | 6 Knives + 2 forks | | 30 |
| 40 | cans tomatoes 7¢ | 2 | 80 |
| 1 | lb Hemp seed | | 10 |
| 6 | Lb. Popy-seed 5¢ per-lb. | | 30 |
| 5½ | " W-Mustard seed 5¢ per. lb. | | 28 |
| 3 | " Green Als pice 9¢ " " | | 27 |
| 9 | Boxes Gun-wads 10¢ per box | | 90 |
| 5 | Lb. Olive Cloves 25¢ per lb. | 1 | 25 |
| 1 | Set Knives + forks | | 18 |
| 36 | Lb Crown baking powder 12¢ per | 4 | 32 |
| 4½ | Lb Royal baking-powder 35¢ lb | 1 | 57 |
| 32 | Boxes London pepper | | 57 |
| 53 | Lb. Kenton Baking powder. 12¢ per | 6 | 36 |
| 107 | " Soda 4¢ per lb. | 4 | 28 |

| | | | |
|---|---|---|---|
| 2 | Lamps 75¢ | 1 | 50 |
| 2 | lbs Almond 12¢ | | 24 |
| 3 | Box Chewing Gum 50¢ | 1 | 50 |
| 2 | Boxes Big-Hart C-9. 50¢ | 1 | 00 |
| 2 | Boxes Red Rose C-9. 40¢ | | 80 |
| 2 | Boxes Yucatan Chewing Gum 80¢ | 1 | 60 |
| 24 | lb. Ground Coffee 7¢ | 1 | 68 |
| 3 | W. W. brushes 40¢ | 1 | 20 |
| 4 | " " " 20¢ | | 80 |
| 10 | W. W. brushes 5¢ | | 30 |
| 4 | Shoe-brushes 25¢ | 1 | 00 |
| 4 | Clothes " 20¢ | | 80 |
| 4 | Shoe " 10¢ | | 40 |
| 4 | Floor " 8 1/3¢ | | 33 |
| 7 | lbs Sealing wax 3¢ | | 21 |
| 20 | lbs dried-peaches 8¢ | 1 | 60 |
| 3 | doz Lemons 10¢ | | 30 |
| 23 | lbs Apricots 8¢ | 1 | 84 |
| 20 | lbs prunes 2¢ | | 40 |
| 4 | " Home made sugar 8¢ | | 32 |
| 3 | gal. Maple Syrup 75¢ per | 2 | 25 |
| 11 | lbs O. Mug Tobacco 20¢ per lb. | 2 | 20 |
| 13 | lbs Old Pledge Tob. 25¢ per lb | 3 | 25 |

| | | | |
|---|---|---|---|
| 4 | Doz No 2 Chimneys 30¢ | 1 | 20 |
| 22 | Covered Baskets 12½ | 2 | 75 |
| 8 | Bu. Baskets 25¢ | 2 | 00 |
| ½ | Doz bu. baskets $1.75 per doz. | | 87 |
| ⅔ | " " $1.50 " " | 1 | 00 |
| ⅙ | " Hampers $1.50 " " | | 25 |
| 8 | " Stone Fruit Jars 50¢ per doz. | 4 | 00 |
| 9 | Doz Split Baskets 30¢ | 2 | 70 |
| 5 | Clothes baskets 25¢ | 1 | 25 |
| 2¾ | Gross Fruit Jars $5.00 per gross | 13 | 75 |
| | Lot Potatoes | 15 | 00 |
| 40 | lbs powder 20¢ | 8 | 00 |
| 3 | B Counter Scales $2. | 6 | 00 |
| 6 | Glass show cases. | 25 | 00 |
| 21 | Glass Candy Jars | 2 | 00 |
| 1 | Coffee Mill | 2 | 00 |
| 1 | Coal-oil Tank | 9 | 00 |
| 1 | Broom Rack | 1 | 00 |
| 1 | Molasses Gate | 1 | 00 |
| 1 | Sugar Auger | | 25 |
| 1 | Large pair Scales | 10 | 00 |
| 1 | Step Ladder | | 25 |
| 1 | Iron Safe (Burgular Proof) | 35 | 00 |

| Qty | Item | | | $ | ¢ |
|---|---|---|---|---|---|
| 14 | lbs Dried Beef 8¢ | | | 1 | 12 |
| 120 | " Cal. Ham 7¢ | | | 8 | 40 |
| 216 | " Ham 10½¢ | | | 22 | 68 |
| 130 | " Bacon 7½¢ | | | 9 | 75 |
| 159 | " Cheese 8¢ | | | 12 | 72 |
| | Job lot Baskets | | | 2 | 50 |
| 156 | gal oil 7¢ | | | 10 | 92 |
| 9 | bbl salt 90¢ | | | 8 | 10 |
| | Tar – – – – – – | | | 1 | 25 |
| 500 | lbs short 75¢ per 100. | | | 3 | 75 |
| 6 | doz No. 2 lamp flues 30¢ | | | 1 | 80 |
| 300 | lb Brand 75¢ per 100. | | | 2 | 25 |
| 260 | lb Wool twine 7¢ | | | 18 | 20 |
| 15 | gal mustard 8¢ | | | 1 | 20 |
| 2/3 | Doz tubs $5.50 per doz. | | | 3 | 67 |
| 1/2 | " " $6.50 " " | | | 3 | 25 |
| 3/4 | " " $7.50 | | | 5 | 62 |
| 17 | Brooms 10¢ | | | 1 | 70 |
| 6 | doz " $1.50 per doz. | | | 9 | 00 |
| 3 | Churns 50¢ | | | 1 | 50 |
| 100 | lbs paper $1.75 per cwt. | | | 1 | 75 |
| 30 | " carpet twine 4¢ | | | 1 | 20 |
| 11½ | doz No. 1 Hoop $1.25 per doz. | | | 14 | 38 |
| 8 | Doz. No. 1. lamp flues 25¢ | | | 2 | 00 |
| 3 | " Rochester chimneys 66 | | | 2 | 00 |

| Qty | Item | | $ | ¢ |
|---|---|---|---|---|
| 950 | Cigars (C. Walk) $1.00 per 100. | | 9. | 50 |
| 850 | Stogas (Standard) 80¢ per 100. | | 6 | 80 |
| 200 | Cigars (Pure Stuff) $1.80 per 100. | | 3 | 60 |
| 550 | Cigars (Famous) $1.00 per 100. | | 5 | 50 |
| 50 | Cigars (Capitol) $1.00 per 100 | | | 50 |
| 50 | Cigars (C. Greys) $3.50 per 100. | | 1. | 75 |
| 50 | Cigars (Cuban Puff) $3.00 per 100 | | 1 | 50 |
| 100 | Cigars (Menus) $2.20 per 100 | | 2 | 20 |
| 100 | Cigars (R. R. $1.50 per 100. | | 1 | 50 |
| 100 | Cigars (F. Prize) $1.00 per 100 | | 1 | 00 |
| 250 | Cigars (W. way) $1.80 per 100. | | 4. | 50 |
| 200 | Cigar (Lady) $2.00 per 100. | | 4 | 00 |
| 1100 | Cigars (Galena) with gun | | 25 | 00 |
| 500 | Stogas 3.50 | | 3 | 50 |
| 60 | lbs Bologna 5¢ | | 3 | 00 |
| 50 | " Raisins 4¢ | | 2 | 00 |
| 3 | Bbl Crackers | | 8 | 00 |
| 18 | Assorted Buckets 25¢ | | 4 | 50 |
| 50 | gal N. O. Molasses 33¢ | | 16 | 50 |
| 284 | lbs Rice 5¢ | | 14 | 20 |
| 295 | lbs Beans 3¢ | 38.57 | 8 | 85 |
| 1 | Shaving Cup & brush | | | 25 |

| Qty | Item | Rate | $ | ¢ |
|---|---|---|---|---|
| 60 | lbs A.A. Tobacco | 20¢ | 12 | 00 |
| 40 | lbs Sal Soda | 1¢ | | 40 |
| 12 | lbs Crown Baking Powder | | 1 | 44 |
| 50 | lbs Lump Starch | 2½¢ | 1 | 25 |
| 1 | Case D. Tomatoes | | 1 | 60 |
| 6 | Doz Cove-oysters | 65¢ | 3 | 90 |
| 20 | Scouring Brick | 2½¢ | | 30 |
| 2 | Sacks Salt | 10¢ | | 20 |
| 9 | Roll. Pins | 5¢ | | 45 |
| 48 | lbs Gloss Starch | 4¢ | 1 | 92 |
| 1 | Doz W. Boards | $1.50 | 1 | 50 |
| 7 | Wash Boards | 12½¢ | | 88 |
| 9 | Wash Boards | 16⅔¢ | 1 | 50 |
| 35 | lbs currants | 4¢ | 1 | 40 |
| 50 | Gal Syrup | 20¢ | 10 | 00 |
| 5 | Gal Vinegar | 15¢ | | 75 |
| 4 | Gal N.O. Molasses | 30¢ | 1 | 20 |
| 6 | Doz Horse Powders | 60¢ | 3 | 60 |
| 1 | Bbl Pickled Pork | $12.00 | 12 | 00 |
| 6 | Kegs Holland Herring | 60¢ | 3 | 60 |
| 4 | Qrs Family White | 75¢ | | |
| 4 | Qrs White Fish | $1.50 | 3 | 00 |
| 4 | Buckets White " | 65¢ | 6 | 00 |

| | | | | | |
|---|---|---|---|---|---|
| 52 | lbs Young Hyson 12½ | | | 6 | 50 |
| 10 | bbl Flour @ $4.60 per bbl | | | 46 | 00 |
| | | | | | |
| 5 | Tubs | | | 1 | 00 |
| | | | | | |
| 20 | Ax Handles | | | | 25 |
| 18 | pr. Suspenders 12½¢ | | | 2 | 25 |
| 3 | Boxes Envelopes 20¢ | | | | 60 |
| 16 | Halters 10¢ | | | 1 | 60 |
| 22 | " 8¢ | | | 1 | 76 |
| 5 | Halters 8¢ | | | | 40 |
| 20 | " 8¢ | | | 1 | 60 |
| | | | | | |
| 3 | 2 gal. Oil cans 20¢ | | | | 60 |
| | | | | | |
| 55 | lbs Tea 20¢ | | | 11 | 00 |
| 51 | lbs Young Hyson 12½ | | | 6 | 38 |
| 40 | lbs. Young Hyson Tea 30¢ | | | 12 | 00 |
| 35 | " Japan " 25¢ | | | 8 | 75 |
| 40 | " G.P. Hyson " 38¢ | | | 15 | 20 |
| 14 | lb Tea Siftings 6¢ | | | | 84 |
| 20 | lbs Oolong Tea 18¢ | | | 3 | 60 |

| | | | | | |
|---|---|---|---|---|---|
| 5 | Doz whisky glasses 25¢ pr. | | | 1 | 25 |
| 5 | Doz Beer Glasses 50¢ per d | | | 2 | 50 |
| 20 | " Lamp Chimneys. 25¢ pr | | | 5 | 00 |
| | Job lot Potato mashers &c. | | | 2 | 00 |
| 2 | Jugs 1 pitcher | | | | 15 |
| 2 | Doz Milk crocks 60¢ | | | 1 | 20 |
| 3 | large " 15¢ | | | | 45 |
| 1½ | Doz Ink | | | | 25 |
| 5½ | Doz Coffee Essence | | | | 50 |
| 10 | Boxes Starch 10¢ | | | 1 | 00 |
| 10 | lbs Sweet Chocolate 20¢ | | | 2 | 00 |
| 10 | lbs Tea 18¢ | | | 1 | 80 |
| 1 | Case Can Corn | | | 1 | 20 |
| 80 | lbs Corn Starch 5¢ | | | 4 | 00 |
| 144 | lbs Gloss Starch (Lump) 2[illegible]¢ | | | 2 | 16 |
| 3 | Boxes No. 2. Soapine $3.80 | | | 11 | 40 |
| 1 | " " " 3.60 | | | 3 | 60 |
| 24 | lbs C. S. Tobacco 31¢ per lb. | | | 7 | 44 |
| 24 | lbs Star Tobacco 38¢ per lb. | | | 9 | 12 |
| 24 | lbs Merry War Tobacco 30¢ per lb | | | 7 | 20 |
| 300 | " Coffee 24¢ | | | 72 | 00 |
| 12 | lbs J. T. Tobacco 32¢ per lb. | | | 3 | 84 |
| 48 | lbs Marine Tobacco 35¢ per lb. | | | 16 | 80 |
| 84 | lbs A. B. C. Tobacco 24¢ per lb | | | 20 | 16 |
| | Job Lot Ladder, S. Brush Yokes. | | | 1 | 50 |
| 25 | lbs Prunes 6¢ | | | 1 | 50 |
| 75 | lbs Pea nuts 6¢ | | | 4 | 50 |

| Qty | Item | | | | |
|---|---|---|---|---|---|
| 5 | lbs Stick cinnamon 6¢ | | | | 30 |
| 45 | Packages mixed spice 2¢ | | | | 90 |
| 45 | Boxes French Blacking 5¢ | | | 2 | 25 |
| 19 | " " " 2½¢ | | | | 47 |
| 12 | " Masons " 2¢ | | | | 24 |
| 6 | 1 gal Coffee Pots 15¢ | | | | 90 |
| 7 | Boilers 50¢ | | | 3 | 50 |
| 6 | ½ gal Coffee Pots 10¢ | | | | 60 |
| 5 | ½ gal Tin oil cans 10¢ | | | | 50 |
| 6 | Sprinklers 25¢ | | | 1 | 50 |
| 12 | Buckets (Tin) | | | 2 | 00 |
| 1 | Doz Tin buckets | | | 1 | 50 |
| 4 | Strainer buckets 25¢ | | | 1 | 00 |
| ½ | Doz 1 gal buckets | | | | 30 |
| 4 | Buckets (Tin) | | | | 20 |
| 6 | Small covered Buckets 3¢ | | | | 18 |
| 3 | Dish-pans 20¢ | | | | 60 |
| | Job lot Tin Ware | | | 8 | 00 |
| 51 | Lbs Lard in small can 8⅓¢ | | | 4 | 25 |
| 1 | 20 Gal-Jar. | | | 1 | 00 |

| Qty | Item | | |
|---|---|---|---|
| 9 | Buckets (2 hoops) 10¢ | | 90 |
| 2 | Churns 50¢ | 1 | 00 |
| 4 | Gal Lubricating oil $1.00 per | 4. | 00 |
| | Lot Lot Brush sugar & meat | 4 | 00 |
| 64 | ~~Cotton~~ Lot Soap 2¢ | 7 | 88 |
| 168 | Cakes Soap. 3¢ | 5. | 04 |
| 60 | Boxes Jim Axel grease 4¢ | 2 | 40 |
| 48 | Cans Pine Tar 5¢ | 2 | 40 |
| 1 | Bu white beans | 1 | 50 |
| 75 | Stew Kettles | 10. | 00 |
| | Queens Ware & Yellow Ware | 35. | 00 |
| 2 | Dinner Pails 20¢ | | 40 |
| 1 | Lot vases | 1 | 00 |
| 6 | Doz iron table spoons | | .25 |
| 7 | Glass Oil cans 30¢ | 2 | 10 |
| 4 | Tin " " 20¢ | | 80 |
| 11 | Lanterns 35¢ | 3 | 85 |
| 7½ | doz tea spoons | | .25 |
| 2 | 5 gal oil cans 25¢ | | 50 |
| 34 | Lamps 10¢ | 3 | 40 |
| | Sal Soda | | .25 |
| 16 | Small lamps (hand) 5¢ | | 80 |
| 6 | Reflector lamps 25¢ | 1 | 50 |
| 70 | Gal Coal oil (headlight) 7¢ | 4 | 90 |
| 3 | corn poppers 5¢ | | 15 |
| 13 | Glass pitchers. 12½¢ | 1 | 62 |
| 7 | Set glass ware 25¢ | 1 | 75 |
| 6 | Cake stands 15¢ | | 90 |
| 12 | Pepper boxes 5¢ | | 60 |

| Qty | Item | | | $ | ¢ |
|---|---|---|---|---|---|
| 18 | lbs Choc- drops 12¢ per lb. | | | 2 | 16 |
| 4 | " Rozin 2¢ per lb | | | | 8 |
| 1 | Box clothes pins 70¢ | | | | 70 |
| 2 | Kegs Sardells 20¢ | | | | 40 |
| – | Fire Works | | | | 00 |
| 5 | Bags shot $100 | | | 5 | 00 |
| | | | | | |
| – | Job Lot Lamp burners | | | 1 | 00 |
| 1 | lb Cuttle bone 15¢ | | | | 15 |
| 30 | " Mixed nuts 10¢ per lb. | | | 3 | 00 |
| 137 | Brushes & Curry Combs Job Lot 5¢ | | | 6 | 85 |
| 46 | Boxes Matches 5¢ | | | 2 | 30 |
| 48 | Package Matches 10¢ | | | 4 | 80 |
| 32 | lbs Concentrated Sal. Soda 2¢ | | | | 64 |
| 68 | box " Lye 6¼¢ | | | 4 | 28 |
| 73 | Packages Soapine 3¢ | | | 2 | 19 |
| 45 | " " 6¢ | | | | |
| 5 | lbs Maple City tobacco smok. 20¢ per lb. | | | 1 | 00 |
| 40 | lbs Long cut Tobacco. 25¢ per lb. | | | 10 | 00 |
| 16 | Boxes Niagra Gloss Starch 12¢ per box | | | 1 | 92 |
| 43 | Packages Corn Starch 4¢ | | | 1 | 72 |
| 56 | " Amer. Gloss Starch 4¢ | | | 2 | 24 |
| 50 | lb Horse Powder 12½¢ per lb | | | 6 | 25 |
| 29 | packages Ivory Starch 7¢ | | | 2 | 03 |
| 30 | Boxes Bird seed 4¢ | | | 1 | 20 |

| Qty | Item | $ | ¢ |
|---|---|---|---|
| 9 | " A.B.C. Tob. 20¢ per lb. | 1 | 80 |
| 10 | lbs J.T. tobacco 32¢ per lb. | 3 | 20 |
| 2 | " Premium Fine Cut Tob. 50¢ per lb | 1 | 00 |
| 4½ | " Leo " " " 20¢ " " | | 90 |
| 3 | " Rose " " " 20¢ " " | | 60 |
| 10 | " All-right " " " 20¢ " " | 2 | 00 |
| 6½ | " Wedge " " " 22¢ " " | 1 | 43 |
| 23 | " Peppermint Lozenges 10¢ per lb | 2 | 30 |
| 15 | clothes lines 10¢ | 1 | 50 |
| 14 | Clothes line 10¢ per piece | 1 | 40 |
| 29 | lbs. Wintergreen Lozenges 10¢ per lb. | 2 | 90 |
| 19 | " Stick candy 6¢ per lb. | 1 | 14 |
| 45 | " Prize (Sun) baking powder 30¢ | 13 | 50 |
| | Lot candy | 3 | 18 |
| 3 | lamps on show case | 3 | 00 |
| 7 | " in use | 5 | 00 |
| 50 | lbs ground pepper 15¢ | 7 | 50 |
| 16 | 3 lbs Niagra Starch 12¢ per box | 1 | 92 |
| 10 | lbs Citron 20¢ | 2 | 00 |
| 1 | Doz jugs catsup | 1 | 50 |
| 4 | lbs Ginger 8¢ | | 32 |
| 27 | Cakes Grand R. soap 6¢ | 1 | 62 |
| 7 | Small brooms | | 50 |
| | Crock & [illegible] | | 10 |
| | 72 11 | | |
| 1 | Doz Knives & forks | | 25 |
| 1 | " Harks? | | 60 |

| | | | | |
|---|---|---|---|---|
| 681 | lbs Extra C. sugar 7¼¢ per lb. | | 48 | 37 |
| 347 | " Winsor A. " 8¼¢ " " | | 28 | 63 |
| 313 | " Prunes 2½¢ " " | | 7 | 82 |
| 85 | " Dried apples 3¢ " " | | 2 | 55 |
| 147 | " Java Coffee 20¢ " " | | 29 | 40 |
| 148 | " Santos " 18¢ " " | | 26 | 64 |
| 114 | " Rio " 18¢ " " | | 20 | 52 |
| 80 | " " " 15¢ " " | | 12 | 00 |
| 17 | " Golden Rio " 22¢ " " | | 3 | 74 |
| 580 | " C- sugar 7¢ " " | | 40 | 60 |
| 165 | " Extra C. " 7½¢ " " | | 12 | 38 |
| 275 | " Soft A. " 8¼¢ " " | | 22 | 69 |
| 175 | " Granulated " 8¾¢ " " | | 15 | 31 |
| 70 | " Rost grain Coffee 21¢ " " | | 14 | 70 |
| 70 | " Rice 5¢ " " | | 3 | 50 |
| 40 | " Oat meal 2¢ " " | | | 80 |
| 326 | " Granulated sugar 8¾¢ " " | | 27 | 52 |
| 310 | " Lard 7½¢ per lb. | | 23 | 25 |
| 90 | " Pickled Pork 6¢ | | 5 | 40 |
| 334 | " Extra C. sugar 7¼¢ " " | | 24 | 22 |
| 30 | " Cheese 10¢ | | 3 | 00 |
| 120 | lbs Buckeye flour 1¢ | | 1 | 20 |
| 75 | " ground coffee 7¢ per lb. | | 5 | 25 |
| 50 | lb Rye flour | | | 00 |
| | Job Lot Pipes &c (Show case No. 2) | | 1 | 50 |
| 5 | Revolvers $1.20 | | 6 | 00 |

| Qty | Item | | Amount | |
|---|---|---|---|---|
| 65 | lbs Mixed candy 8¢ per lb | | 5 | 20 |
| 185 | lb Rag paper 1¾¢ per lb. | | 3 | 24 |
| – | Lot Paper Sacks | | 3 | 00 |
| 4 | lb. Candle wick 15¢ | | | 60 |
| – | Job Lot Pipes | | | 75 |
| 3 | Doz Shovels 60¢ per doz | | 1 | 80 |
| 277 | Bars Flag soap 3½¢ | | 9 | 69 |
| 504 | Bars Star Soap 3¾¢ | | 18 | 90 |
| 462 | Bars Town talk soap 3¢ | | 13 | 86 |
| 249 | Bars Small Ivory soap 4¢ | | 9 | 96 |
| 98 | Bars Large Ivory Soap 6½¢ | | 6 | 37 |
| 206 | Bars Lenox Soap 3½¢ | | 7 | 21 |
| 488 | Packages T. D & H. 6¢ per packages | | 29 | 28 |
| 25 | lbs Fine candy 10¢ | | 2 | 50 |
| 17 | papers Rockwoods Chocolate 3¢ | | | 51 |
| 12 | Barn Boo 5¢ | | | 60 |
| 22 | Cane Pole 2¢ | | | 44 |
| | Job lot Chewing gum | | | 50 |
| 10 | lbs Bengal Fine Cut Tobacco 40¢ per | | 4 | 00 |
| 5½ | lb citron 10¢ per lb. | | | 55 |
| 7 | " Star tobacco 35¢ " " | | 2 | 45 |
| 24 | " Corner Stone 30¢ " " | | 7 | 20 |
| 25 | " Sweet Russell Tob. 25¢ per | | 6 | 25 |

| Qty | Item | Dollars | Cents |
|---|---|---|---|
| 24 | Sacks salt 4¢ | | 96 |
| | Job lot butter bowls | 2 | 00 |
| | Job-lot Sieves & measures | | 50 |
| 22 | lbs Sweet cakes 8¢ | 1 | 76 |
| 19 | lbs Sweet cakes 8¢ | 1 | 52 |
| 26 | " Ginger snaps 8¢ | 2 | 08 |
| 26 | lbs Ginger cakes 8¢ | 2 | 08 |
| 30 | lbs candles 6¢ | 1 | 80 |
| 1 | case Sardines $4.00 | 4 | 00 |
| 17 | Packages Yeast Powd 3¢ | | 51 |
| 28 | Packages Yeast 3¢ | | 84 |
| 10 | lbs White Whole pepper 18¢ | 1 | 80 |
| 10 | " Rock Candy 10¢ | 1 | 00 |
| 1 | Gross Carpet Tacks | 1 | 50 |
| 3 | Doz. Small Mason Flack 24¢ per | | 72 |
| 4 | Boxes Dried Herrin 20¢ | | 80 |

| | | | | |
|---|---|---|---|---|
| 6 | Watch chains 5¢ | | | 30 |
| 4 | " " 5¢ | | | 20 |
| 6 | pr. Sleeve buttons 6¼¢ per pr. | | | 37 |
| | | | | |
| 10 | Prs Specks 10¢ per pr. | | 1 | 00 |
| 124 | Cakes Toilet Soap 3¢ | | 3 | 72 |
| | Job Lot in Show case No. 5 | | 9 | 00 |
| 100 | lbs Lard 8¢ per lb | | 8 | 00 |
| 28 | " Fipp-baking-powder 30¢ | | 8 | 40 |
| 6 | Boxes Star Soap 3.75 a Box | | 22 | 50 |
| 2 | " Flag Soap 3.50 | | 7 | 00 |
| 6 | Coffee mills 25¢ | | 1 | 50 |
| 3 | " " 35¢ | | 1 | 05 |
| 16 | Dinner Pails 25¢ | | 4 | 00 |
| 4 | lbs. Common Rope 7¢ | | | 28 |
| 20 | " Cotton " 15¢ | | 3 | 00 |
| 30 | Bars Sodsalo Soap 6¢ 6¼¢ | | 1 | 88 |
| 5 | Doz Rising Sun Stove polish 48¢ | | 2 | 40 |
| 38 | Cakes Pride of K. soap 3¢ | | 1 | 14 |
| | Job Lot Butter dishes & Oyster pails | | 2 | 00 |
| 30 | lb. Cream nuts 5¢ per lb. | | 1 | 50 |
| 45 | " Lima Beans 5¢ " " | | 2 | 25 |
| 17 | Grain Sacks 10¢ per piece | 19 | 1 | 70 |

| | | | | |
|---|---|---|---|---|
| 5 | lbs | Allspice 8¢ per lb | | 40 |
| 5 | lb | Poppy seed 5¢ | | 25 |
| 17 | lbs | Sulphur 2¢ | | 34 |
| 6 | lb | Allum 2¢ | | 12 |
| 13 | lbs | Salt-peter 6¢ | | 78 |
| 6 | lb | Cera-seed 5¢ | | 30 |
| 9 | lb | Twine 20¢ | 1 | 80 |
| | | Job Lot Lamp wick | | 75 |
| – | | Job Lot Insect Powder & Pills | 2 | 50 |
| 2 | lbs | Maple Smoking tob 20¢ | | 40 |
| 1½ | lbs | Virginia Smoking Tob. 12½ | | 19 |
| 7½ | lbs | Climax Tob. 35¢ per lb | 2 | 62. |
| 6 | " | Piper Heidsieck Tob. 60¢ | 3 | 60 |
| 9¾ | " | Twist (Daisy) Tob. 10¢ per | | 97 |
| 13 | lbs | Horse-shoe tobacco 35¢ per | 4 | 55 |
| 19 | " | 2 & 2. " 24¢ " | 4 | 56 |
| 13 | " | State seal " 28¢ " | 3 | 64 |
| 7 | lbs | Happy Thought " 35¢ per | 2 | 45 |
| 6 | " | Marine Tobacco 35¢ " | 2 | 10 |
| 15 | " | Proof $1.50 | 22 | 50 |
| 8 | " | Port Wine $1.00 | 8 | 00 |
| 29 | " | 90 Proof Whisky $1.00 | 29 | 00 |
| 8 | " | Brandy 1.25 | 12 | 00 |
| 1 | | Lamp | 1 | 50 |

| | | | |
|---|---|---|---|
| 59 | Packages Mandarine Tea ½ lbs. 6¢ per p. | 3 | 54 |
| 24 | ½ lb " " " 12¢ " | 2 | 88 |
| 5 | Boxes Pepper tin 5¢ per box | | 25 |
| 7 | " " 5¢ " " | | 35 |
| 00 | Rulios | | 00 |
| 19 | lbs Cod-Fish | | 00 |
| 34 | Boxes Mustard sardines 8¢ per box | 2 | 42 |
| 35 | Cans White fish 8¢ " " | 2 | 80 |
| 183 | Spools Thd 3¢ | 5 | 49 |
| 15 | Cans Peaches 6¼¢ per piece | | 94 |
| 23 | " Corn-beef 12½¢ per can | 2 | 88 |
| 3 | Doz Lima beans 75¢ | 2 | 25 |
| 22 | Cans Salmon 10¢ | 2 | 20 |
| 3¾ | Doz. Corn oysters 60¢ per doz. | 2 | 25 |
| 197 | Cans Sardines 4¢ per can | 7 | 88 |
| 17 | Bottles Ammonia 10½¢ per bottle | 1 | 78 |
| 4 | Glasses Jelly | | 00 |
| 11 | Boxes blacking-brushes 5¢ per piece | | 55 |
| 13 | Cans Sugar corn 5¢ can | | 65 |
| 3 | Boxes Marbles | | 35 |
| ¾ | Doz Pine Apple 75¢ per doz. | | 56 |
| 15 | Lbs West. Vir. Mail Pouch Tobacco 24¢ per lb | 3 | 60 |
| 135 | Spools Thread 3¢ per Spool. | | 5 |
| 1½ | Doz Booth Pie-peach 60¢ per doz. | | 90 |
| 133 | Spools Thread 3¢ per Spool | 3 | 99 |
| 40 | Cans pumpkin 6¼¢ per can | 2 | 50 |

# Leopold Haymann

## *It's Haymann not Hyman*

**Leopold Haymann** lived in Mount Vernon just long enough to confuse townspeople, newspapers, mid-century local historians, and current genealogists about who he was. Was he Leopold Haymann or Hyman or Hayman or Heyman, and was he the same man as L. Hyman? Both L. Haymann and L. Hyman spoke with German accents and were part of the liquor business in Mount Vernon. It is no surprise that many times local newspapers confused L. Haymann and L. Hyman.

Leopold Haymann was born around 1845 in Baden, Germany. He arrived in Mount Vernon in 1878, found a room at a boarding house on Gay Street, and placed an announcement in the *Banner* on November 22 saying that he was the sole agent for Bond & Lillard Distillery out of Anderson County, Kentucky. He rented a storeroom at 77 Main Street and advertised that as a wholesale dealer in bourbon, brandies, wines, and cigars, he stocked "only the very best brands" and sold at the lowest prices. At the end of that year, an early-morning fire broke out in his liquor store. The damage could have been catastrophic to both him and downtown, but the fire was quickly put out, and Haymann's business suffered only slight losses.

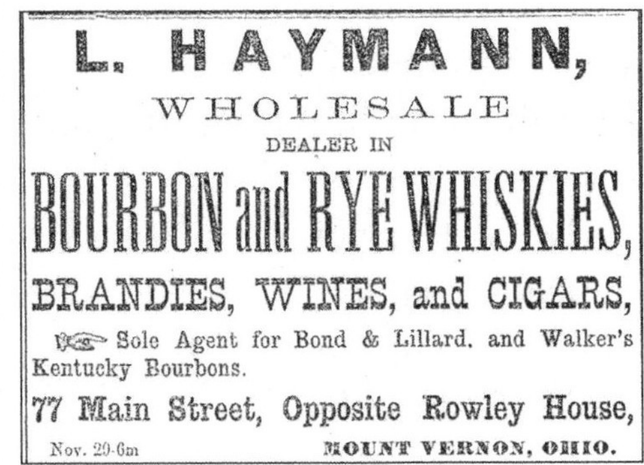


**Above**
L. Haymann, often confused with Louis Hyman, sold his business to Max Hyman.
*Democratic Banner*

Because Leopold was a wholesale distributor, he traveled throughout the state personally collecting money for the liquor he sold. Once in Shawnee, Ohio, he collected about $600. Standing at the bar in one saloon, he laid his "pocket book" (large wallet) on the counter and turned his back as he completed his business. After he left the saloon, he realized that his money was gone. Racing back, he interrogated all the patrons about the missing cash. No one knew or admitted anything so Haymann hired a detective. His money, however, was never recovered.

In April 1881, thirty-year-old Leopold Haymann married twenty-four-year-old Amelia Plautt in Cincinnati. Leopold continued traveling throughout the state invoicing and collecting money for the liquor being drunk legally in Ohio saloons and bars.

And Amelia? What was she doing? Having children--eight of them in thirteen years.

1882--Martha

1884--Hattie

1886--Milton

1887--Julius, who died at eight months from *cholera infantum*. This disease was prevalent in the summer, and Julius, indeed, died on June 4. In 1837, Dr. David King wrote that *cholera infantum* had not "received that attention which its prevalence and fatality demand." The symptoms, which appeared suddenly, began with vomiting and diarrhea and then dehydration and fever. (His descriptions of the discharge "matters" are really too disgusting to list.) Julius's parents would have been frantic trying to keep the baby clean and nourished. If the child survived the first twenty-four hours, he might recover. "The doctors . . . did not pretend to cure these children; they congratulated themselves on being very successful if they could keep the little ones alive until the frost came."

Following Julius's death, four more children were born to Leopold and Amelia:

1888--Henrietta

1890--Daniel

1892--Minnie

1895--Joseph

Four months before Daniel was born, L. Haymann sold his wholesale liquor establishment to M. (Max) Hyman, brother of L.

(Louis) Hyman. The Haymanns moved to Columbus after living in Mount Vernon for about twelve years. Amelia died eleven years later from liver cancer at the age of fifty-four. Leopold lived until he was seventy-one. There was no further connection between the Haymanns and Mount Vernon.

**Above**
Leopold Haymann's tombstone.
*Findagrave*

**Samuel Weill – Hyman Families**

Samuel Weill m. Caroline (1)
no issue
Samuel m. Fannie (2)
Louis
Julius
Harry
Morton

Jennie Weill m. Joesph Levy(1)
David
Jennie m. ????Beer(2)

Bertha m. Herschel Weill
Eli
Henry
Ernestina
Sophia m. Louis Hyman
Ricka m. Marcus Hyman

**Hyman Family Tree**

Father Solomon Hyman m Mother Sarah Fryborn

Three sons lived in Mount Vernon.

Isadore m. Theresa Altman
Morris
Harry
Sadie
Eddie

Marcus m. Ricka Weill (1)
Stella m. Sam Hantman
Henry
Marcus m. Clara (2)
No issue

Louis m. Sophia Weill
Ricka and Sophia were sisters.
Harry
Arthur

**Above**
Samuel Weill – Hyman Family Tree.
You will need this for the next four chapters.

# Louis Hyman

## *Unsuccessful Clothier – Successful Family Man*

Once upon a time there were two brothers who married two sisters. Marcus (aka Max) and Louis (anglicized to Lewis by local newspapers) Hyman were born in Prussia. **Louis**, born in 1848, was the older brother by about five years. He probably arrived in the United States around 1869.

The brothers lived in Newark for a time, and they arrived on the Mount Vernon scene in July 1878 when Louis married Sophia Weill at the home of her uncle, Samuel Weill. Then in 1883 brother Marcus married Sophia's sister, Ricka. Rabbi Felix Jesselson from Columbus married the couple at Uncle Samuel's house. Because another brother, Isadore, and his wife Theresa also lived in Mount Vernon at that time, there were three Mrs. Hymans in town in addition to Mrs. Haymann, wife of Leopold. All were Jewish and spoke with German accents. No wonder the newspapers confused their names, husbands, and

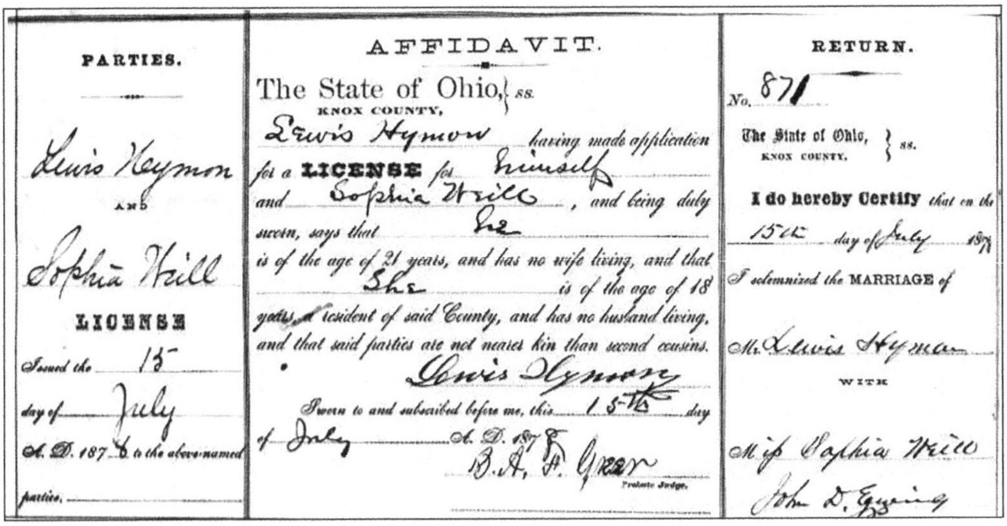
PARTIES.

Lewis Heymon AND Sophia Weill

LICENSE Issued the 15 day of July A.D. 1878 to the above-named parties.

AFFIDAVIT.

The State of Ohio, Knox County, ss.

Lewis Hymon having made application for a LICENSE for himself and Sophia Weill, and being duly sworn, says that he is of the age of 21 years, and has no wife living, and that She is of the age of 18 years, a resident of said County, and has no husband living, and that said parties are not nearer kin than second cousins.

Lewis Hymon

Sworn to and subscribed before me, this 15th day of July A.D. 1878

B.A.F. Greer, Probate Judge.

RETURN.

No. 871

The State of Ohio, Knox County, ss.

I do hereby Certify that on the 15th day of July 1878 I solemnized the MARRIAGE of Mr. Lewis Hyman WITH Miss Sophia Weill

John D. Ewing

**Above**
Louis (Lewis) Hyman and Sophia Weill's marriage license.
*Knox County Records Center / Mount Vernon*

sometimes even their genders. Writing about Ricka's wedding, the local newspaper said that she and Sophia Weill were Samuel's sisters. They weren't. They were Samuel's nieces; Bertha and Hertzel Weill were the girls' parents.

Sophia Weill was born in Emmendingen, Germany, around 1858 and immigrated around 1874. Younger sister Ricka was born around 1861 or 1862, and she came to America about 1880. A caveat about the dates. Do I believe that they are accurate? No. They are taken from federal censuses where dates, countries of birth, and names changed with confusing regularity. *Ricka* transformed into *Rebecca* in 1900, and *Eureka* on later documents.

Louis Hyman was Banquo to Max's Macbeth. "Lesser than Macbeth and greater. Not so happy yet much happier." Louis owned his own business for just over a year, but after that he was a traveling salesman for the rest of his life. When Max's name was splashed all over the papers for breaking temperance laws, Louis's name was in the newspapers as the proud father of Harry Hyman, collegiate athlete.

The year was 1879. Louis and Sophia had been married just six months when he opened the County Dry Goods House in a room in the Rogers Arcade on the east side of Main Street. Notions, women's clothing, shawls, "dress goods," linen suits, two-button kid gloves, muslins and prints, "ladies', gents' and children's hose," and gentlemen's furnishings--all were in stock and for sale at "bottom prices."

The store opened in April and sometime within the next twelve months, Louis had significant financial problems--so much so that either his uncle-in-law

**Above**

An 1879 advertisement for Louis Hyman's dry goods store. By the end of the year, Louis was in assignment, and his uncle by marriage, Samuel Weill, was the owner.

*April 1879 – Democratic Banner*

Samuel Weill or his brother Max bought the business. In December 1880, Louis went into assignment; he owed $5,000 and had only $1,500 in assets. Louis assigned his business to David Ewing but continued working in the store until his debts were paid.

In May 1881 Louis walked downtown smiling broadly and announced to all that "It's a boy!" Within a week, thirty men gathered at the Hyman house to witness the *bris*. Rabbi Bonnheim arrived from Columbus to perform the delicate operation. Justice of the Peace John Ewing, who had married Sophia and Louis, attended as did Louis's landlord Colonel Rogers, Drs. J. C. Gordon and E. J. Wilson (just in case), Samuel Weill, Isaac Rosenthall, and Lieutenant Joseph Levy, a Weill cousin. The *Republican* stated, "At the conclusion, a beautiful and impressive prayer in Hebrew was offered and the young Israelite duly *christened* [my emphasis] Harry Abraham Hyman." The men walked to Mrs. Murphy's, "the prince of caterers," parlor, where she had set a "magnificent spread."

If only the joy of a new child and the toasts to health and happiness could have influenced the rest of the year. But that was not to be. In June the *Mount Vernon Republican* ran a notice that all the claims against Lewis [*sic*] Hyman, "an insolvent debtor," would be sold at the south door of the courthouse. The sale commenced at two o'clock, and only cash was accepted. David Ewing testified, "I could get no bidders for the claims separately." He bundled all of them together, and the auction began. The highest bid was $10.50. The winning bidder? Louis Hyman. By the end of the year Louis's creditors received only 4.6 percent on the dollar, and the store was back in business.

By now brother Max owned the business, and in 1883 when the sheriff walked to the County Dry Goods House on a Monday evening to shut it down, the papers reported that M. Hyman owed money to Samuel Weill, Louis Hyman, and a Cincinnati company. The same day that the store permanently closed, Louis won a judgment against his brother Max for $576.25.

Louis had a wife and a child to support, and in 1885 another son, Arthur David, was born. Every document pertaining to Arthur states that he was born in Seward, Nebraska. Either Sophia was pregnant and visiting kin in Nebraska when Arthur was born or the family had moved there.

If the latter, by June 1888 the family was back in Mount Vernon, where another son, Julius, was born; the baby was either eight or ten months when he died from "infant troubles."

The family lived in Room E in the Cooper Block, and Louis supported his wife and two surviving sons as a traveling salesman. His itinerary over several months was Utica, Centerburg, Brinkhaven, Millersburg, Johnstown, and Gambier. He lived a low-key life out of the public. And he would have disappeared from the public record were it not for the athletic prowess of his first-born son, Harry Abraham.

**Above**
Harry Hyman - sitting on the floor - far right - staring at the camera - with the Mount Vernon High School football team, was Louis and Sophia Hyman's son.
*Mount Vernon News Sesquicentennial newspaper July 5, 1955 / Public Library of Mount Vernon and Knox Co.*

Harry could run. He could run fast. He was on the Mount Vernon High School 1898 and 1899 football team. In the team photograph of 1899 he looked dapper as he lounged on the floor in the front row--his long dark hair parted in the middle, hands clasped in front, and eyes staring fiercely at the camera. He was the "breakaway" touchdown runner, the "flyman." When he had the ball and was in the clear, he was never caught.

It was no surprise that when he attended The Ohio State University he was on the track team; he was one of the stars and then captain of the 1901–1902 team. He was a sprinter and set a school record for the 100-yard dash (9.8 seconds) which stood until Jesse Owens and George Simpson broke it. The newspapers followed his wins with laudatory articles.

May 14, 1901: "Fleet Footed Young Wonder" won all his events with ease. He won the 220 dash in 21 seconds and the quarter mile in 58 seconds.

May 20, 1901: "Mt. Vernon Boy Made a Record in Cincinnati." He won all his events, the 100, the 220, and the 440, easily.

May 27, 1901: Hyman "distinguished himself at Oberlin," winning the 100 in 10 seconds and the 220 in 22.6.

Harry transferred to the University of Pennsylvania as a junior and continued to set track records.

October 1902: He won the 60- and 150-yard dashes in the fall Novice Games. "Good for Harry," stated the *Banner.*

March 1903: "Mt. Vernon Boy Assists in Breaking World's Record" in a relay race between the University of Pennsylvania and Georgetown, shouted the *Banner.* Each man ran 320 yards and the Penn team set a new record of 2:47. The local paper erroneously cited Harry's parents as Mr. and Mrs. R. Hyman, which was wrong on so many levels. (His parents were Louis and Sophia, and R. Hyman was not a man but his aunt, Ricka.) Louis must have corrected the paper because that was the last time Harry's parents were misnamed. Harry brought home a gold medal mounted with diamonds from that meet.

The next month he won more prizes for the 220 (25 seconds) and

**Above**
Harry Hyman on The Ohio State track team – sitting in the first row - third from the left.
*Mount Vernon News Sesquicentennial newspaper July 5, 1955 / Public Library of Mount Vernon and Knox Co.*

the 440 (55 seconds). He sent home a silver loving cup, two gold medals, and another loving cup (obviously not a silver one). One can imagine how proud Louis was as he informed the *Banner* about this win.

January 1904: Harry set an indoor record for the 300-yard handicapped race in 43.4 seconds.

February 1904: At Madison Square Garden he ran his "most exciting race" against Amherst and won another medal.

February 19, 1904: Harry sent another loving cup home after yet another relay win.

March 11, 1904: "Hyman Defeats World's Record in Relay Race and Gets a Beautiful Gold Medal" was the next headline. In a relay against Yale and Columbia, the U of Penn team easily won first prize. Harry wrote his parents that the "world's record was broken in the relay race" for the five-mile run. The gold medal he received was the "finest in [my] collection" and the "most prized" because the late Senator Marcus A. Hanna had donated it.

**Above**
Harry Hyman on The Penn State track team – standing second from the right.
*Penn State Archives*

In the summer of 1904 Hyman sailed from New York with the American track team to compete throughout the United Kingdom. The passengers on the six-and-a-half-day voyage on the *Oceanic* had fine weather interrupted with whale sightings until the third day, when a passenger jumped overboard. The ship stopped, and lifeboats were lowered, but the man was not found.

The team disembarked in Manchester where, later in the week, Harry ran before of a crowd of ten thousand fans. Amateurs were handicapped, and Harry broke the Manchester 220-yard track record even as he ran against a strong wind. His prize, a large clock, was too big to send home.

After the Manchester meet, Harry wrote a letter to the *Banner* about his travels, thinking that a "short description of our trip to date might be of interest to some . . . readers." Perhaps it was his civil engineering studies, but much of the letter lectured about British trains (not as crowded as in the United States), which traveled over fifty miles per hour, and their engines. British double-decker street cars and bicycles also warranted descriptions.

Hyman's favorite place was Ayr, Scotland. The scenery was beautiful, and he and two British runners were "treated like lords" in the Dalbari Hotel, one of the finest in the country. Many of the town's prominent citizens called on the runners every day and became their tour guides to sites associated with poet Robert Burns. In September Harry telegraphed his parents that he was back in Philadelphia and

HARRY ABE HYMAN, "*Hy*"

Mt. Vernon, Ohio — Civil Engineering

Born May 4, 1881, at Mt. Vernon, Ohio.

Entered Junior Year; Mt. Vernon High School; Ohio State University. Civil Engineering Society (3) (4); Secretary (4); Ohio Club (4). Varsity Track Team (2) (3) (4). First 220-yard Dash, Second 440-yard Run, Varsity Inter-class Games, Franklin Field; First 360-yard Run, Varsity Handicap, Franklin Field; Inter-city Relay Team vs. New York A. A. U. Meet; Winning Relay Team vs. Yale and Cornell G. N. Y. I. A. A. Games, Madison Square Garden, N. Y. Winning Relay Team vs. Harvard, Boston, Mass., B. A. A. Games; Relay Team N. Y. A. C. Games, Madison Square Garden, N. Y.; One Mile Relay Team, Columbia Games, Madison Square Garden, N. Y.; One Mile Relay Team, Relay Races, Franklin Field; Second 440-yard Run, Columbia-Penn Dual Meet, N. Y.; Second 440-yard Run, Cornell-Penn Dual Meet, N. Y.; Represented Pennsylvania in Track Meets during the Summer of 1904 in England, Ireland, Scotland and Wales, breaking the 220-yard Track Record at Manchester, Eng.

**Above**
Harry Hyman's senior class entry in the Penn State yearbook.

would be home in a few days.

The 1905 track season and Harry's senior year were filled with more records set and trophies won. He triumphed against Cornell at a meet in Madison Square Garden and against teammate John Baxter Taylor in the spring handicap races. Harry graduated in June 1905 and his mother and brother Arthur traveled east for the occasion. Did Louis go and the newspaper just didn't include his name? I can't imagine what would have kept the proud father from attending the graduation.

Harry then left for another summer running abroad. The hardest and what turned out to be his last race took place in Glasgow. He ran against C. H. Jupp, the British title holder, whom he had defeated a few weeks earlier. Jupp was in the lead, and Hyman ran a few yards behind. As Harry fought his way to the front, he was crowded into a wooden curb lining the track. He stepped on it and twisted his knee. Harry probably didn't finish the race and was using a cane when he returned to the United State. "Track stunts are over for me now," he told the *Ohio State Journal.*

He started his first job as a civil engineer. In 1906 he was invited to represent the United States in the 1908 Olympics. His knee, however, still bothered him, and he was reluctant to leave his new job to devote the necessary time to train.

After Louis and Sophia moved to Columbus in 1910, Harry Hyman's reputation as "the fastest human" in Mount Vernon's history was mostly forgotten until the town's sesquicentennial in 1955,

ARTHUR DAVID HYMAN, *Z B T*
*"Art" "Artie"*
Mount Vernon, Ohio — Civil Engineering
Born August 21, 1886, at Seward, Neb.
Entered Freshman Year; Mt. Vernon, Ohio, High School. Civil Engineering Society (2) (3) (4); Ohio Club (1) (2) (3) (4). Freshman Track Team.

**Above**
Arthur's entry in The Ohio State yearbook.

when the *Banner* created a special newspaper, and the front page of Section H was devoted to "Harry Hyman Mount Vernon Track Star, Won Athletic, Construction World Fame." Naming him the "fastest human" in Mount Vernon High School athletic history, the paper brought Hyman once more to the town's attention.

**Above**
Mount Vernon High School senior class 1904 – Arthur Hyman, Louis and Sophia's second son, is in the second row, third from the left. Note how much he looks like his older brother.

*Centennial 1958 Forum / Mount Vernon High School Yearbook*

# Marcus (Max) Hyman

## *The Liquor Salesman and the Temperance Movement*

Like Gaul, Marcus Hyman's life in Ohio divided into three parts. There was the first part, the "I'm just an ordinary German-Jewish immigrant in Mount Vernon" section, until he purchased Leopold Haymann's liquor business in 1890 and immediately ran afoul of the temperance movement (part two). In the final, third section, he morphed into one of the town's well-known citizens who sold, among other products, "confectionaries."

**Marcus (Max) Hyman** was born in Prussia on or about June 7, 1853, immigrated to the United States in 1870, lived in Newark, Ohio, where he became a naturalized citizen in 1876, and finally settled in Mount Vernon. In 1880 he was entangled in brother Louis's County Dry Goods House's failure (see chapter on Louis Hyman) but later found a steady job in Samuel Weill's (his uncle by marriage) grocery store.

When Max married Ricka Weill he became *paterfamilias* to her family. He provided for her widowed mother Bertha and her two sons Henry and Eli. Max vouched for both of them at their naturalization hearings. Ricka and Max had two children of their own. Henry was born in 1885 and his *bris* was attended by twenty family friends a few days later. A daughter, Stella, was born in 1887.

A description of Max exists from 1895 when he applied for a passport to visit Germany. He was short--only five feet, six inches tall--and had a round, fair face with dark hair and blue eyes. His nose, described as Roman, was long and sloped downward.

On February 15, 1890, Max bought and took possession of Haymann's wholesale liquor establishment at 216 South Main Street. He sold whiskies, brandies, wines, cigars, and tobaccos both wholesale and retail. The saloon received bottled beer every morning from two breweries--one in Columbus and one in Cincinnati--and Max delivered throughout the city. The owner of the business, at least according to all the newspaper ads, was R. Hyman. That was Ricka, Max's wife. (About her name. Rivka or Rifka is the Hebrew name for Rebecca, which appeared as Ricka's name in the 1900 census. In one document her name even appeared as Eureka. I believe her name was Rebecca but she became Ricka in Mount Vernon. Because the name on her tombstone is Ricka, I use that spelling.)

The business was in her name. Why? Perhaps Uncle Samuel Weill put up the money and recalled the financial problems that Louis Hyman had encountered. Perhaps Max had some legal or financial reasons why it was better to have the business in his wife's name. No information exists explaining this uncommon setup. Regardless of the title, seven months later, it was Max who was arrested for violating the city's Sunday saloon closing ordinance.

Mount Vernon passed an ordinance which seemed to contradict the Owen Law about Sunday saloon closings. Max was open on Sunday and arrested. He was "at a loss which (law) to obey," said his lawyer. The court handed him an answer. Whatever he was doing was illegal; he was guilty. He

R. HYMAN
SELLS BETTER AND PURER
WHISKIES, BRANDIES,
WINES, CIGARS
AND TOBACCOS,
AT WHOLESALE OR RETAIL,
THAN ANYBODY ELSE IN THE STATE. GIVE ME A CALL AND BE CONVINCED.

We buy all our goods for the WHOLESALE TRADE, and in large quantities, and PAY CASH FOR THEM. We can therefore sell BETTER GOODS at a LOWER RATE than any ordinary retail dealer.

We keep BOTTLED BEER, always FRESH BOTTHED, received every morning from the Windisch, Muhlhauser, Brewing Co., Cincinnati, O., and also the Hoster Brewing Co., Columbus, Ohio.

We deliver goods to any part of the city.

Haymann's Old Stand. R. HYMAN.

**Above**
Max Hyman bought Louis Haymann's liquor business in 1890. Note that Max is not listed as the new owner; R. Hyman (Max's wife) was.
*Democratic Banner*

**A Short History of Pertinent Temperance Laws**

**1886:** The Dow Law was a state law requiring saloon owners to pay $200 per year for a liquor license. The tax increased over the years until it was $1,000 in 1906.

**1888:** The Owen Law prohibited selling liquor on Sunday and made it a criminal offense for any place that sold liquor to be open on Sunday.

**1902:** The Beal Local Option Law allowed municipalities to vote whether to sell liquor or not.

**Photos This Page**
Max quickly ran afoul of the temperance laws and ladies.
*Ohiomemory.org*

paid the $25.00 fine and court fees. Speaking of lawyers, D. F. Ewing defended Max in most cases, and Max's cases kept the attorney quite busy.

Max was arrested again the next year. He insisted that his *bar* wasn't open on Sunday. His wholesale tobacco and cigar section was separate from the bar. It was open, and there was no law prohibiting the sale of tobacco on Sunday. Max vowed to "vigorously defend his right to open or enter his store" on a Sunday. The case was dismissed for lack of evidence. Hyman was also accused of selling liquor to a minor, but that case, too, was dismissed when a key witness failed to appear in court.

November 1891 was not a good month, publicity-wise, for Max. He was again found guilty of violating the Owen Law. A week later he was indicted for bribing a witness, Harry Green, who swore that Max had paid him not to appear and testify against him in the selling-liquor-to-a-minor case.

Despite all the bad press, Hyman took the advertising offensive and announced that his business was "Still on Deck." Then he listed his stock of Yellow Brand lager beer, Imperial rye and bourbon (selling for $2.00 per gallon), Golden Wedding rye, Old Jim Crow bourbon, Old Hume rye, and imported and domestic wines and brandies. His business was good, and he moved to a new, larger room. He wanted his customers to remember that whiskey was "stimulating and nourishing to the consumptive, the old, and the feeble." Between court appearances, Hyman found time to move his store to 206 South Main Street.

Throughout 1892 and 1893 Hyman's name often appeared in the papers when he was arrested and appeared in court for selling alcohol on Sunday. Max always pleaded not guilty in the Mayor's Court, and his lawyers always argued that the saloon portion of the room was securely closed and that no liquor was being served. He lost all the cases except one when a "prejudicial error" against him on the Mayor's record gave him an acquittal.

Cigarettes, not liquor, were the topic of conversation in the summer of 1893. A new state law mandated that wholesale cigarette dealers be licensed. The $300 fee convinced two local merchants to get out of

HYMAN'S

Place Of Business Closed By Sheriff

Shortly Before Noon On Saturday.

Alleged that Hyman Sold Intoxicating Liquor

Without Paying Dow Tax To The County.

Other Items Of Interest Gathered At The Knox County Court House On Saturday.

HYMAN

Found Guilty Wednesday Afternoon

For Selling Liquor Under Beal Law.

Copper Case Comes Up For Second Time.

Witnesses Present from Bellefontaine.

Other Items Of Interest Gathered At The Knox County Court House On Thursday.

**Above**
Headlines like these were in the papers almost weekly. Max was always charged with violating liquor laws and always found guilty.
*Democratic Banner*

---

the tobacco business because they knew they could not sell enough cigarettes to recoup the license fee. Hyman, however, sold the bulk of all cigarettes locally; he estimated sales of over fifty thousand units per month. He was the first to pay the fee and said, "There is one thing certain; the retail price of cigarettes will just be doubled and those who indulge in this production of the weed will have to pay for the luxury." In October the Hymans went to the Chicago World's Fair before the winter arrests began.

And then liquor was the focus again.

**November 1893:** Max was arrested for selling liquor on Election Day. He claimed that Frank Willyerd, who swore out the affidavit, had lost an election bet with Max and this was his way of getting even.

**November 1893:** Max was charged with selling liquor to a minor named Chapman. Max denied even being in the store when the transaction occurred.

**July 1894:** Max was arrested for selling liquor on Sunday. He said that the front part of his store, where he sold tobacco, was open and that was legal. The prosecution said that since the room led to the bar, Max was guilty of having a saloon open. The mayor found him guilty.

**February 1897:** Max and Ricka were sued for $2,000 for selling liquor to Charles Wolford, a minor, on the night he died. This is the first time Ricka's name was mentioned in an arrest or suit. The case was dismissed.

**March 1897:** A woman sued Marcus and Ricka for $2,000 for selling liquor to her husband. She alleged that "being liable to be injured by sale of liquor to her husband," she had filed a notice to all liquor dealers two years earlier not to sell to him. The suit alleged that Hyman had ignored the notice and sold intoxicants to him on February 12 and many other times."

**July 1897:** Max was arrested for violating the 10:00 p.m. closing ordinance.

Finally in 1901 Max's name and the word *arrest* appeared in reference to someone else. Max appeared before Mayor Harter and asked that a warrant be issued against Carl Bartell, who with "malicious destruction of property," had torn pieces of spouting from the new veranda on Max's house on East Front Street and then thrown them in the street.

As the year and the century turned, anti-saloon laws and protests increased, and Max must have worried about how things would develop. He surely did not expect personal tragedy.

Ricka Hyman did not feel well in the fall of 1902. She was tired and achy and had a severe headache. When her symptoms worsened, a doctor diagnosed typhoid fever. She was bedridden for about five weeks but finally improved enough to get up and "be around the house." Daughter Stella was sixteen and still in school, but surely sister Sophia helped as her sister lay in bed. At some point an abscess formed on her side, and a physician operated. The patient did not improve, and a second physician came from Columbus to operate again. Ricka never regained consciousness and died at home in the morning of April 30, 1903. Her family accompanied her body to Cincinnati where her mother lived. Ricka was buried in the Price Hill Jewish cemetery there. She was just forty years old.

And then, two weeks later, "Mount Vernon Goes Dry! Saloon Doors Closed!" the headlines shouted on April 14, 1903. Mount Vernon citizens had voted for local prohibition under the Beal Law; the city would be dry. At midnight every saloon closed its doors. The next day Max and all the other "saloonists" walked to the county auditor's office for a refund of $43.20 from the Dow tax they had paid.

Once the dust settled, agents of the Ohio Anti-Saloon League arrived in town and went undercover to gather evidence against any saloons still selling beer. They listed fifteen places that they claimed violated the Beal Law and, presumably, gave the names to city officials before promptly leaving town.

Max had lost his wife, but he was damned if he was going to lose his business too. For the next two years it was Max vs. the Beal Law.

He was charged with selling liquor--and not just bishop's beer of 2 percent alcohol which was allowed--four times and paid $200 per charge. Once his lawyers argued that Dr. L. L. Willikams said Max was too ill to appear in court. The judge subpoenaed the physician, who testified that Max was suffering from a tumor on his neck and would be unable to appear in court for several days. The case was delayed, but when it was taken up again, Max lost again.

Max's business was closed twice on the same charge. He was held in contempt of court once. He was jailed three times. His business was declared a nuisance, and he was ordered to abate, to close his business. Max didn't and was arrested for contempt. He was fined $100 and sentenced to thirty days in the Columbus workhouse. The sentence was suspended when Hyman paid a $500 bond assuring his appearance in October in the circuit court.

In January, Max was in the county jail for contempt. His lawyer needed two judges' signatures to secure Max's release. Knowing that the judges would pass through Mount Vernon en route to Mansfield, the attorney took the train to Utica, met the northbound train, found the judges who signed the release order, disembarked in Mount Vernon, and got Max's release. To be sure, Max wasn't the only liquor dealer breaking the law. In November there were nineteen indictments against different "saloonists."

Max's December court appearance was a piece of theater. For the first time he pled guilty. The judge took the opportunity to recount all of Hyman's arrests and lecture him about his "unlawful actions." Max had to pay a fine and court costs. He flamboyantly pulled out his checkbook and paid the $200. Then he walked to the treasurer's office and wrote another check to pay for the Dow tax. The newspaper breathlessly totaled that his costs that day were over $700.

In the two years under the Beal Law, Knox County lost over $16,000 in revenue from the Dow tax. The cost to the county was $30.00 every time the grand jury convened to hear evidence about liquor violations. Prosecuting Beal Law violators cost about $2,000 per case. And, most tellingly, the law was a failure. There was a whole lot of drinking still going on in Mount Vernon and immediately outside the city limits. A special election was held on April 13, 1905, to repeal the Beal Law. The drys only carried two precincts (Third Ward B and Fourth Ward A). The city was "wet" again, and Max Hyman was back in business.

Stella Hyman was sixteen when her mother died; Henry was eighteen and on his way to OSU to study civil engineering. Stella came home from high school to a motherless house. In her junior year she became so ill that she couldn't sit up. This must have terrified her father until she recovered. And when Henry became ill with typhoid fever at Ohio State and his condition worsened, Max stayed in Columbus until he could report that his son was somewhat improved. Henry recovered enough to visit Yellowstone National Park in June with thirty-six other students for practical instruction in bridge building and roadwork.

Max decided he wanted or needed a wife. According to local Jewish legend, he sailed to Germany in 1905, found Clara Wolf who was fifteen years his junior, married her, and brought her back to Mount Vernon. It's a lovely story but doesn't agree with Max and Clara's marriage certificate. Clara was thirty-two and a German immigrant. She lived with her parents, Baruch and Caroline, in Cleveland. A rabbi performed the ceremony on April 23, 1905.

Where did the trip to Germany come from? Perhaps a visit that Clara and her stepdaughter Stella took to Germany in 1907 was confused with Max's search for a wife. We know the two women were in Germany in August 1907 because they boarded the *President Lincoln*--second class cabin--in Cuxhaven, Germany, on August 24, 1907. After ports in Boulogne and Southampton, the steamer arrived in New York City twelve days later on September 5.

Perhaps it was Clara's influence or the repeal of the Beal Law, but Max's life calmed. He sold cigars and soft drinks now. His name appeared in the papers only when relatives--Ricka's sister-in-law and her sons from Williston, North Dakota, or her brother and his wife visited or when a family member, Ricka's Aunt Fanny or Bertha, Max's former mother-in-law, died.

There was one "stupendous raid of alleged speakeasies" in 1916 when a single pint of whiskey was found in Hyman's place, but Samuel Hantman, Max's son-in-law, said the whiskey was his personal property.

Ten days before Christmas 1916 temperatures dropped to below zero. Max woke up around 6:30 and found a man either dead or dead drunk on his front porch at 100 Ohio Avenue (Front Street was now called Ohio Avenue). He called police (Max had had a telephone for over twelve years), who determined that the man was drunk and nearly frozen. They took the "prominent Fredericktown farmer" to a nearby paint store and put him in front of a warm fire where he revived but could not recall how he ended up on Max's doorstep.

Prohibition was the law of the land beginning in 1920, and Max was out of the whiskey business. He sold different kinds of cheeses in his store and opened the town's first temperance saloon, where he sold "near beer" for ten cents a bottle or on tap. The bar looked like a real saloon with its long mahogany bar and brass foot rail still dominating the room. Light and dark "near beer" flowed from the two brass faucets. The "near beer" sparkled, foamed, looked, and tasted like beer but without any alcohol or "kick." This business must not have been a success because in 1927 Max only sold wholesale tobacco, cigars, and confectionaries--no "near beer."

Max was seventy-six years old. His daughter Stella was married to Sam Hantman. She and her family lived with her parents on Ohio Avenue. Son Henry was a civil engineer in Miami, Florida. Max fell ill and was bedridden for seven weeks. Doctors said his condition was improving, but early Thursday morning on May 31, 1928, he had a fatal heart attack. Funeral arrangements waited until Henry arrived

Loaned by Ruby Vance — Identified by Laura Koons

FIRST ROW: Francis Anderson, Kenneth Campbell, Henry Hyman.

SECOND ROW: Laura Koons, Lillian (Rush) Pettit, Ruby Vance, Bertha (Ellis) Morris, Bessie (Ringler) Camp, Clara Wood, Hattie (Jupiter) Perry, Pearl (Severns) Cole, Coreta (Robinson) Taylor, Grace (Blocher) Rawlinson, Mae (Bryan) Stump.

THIRD ROW: Beatrice Stradler, Armistead Waight, Ralph Gallimore, Paul Ashbaugh, Mr. Leland (Principal), Ralph Sellers, Charles Jennings, Dwight Lafever, Carl Skeen, Ethel Hagaman.

**Above**

The senior class of 1903 had two Jewish students. Beatrice Stadler (with misspelled surname) is standing in back row, far left. Max and Ricka's son Henry is sitting in the front row on the far right.

*Centennial 1958 Forum / Mount Vernon High School Yearbook*

from Florida, and then Max's body was taken to Cincinnati to lie beside Ricka. Clara stayed in Mount Vernon until her death in 1950. She, too, was buried in Cincinnati near Max and Ricka. Stella Hyman Hantman now became the last of the Hyman-Weill clan who still lived in Mount Vernon.

**Above**
Max and Ricka's tombstone in Cincinnati, Ohio. Second wife, Clara, is buried nearby with her own, small headstone.
*Findagrave*

# Isador Hyman

## *The Forgotten Hyman Brother*

**Isadore** was the least known of the three Hyman brothers who lived in Mount Vernon. All the brothers were born in Germany to Solomon and Sarah (née Fryborn) Hyman. Available records indicate that Isadore was born around 1852 and immigrated around 1871. (I question this date because his first child, Morris, was born in Ohio sometime around 1871.)

He was twenty-eight, married, and living in Mount Vernon when the census enumerator found him on the west side of town in 1880. His name was totally mangled in that interview, and he has been immortalized in the record as Iedell Heyman. The rest of the census information proved more accurate. His wife, Theresa (née Altman or Aultman), was three years younger and also a German immigrant. There were four children in the family: Morris (b. 1871--age 8), Sadie (b. 1875--age 5), Eddie (b. 1878--age 2), and Harry (b. 1880--age 1 month).

Unlike his siblings, the third child, Edward, was not born in Ohio; he was born in Schuetz, Prussia (according to the 1880 census), or Nuremberg, Germany (his 1926 wedding license). Was Theresa pregnant and in Germany when Edward was born? Possibly. A Hyman descendant referred to Edward as a half-brother to the other children. One document stated that Edward immigrated in 1882, which can't be correct because he was in the 1880 census. He became a naturalized citizen, which confirms his birth outside the country. Theresa always stated that she had four children. Perhaps she had been visiting family when Edward was born or perhaps he was adopted from a branch of the family still in Germany. Whatever the answer, he was part of the family whom Isadore supported as a dry goods peddler--probably working for his brother Louis's store.

In 1883 Isadore and his wife were among the guests at Samuel

Weill's house for brother Max's wedding to Ricka Weill. Two years later three cases of diphtheria were reported in Mount Vernon. One of the sick children was eight-year-old Edward Hyman. He was bedridden for three weeks but survived.

What the family's life was like for the next thirteen years is hidden. By 1893 this branch of the Hyman family had moved to Columbus, and Isadore was a junk man. His son Morris was a merchant, and Edward and Harry were plumbers. Sadie and her mother kept house.

And then in 1905 the following article--taken from the *Ohio State Journal*--appeared in the *Banner.* "Ended Her Life / Did Miss Sadie Hyman / a Former Resident of Mt. Vernon." Sadie lived with her mother and brother at 1285 Highland Street in Columbus. (I believe Isadore had died because he's not mentioned as living in the house.) Late in the evening of July 2, Sadie wrote two "despondent" letters and then drank carbolic acid. Two women, a Mrs. Beekman and a Mrs. McClure (nurses? neighbors?) were summoned but were not able to save the thirty-year-old woman. Sadie died at 1:20 a.m. on July 3. The article was reprinted locally because she was the niece of "Messrs. Max Hyman and L. Hyman of this city."

The story the family handed down was that Sadie had had an illegitimate son, and that brother Harry and his wife Bertha, who had been married just the year before, raised the boy. In their lifetime, they had only that one child, Albert Edward.

# Samuel Hantman and Stella Hyman

## *The Last of the Weill-Hyman Family*

Where were you born should not be a difficult question for an adult to answer, even for a nineteenth-century immigrant who could not swear to the exact year of his birth. Country of origin shouldn't be a challenge--unless you were Jewish and came from Eastern Europe. **Samuel Hantman** was born around 1879 in Volkovinitz, Finland, when czarist Russia controlled the country. For several decades Hantman's birth country changed with the political winds--several times he said he was from Russia and sometimes from Finland. He spoke Russian growing up and in the latter part of his life claimed Finland as his homeland. He came to the United States when he was about seventeen. In 1910 he said he immigrated in 1883. In 1920 he said he came to the United States in 1887. Ten years later he said he arrived in 1895.

What is certain is that he settled in Pittsburgh with his parents Joseph and Augusta and his siblings. While there he married and had two sons, but when he moved to Mount Vernon in 1908 to manage the Cooper Theatre, he was divorced and a naturalized citizen. He moved several times in Mount Vernon, perhaps seeking the right place for the right rent. He lived at 206 South Gay, then boarded at 305 South Main Street, and in 1910, he lived with the William Simpkin family on West Front Street. As the theater manager, Sam traveled to Newark, Columbus, Cincinnati, and Cleveland to book all the acts for the vaudeville theater--comedians, singers, contortionists, and magicians. He hired employees and paid the workers weekly, usually on Saturday night after the theater closed.

On a balmy May in 1910, several of the Cooper Theatre employees walked to the west side of town to shoot pool. They left around 1:00

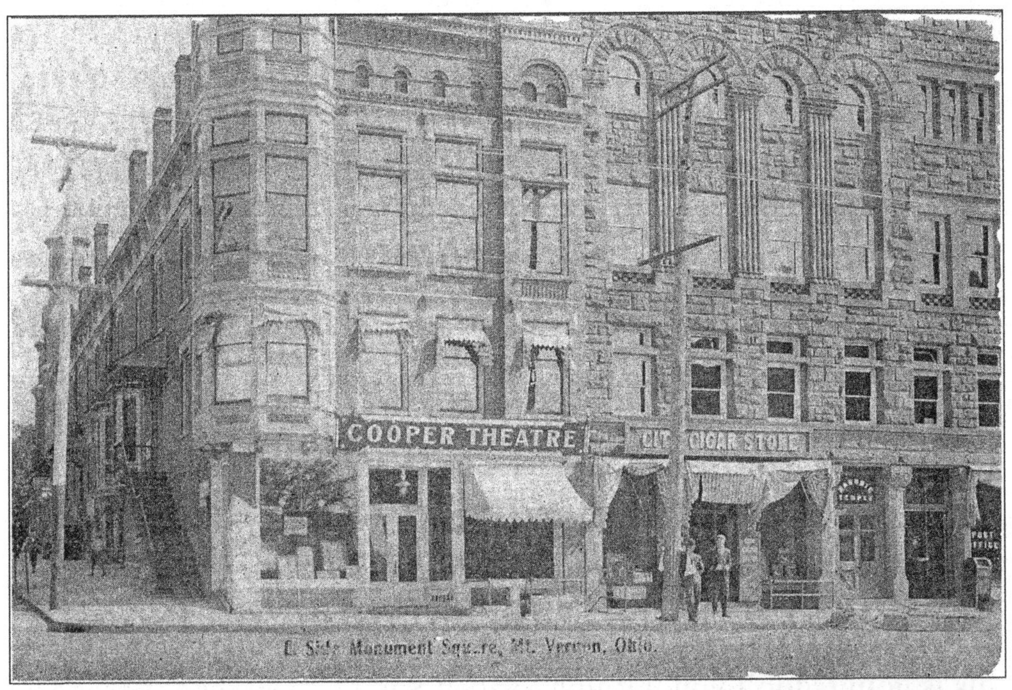

**Above Photos**
Sam Hantman managed the Cooper Theatre.
*Private Collection*

a.m. and two of the men, Earl Croston and Ralph Beach, headed home. They separated around Harrison Street, and Ralph walked towards Vine. Near a large walnut tree on the southeast corner of the street, two masked men stepped out from its shadow and ordered Beach to "hold up his hands." He did so because a large revolver was pointed at his face. The men told him to "keep his mouth shut" as they took twelve dollars from his pocket. He was then ordered to "beat it," which he did. As soon as he was home, he called the police. Even though Patrolman George hurried to the scene, the men were never caught.

Ralph Beach no longer felt safe and purchased a small revolver. He brought it with him when he showed up to work on Monday. He also had a prop revolver that had been damaged in Saturday night's performance, and which he had fixed. Sam asked for the prop pistol to make sure it would work in the next performance. (You know where this is going, don't you?) Ralph handed Sam the real revolver, and he pulled the trigger. The bullet narrowly missed both Hantman's hand and Beach's head and buried itself in a wall.

Over the next few years, the theater changed from vaudeville to movies but Hantman still had to hire acts to entertain the audience before the main "moving picture." The year 1911 started slowly for the Cooper Theatre. Hantman booked the Sanford Stock Company for two weeks, believing that it was a "first class company." It wasn't. Sam called it a "failure" and canceled the remaining shows. He was unable to find a "good bill" for the open dates; the Cooper "went dark" for several days.

Later that year, Sam received a telegram that his father Joseph was seriously ill in Pittsburgh. He left immediately. His father survived, and Sam returned to Mount Vernon. It might not have been a surprise a year later when he received another telegram about his father. He again rushed to Pittsburgh and was with his father when he died. The shock probably occurred when he returned to Mount Vernon only to be handed another telegram that his mother was seriously ill. This time there was a happier ending. His mother, Augusta, survived.

When the Cooper Theatre became the Grand movie theater, Sam was still the manager. In fact he also managed the White Palace and

# Programme
# COOPER THEATRE

**STAFF**

A. Kerner............Lessee Sam Hantman............Manager
Fred L. Glosser.......Stage Manager B. Kerner............Treasurer
R. E. Harrington....Musical Director Russell Robison.......Chief Usher

THURSDAY, FRIDAY AND SATURDAY, DEC. 24, 25, AND 26

| | |
|---|---|
| A | OVERTURE,<br>Prof. R. E. Harrington |
| B | J. W. LETTON,<br>Funny Comedian. |
| C | ELSA STRAUSS,<br>In illustrated Songs. |
| D | DILLA AND TEMPLETON,<br>Contortions, "The Goblin's Den." |
| E | Miss Strauss, in an Xmas Song,<br>"TO VICTORY." |
| F | THE IMPERIAL MUSICAL TRIO,<br>Songs and Music. |
| G | MOVING PICTURES—"THE BLUE AND THE GRAY<br>OF THE DAYS OF '61." |

FRIDAY TWO SPECIAL MATINEES, 2:30 AND 4:00;

EVENING, 7:00 AND 8:30

BOTH PHONES 605

**1908 MOVIE PROGRAM—Christmas playbill of the Cooper Theater. "Moving Pictures constituted only a portion of the program in those days. The Cooper was in the present Chamber of Commerce rooms. "A Kerner" was August Kerner and "B. Kerner" his wife, Barbara. Elsa Straus, their daughter, is now Mrs. Russell Stillwagon. Sam Hantman was active in theaters here for many years.**

**Above**
A typical program for the Cooper Theatre in 1908 showing a combination of vaudeville acts and a "moving picture."

the Princess theaters. In 1915 he quit "show biz" and took a job as a tobacco salesman for Max Hyman. This was a good decision for both men. Max's reputation was in need of rehabilitation, and Sam had a reputation for fairness and honesty. When Samuel registered for the draft in World War I (between 1917 and 1918) he stated that he managed the Vine Theatre. Perhaps he had two jobs, one for Max and one as the theatre manager working for Harrison Smoots.

REGISTRATION CARD

SERIAL NUMBER 2059 ORDER NUMBER 2748

Samuel Hartman

PERMANENT HOME ADDRESS: 100 E. Ohio ave, Mt. Vernon, Knox, Ohio

Age in Years 41 Date of Birth Aug. 28 1877

RACE: White X

U. S. CITIZEN: Naturalized X

PRESENT OCCUPATION: Manager Vine Theatre EMPLOYER'S NAME: Harrison Smoots

PLACE OF EMPLOYMENT OR BUSINESS: W. Vine Mt. Vernon Knox Ohio

NEAREST RELATIVE: Mrs Stella Hyman Hartman, 100 E. Ohio Ave Mt Vernon Knox Ohio

I AFFIRM THAT I HAVE VERIFIED ABOVE ANSWERS AND THAT THEY ARE TRUE

Samuel Hartman

P. M. G. O. Form No. 1 (Red)

**Above**
Sam's World War I draft registration showing he managed the Vine Theater.
*Ancestry.com*

Sam courted **Stella Hyman**, Max's daughter, for more than four years before their engagement was announced. In June 1912 she accompanied him to a family wedding in Connellsville, Pennsylvania. Sam often attended Friday night dinners at the Hyman household. In 1915 Sam's mother visited Mount Vernon as the guest of Mr. and Mrs. Max Hyman. Something was definitely afoot.

In 1916 a wedding announcement appeared. Mr. and Mrs. Max

**Above**
Vine Theatre advertisement.

**Above**
Senior class photograph 1905 – Stella Hyman, second row, far right, was the daughter of Ricka and Max Hyman.
*Centennial 1958 Forum / Mount Vernon High School Yearbook*

---

Hyman announced the approaching marriage of their daughter Stella to Samuel Hantman. The local Sorosis honored Stella at its March meeting. There was lively conversation and Victrola music. A buffet lunch was served, and the women entertained the bride-to-be with speeches, recitations, original poetry, and household hints. Martha Irwin thanked Stella for all her years as the Sorosis secretary and wished her happiness and prosperity in the years to come. Stella's reply was "neat and happy," and she invited all to enjoy the "web-footed fowl" as she sliced it with a carving set the women had just given her. A month before her March wedding, Stella visited relatives in Cincinnati for two weeks.

On the Thursday before the Sunday wedding, Sam's bachelor dinner was held in a private banquet room of the Wisner Hotel. The tables were arranged in a T to seat the thirty guests who honored and roasted Sam. Before the dinner began, Mayor Charles Mitchell gave Sam a "handsome wicker chair with a tapered back." The groom fought hard to keep back his tears at the generous gift. The men then dined on consommé, a relish tray of celery, pickles, olives, and spring onions, sliced tongue, cold roast beef, smothered chicken, mashed potatoes with gravy, and a tomato salad. The service and the food were outstanding.

Throughout the meal, as the mayor acted as toastmaster, guests stood and spoke about Sam. Sam's future father-in-law and two other Jewish businessman, Joseph Meyer and Jacob Dubinsky, were among the fourteen speakers. Even though the halls of the hotel echoed with laughter during the dinner, all the speakers emphasized that they valued Sam's friendship and wished him great happiness.

Three days later Sam and Stella were married in the Rose Room at the Virginia Hotel in Columbus. Stella's Uncle Louis and his wife and Uncle Edward attended the one o'clock ceremony. Rabbi Joseph Kornfeld united the couple. It wasn't a fancy wedding; Stella wore a "plain traveling suit," not a wedding gown. The wedding party walked into the Virginia dining room, where a special table bedecked with roses and garlands was set up in the middle of the room. After the meal, the couple left for a short honeymoon in New York City. When they returned they lived with Max and Clara at 100 East Ohio Avenue.

In 1917, the Hantmans had their first child; Ruth Josephine was born on July 28. Five years later their second child, Joseph Henry, was born on August 26, 1922.

Imagine a typical American family in prewar Mount Vernon, and the Hantman family qualified. Sam was a salesman. He owned a car and once smashed his finger as he changed a tire. He was an active Republican who recognized his civic obligation by serving as a precinct election official for many years. He attended meetings at the

Elks Lodge and was a member of the Improved Order of Red Men. The children attended East School and then Mount Vernon High School, where they were on the "college track" of classes, and, it seems, were involved in band, orchestra, and almost every club.

In his junior year, Joseph Hantman had a starring role in the class play, *The Merchant of Venice*. And, yes, he played Shylock. My jaw dropped when I found this photo. Was he the only male in the junior class who could play the part? Did the director think that Joseph could bring some cultural history and back story to the role? Did the director think Joseph "looked" Jewish? Did the director think that only a Jew could play the part of the Jewish money lender? Was this irony? Naiviete? Sterotypes of Jews? But there is the photo of Joseph costumed as Shylock holding the money scales in his hands.

Stella stayed at home and continued her active membership in Sorosis. She was a charter member and secretary of the Mount Vernon Branch of the Newark Sisterhood. She inherited the family home when

**Above**
Senior class pictures of the Hantman children, Ruth and Joseph.
*Mount Vernon Forum / 1935 and 1939*

**Above**
Joseph Hantman as Shylock.
*Mount Vernon Forum 1938*

her father died, and her widowed stepmother, Clara, lived there too.

**Above**
Samuel and Stella's tombstone in Price Hill United Jewish Cemetery, Cincinnati, Ohio.
*Findagrave*

In May 1936 Sam entered Mercy Hospital "in failing health." He probably had a brain tumor. He lay in a hospital bed for almost a month and had two operations. Stella probably visited daily and perhaps brought him homemade food and read to him. After two weeks he improved and there was hope that he would soon be home. Then midway through the month, he relapsed and died of a brain abscess on June 19. Samuel Hantman was only fifty-eight when he died. His body was taken to McCormick Funeral home on South Gay Street, and then his family accompanied him to Cincinnati where he was buried in the K. K. Sherith Israel cemetery.

Sometime in the 1940s, Stella moved to Miami, Florida, where she died in 1963. Once she left town, she firmly ended the chapter on the Weill-Hyman-Hantman families.

# Max Meyers

## *The Stove Man*

Charles Meyers became ill first. The four-and-a-half-year-old probably had a sore throat and a fever. When his glands became swollen and he had trouble swallowing, the doctors diagnosed diphtheria. With no vaccine or known treatment, his throat closed and the family watched as Charles suffocated. He died on August 25, 1879. Isabella, the only girl in the family and a year younger than Charles, was already infected with the highly contagious bacterium. She died two weeks after her brother. And a week later, on the second day of the Jewish New Year, the baby Louis died. In the Rosh Hashanah liturgy for the new year, there is a prayer that asks who shall live and who shall die in the new year. For the distraught Meyers family, the answer was all too clear.

Added to their grief was the opinion of two local doctors that the children had caught the disease from the paper and rags which **Max Meyers** bought and handled in his peddler's wagons. Although Meyers had established a store five years prior to his children's deaths, he still had several wagons on the road selling tinware and glassware and trading for junk. Meyers still considered himself a rag merchant; all the junk and rags had to be picked over.

**Above**
Max Meyers.
*Daily Banner 1920*

Max vociferously denied that diphtheria could be carried on

clothes; the doctors stood by their statement as to the cause of the first case. (The CDC now states that although this mode of transmission is rare, objects such as bedding or clothes used by an infected person could spread the disease.) After the first case, however, the other Meyers children had only to inhale some droplets in the air when Charles coughed or sneezed to become infected. The two older children in the family, ten-year-old George and Joseph, a seven-year-old, did not become ill.

The *Democratic Banner,* which at first erroneously wrote that two "bright and promising children" had died of scarlet fever, now intoned, "Sore affliction has visited the family of our worthy townsman Mr. Max Myers [*sic*]. He has the sympathy of the entire community in this sad bereavement." The three children were buried in Temple Israel Cemetery in Columbus. A small standing stone marks the site, engraved with their three childhood names: Charley, Isabelle, and Louie.

Max Meyers's story began near Berlin in 1843. Herman, his father, was a tailor, and his mother Rose cared for their large family of nine sons and one daughter. Max left school at fourteen and clerked for several years until he became a traveling salesman for a tobacco company. Speaking no English, he emigrated to the United States when he was twenty-one. He immediately found a job in a hat factory in New York and worked there a year. With his savings, he boarded a train and rode as far as his ticket would take him. He disembarked at Hornellsville, New York, where he worked in a clothing store and drove a peddler's wagon.

He met and married Sarah Shul (Shaw), and they had their first child, George. In the 1870 census Max was listed as a peddler and the head of a household which included Sarah's widowed mother Amelia and her son Sugman (his name was probably Sigmund or Sigman), who was a rabbi.

When Max's employer moved to Columbus in 1871, Max, wife Sarah, baby George, and mother-in-law Amelia followed. A year later Max struck out on his own and moved to Mount Vernon, where he continued peddling. Within a few years he had eight wagons on the road but didn't feel that they were profitable enough. In 1874 he started a stove and tinware business at 201 West Gambier Street, on the northwest corner of Gambier and Sandusky, but kept the peddling wagons rolling for another twenty years. In White's 1876 city directory, Max was listed as owning a "second hand emporium" that also sold peddlers' supplies. In 1888 one of Max's mule teams broke loose and ran around Public Square several times until eventually stopped.

Max's peddlers bought everything--tin, rags, glass, junk, scrap, and once a revolver. Max wanted to sell it and went to his yard to fire it against an outbuilding. Either the revolver was "sadly deficient" or Max was a poor shot, because the bullet struck his neighbor's home. It ripped through Mrs. Guy Fink's weatherboard, plaster, and small mirror. She was cleaning two feet away from where the bullet hit; she was startled but unharmed.

Knox County appreciated and praised the industrious Germans who settled here. They were lauded for their thrift, honesty, and sound sense that would "enrich any land and place it at the top of the countries of the world in the scale of elevated humanity." This adulation notwithstanding, Max became a naturalized citizen in 1874, renouncing "all allegiance and fidelity to the present reigning Emperor of Germany William."

A decade later Meyers became interested in local politics. He was a Democrat living in the Second Ward. In March 1886 he and two others presented their credentials to the Democratic Committee, which chose who would run for City Council. (There were no primaries at this time.) The three men left the room, and the committee made its decision. It wasn't Max; he became a committeeman for the ward. The next year he was part of the committee to nominate candidates for trustee, constable, and justice of the peace. In 1888 Max was again denied the city council nomination and was again named a committeeman. By 1891, Max had demonstrated his loyalty and was given the Democratic nomination; he was elected to represent Second Ward on City Council.

One of his first proposals was a resolution to issue licenses to vendors to sell peanuts, candies, and fruit on street corners. The measure was adopted. At one meeting Max, the only Democrat, insisted that the appointment of Charles Fredericks to the Tax Board of Equalization was illegal. He asked the clerk to read a recent law that gave honorably discharged soldiers a preference in appointments. And one of Fredericks's opponents, Mr. Stone, was a veteran. Council tried to deny Meyers a chance to bring the question to a vote, but Max persevered and brought it up again during miscellaneous business and moved for a vote. The city lawyer's opinion was that the law did not apply to the Tax Board of Equalization, and the appointment stood.

Max was "hopelessly in the minority" on Council with eleven Republicans to the lone Democrat, but he won his re-elections handily. The *Banner* praised him as "one of the best trustees the city ever had" and wrote that "his views have always been given due consideration . . . and his sound business judgment has won him high esteem." Perhaps his belonging to the Masons, Odd Fellows, and Ancient Order of United Workmen overcame partisan voting in the Second Ward. In 1897 Max spent two dollars on his re-election campaign and won.

In 1881 after the deaths of their three children, Max and Sarah had another child, Cora. Imagine their horror when she was eight years old and they discovered she had swallowed a teaspoon of laudanum instead of cough syrup. (Why was an eight-year-old even getting the medication herself?) The child "fell into a stupor," and Dr. Fulton spent twenty-four hours reviving her.

When the High Holy Days of Rosh Hashanah and Yom Kippur came, Max was often called upon to lead services for Mount Vernon's "Hebrew fellow citizens" in the Knights of Pythias's lodge room. Most of the Jewish men and women would know the liturgy and the prayers, but Max was the one asked to officiate. The attendees probably brought their personal prayer books to the services although most would know the prayers by memory. How much of the service was in Hebrew, German, or English is unknown.

Max bought his mother-in-law a house next to his own on West Gambier Street. She shared it with Eliza Southwick and her daughter Alice, both seamstresses. It was in this house that Amelia died in 1885. Unlike her three grandchildren, who were buried in Jewish cemeteries in Columbus, Amelia was buried in Mound View Cemetery in Mount Vernon.

Max's business continued to grow. He went into partnership

**Above**
Max Meyers with beard and rakishly tilted boater hat stands in the doorway of his store. Perhaps the other gentleman is Elliot, Max's partner in the coal business.
*Knox County Historical Society*

---

with J. Elliott to sell hard and soft coal from his store. When Max's sons became old enough, they joined the store and eventually added plumbing for water or gas pipes, pumps, bathtubs, closets (septic tanks), and tanks to the store's offerings. The boys eventually totally took over the plumbing part of the business. Weekly advertisements stated that Max's stoves--"all kinds, any size, and every design"--reflected prices to "suit the times." Even as he referred to his business as the "mammoth stove store," Max added washing machines, linoleum, oil cloth, window and door screens, and cream separators to his inventory.

However, either Max was a casual employer or he sometimes hired "sticky fingered" workers. Employees twice stole from the store, and Max always prosecuted. One man, Miletus Baker, left town for a year, but when he returned, Max had him arrested for stealing $15.00. The

**Above**

I have no idea who any of the people posing outside Max's store are. The wagon might be one of Max's mule-drawn peddling wagons. You can just make out the words "peddler" and "supply" or "supplies" on the door posts.

*Knox County Historical Society*

---

matter was settled out of court.

Meyers had a large safe in his store, but local burglars were a determined lot. After the safe was blown open and thieves took $36.00 during the third burglary, Max didn't even repair it. Instead he posted a sign saying, "The safe is not locked. To open turn the knob to the right." The sign finally became tattered and was thrown away. The next burglars who broke into the store in 1893 didn't know that the safe was unlocked. They drilled into the iron door, inserted about a pound of powder, and blew the door off its hinges. The 8' x 10' office was wrecked. An upper panel in the front door was knocked out, and plaster was torn from the walls. The coal platform scales skittered across the floor, and wooden shovel handles broke. There was no money in the safe. The culprits were never found, although two men who were approached by the police around midnight took off running west on Gambier Street and escaped.

**Above**
Max Myer's storefront throughout the years.
*Knox County Historical Society / City Directory*

Speaking of safes . . . in 1902 the oldest safe in Knox County was sold for scrap iron. For over sixty years, it had been encased in the wall of a room "now occupied by C. A. Bope's" store at 114 South Main Street. The sides and rear of the safe were built of wood and covered with sheet iron. Its two large doors were locked with a key. It was considered such a safe safe that the keys to the Knox County Bank vault were deposited there every evening because it was more secure than the safe in the bank. The original owner, a man named Miller, had paid several hundred dollars for the safe. Max bought it for two dollars.

**Above**

A typical Myer's advertisement.

*Knox County Historical Society / City Directory*

Where did Max keep his money? Sometimes he stashed a money bag in a stove that was on display. That worked until he sold a stove to John Hall and suddenly remembered where his $46.00 was hidden. He rushed to Hall's house only to find a fire already burning in the stove. Meyers removed the stove pipe and thrust his arm into the hole to retrieve the money. All he recovered were intact coins and "burnt and charred remains" of bills. Max took the paper scraps to First National Bank, which sent them to the Treasury Department. Max's hand was severely burned.

Meyers bought a "sack of rags" and found a musty old plat map that probably helped the city prevent a lawsuit. City officials thought that an 1833 plat map published by county surveyor John Beran existed but had no idea where to find a copy. Max gave the map to the city, which proved that city officials had the right to open up South Norton Street.

Mount Vernon's Jewish community was small. Every family knew every other one; their children were friends. Even after Isadore Hyman's family moved to Columbus, his daughter Sadie often visited Cora Meyers in Mount Vernon.

Max served three terms on City Council and then either decided not to run or was not re-elected. His interest now turned to the Citizens Building and Loan Association of Mount Vernon. In 1914 he was elected to the Appraising Committee and two years later he was president of that institution, which offered 5 percent interest on a certificate of deposit. He continued to work toward improving Mount Vernon. In 1902 two men called on Max and told him their interest in establishing a stove foundry in town. They had the capital and wanted the town to give them two acres of land for the business. Max informed the Board of Trade, which took up the issue at their next meeting. However, nothing came of the idea.

Four years later Max had a stroke which temporarily paralyzed his left side. Within a week he improved enough to sit up in bed. And less

**Above**
Aerial view of West Ohio with Max's store in the lower left-hand corner.
*Author's Postcard*

than four months later he was well enough to be outside his store on the corner of West Gambier and Sandusky. Two strangers approached him one early morning and said they had $5.00 that a third man owed Max. Would he step around the corner for this transaction? He would, and as he reached for his pocketbook to make change for the $10.00 handed to him, one man grabbed the wallet and ran toward the B.&O. tracks. Police Chief Parker tracked the men through "the Jungles" but couldn't find them.

Max became ill again, perhaps with another stroke, because in the 1920 census son George was enumerated as the head of the household and Max was an invalid. He died at 7 p.m. Saturday, February 28, 1920, at his home "after an illness of many weeks' duration. His death was due to diseases incident to an advanced age." He was 77.

His obituary and photograph were on the front page of the *Banner.* A funeral service led by the local Masonic lodge was held at his house. Max, "a prominent citizen of Mt. Vernon," was buried in Mound View Cemetery.

Max's life was a perfect rags-to-riches story. An inventory taken of the goods in his store when he died totaled $10,550 (about $137,000 in today's dollars). Securities, especially stocks in the Citizens Building & Loan Company, totaled $17,873 ($233,000) and real estate $13,140 ($171,000). Money on hand equaled $1,205 ($15,717) and money accounts receivable totaled $2,772 ($36,000). A recapitulation of Max's estate totaled $45,541.84, or in today's valuation about half a million dollars.

Max's first will, signed in 1910, gave his children the business and wife Sarah all the real estate and other property. Son George was named executor. Max changed his mind several times and added four codicils to

**Above**

Although his three young children were buried in a Jewish cemetery in Columbus, Ohio, Amelia (Max's mother-in-law), Max, and his wife Sarah were buried in Mount Vernon.

*Photo by the Author*

the will. The first, added just days after the original will was signed, said that anyone who contested the will would lose any inheritance. Five years later a second codicil revoked George as the executor and appointed Sarah as the executrix. In 1918 Max purchased a house in Columbus for daughter Cora Ackerman for $3,900 and stipulated that at the time of his death, Cora could purchase the home for that amount. The final codicil, made a year before his death, revoked Sarah as the executrix and re-named George. Max also now gave Sarah everything except the investments in the bank which could not be sold as long as she lived. Any earnings from the stocks were to go to Sarah alone.

Max's will stipulated that his tombstone resemble that of John Fowler and that there be no inscription except name, date of birth, and date of death. This meant that there would be no Hebrew inscription or Star of David. He made no mention of the Masonic emblem which can be seen on the stone.

**The Rest of the Meyers Family**

Son Joseph Henry Meyers married Cora Hirsh from Columbus in April 1895. A rabbi from B'nai Israel in Columbus officiated, and they had one child, Lowell Max Meyers. In 1918 Cora divorced Joseph, saying that he had "become cold and indifferent to her and been guilty of extreme cruelty." Within a year he married a woman named Edith. Joseph, who listed himself as a stove salesman, died in Columbus of cancer in 1940. His body was returned to Mount Vernon for burial.

George Meyers never married and was a plumber for Knox Plumbing and Heating. He died of cancer at the age of 81 in 1950.

Cora married Carl Ray Ackerman in 1899 when she was nineteen years old. A justice of the peace officiated, probably because Ackerman wasn't Jewish. The couple rented a house at 105 West Gambier, and Carl worked as a clerk, probably for his father-in-law. The couple had one child, Meyers Ackerman, who was born in 1902. At some time Cora and Carl divorced; Cora remarried on March 7, 1920, and became Mrs. Thomas Carney. In that same year Cora's son Meyers lived with his grandparents in Mount Vernon and worked at the store. (Interestingly enough, a week earlier he had visited his mother on West Patterson Avenue in Columbus and was also enumerated on that census report.)

Sarah Meyers died a year after her husband in 1921 from a hemorrhage in her stomach and was buried beside him. When her will was read, grandsons Lowell and Meyers each received $500.00. But the rest of her estate was not divided equally among her three surviving children. Daughter Cora Carney was given $100 although a codicil in Max's will had given her a house in Columbus. Joseph was left $100, while his ex-wife Cora Hirsh Meyers would inherit $1,000 if she had lived with Sarah and "rendered such service" that Sarah would have required "for her comfort." Older son George was left everything else and was executor of the estate. The will gave him the option of giving money to his sister Cora "for her support and comfort" when and if he deemed. Joseph and Cora, Sarah's two divorced children, did not inherit much. Perhaps Sarah did not approve of divorce. Perhaps she didn't approve of the second spouses. There is no way to puzzle out the reasons behind the inheritances.

Grandson Lowell Max Meyers worked and lived in Mount Vernon in the 1920s and '30s. When he died in Columbus at age 89, his body was brought to Mount Vernon and buried in Mound View Cemetery. Great-grandson Meyers C. Ackerman Jr.'s obituary said that he grew up in the small, farm town of Mount Vernon, and there is a photograph of Meyers in the 1942 *Forum* yearbook to prove he was here. The obituary also said that he loved spending summers working his Aunt Mary and Uncle Otis Mead's farm near Mount Vernon. I've not been able to trace the Meads; there might still be Meyers family in Knox County.

# Marcus Rosenthall

## *Paterfamilias of the Rosenthall Clan*

To understand how Isaac Rosenthall's clothing business became "famous in the retail history" of Mount Vernon, it is necessary to understand the sibling relationships that were the cornerstone of the Rosenthall business model. And that means a detour to meet the patriarch of the family.

**Marcus Rosenthall** was born in Poland around 1800, and in 1832 he and his wife had a baby girl, Priscilla. Sometime and somehow the family arrived in Manchester, England. All but two of their fifteen children were born there. Trying to generate a list of all their names has been a challenge. Born in England were Permelia, David, Louis, Gordon, Solomon, George D., Abraham, Rosetta, and a Priscilla. Isaac was born in Virginia and Aaron in Ohio. That means there are still four unaccounted Rosenthalls. Parents and many children sailed to America and settled in Richmond, Virginia. In the mid-1830s, a hat store, the Southern Hat Emporium, was owned by Messers Garbanati and Rosenthall. This might have been Marcus or a relative whose store had drawn Marcus to Richmond. In 1840 Marcus's family included himself (a free white male between the ages of 40 and 50), perhaps his father or father-in-law (a free white male between the ages of 65 and 70), Marcus's wife (a free white woman between the ages of 30 and 40), and nine children.

2 boys under the age of 5
1 girl under the age of 5
2 boys between 5 and 10
2 girls between 5 and 10
1 boy between 10 and 15
1 girl between 10 and 15

If the census that year had asked for the names of all the people in a household, at least we would know the names of the nine children.

There was one more household member--a female slave between the ages of 35 and 54.

According to the 1850 census Marcus still lived in Virginia, but there were no adult woman listed, and only three children were enumerated--Priscilla, David, and Isaac. There was no mention of a slave. Marcus was a widower now, and eighteen-year-old Priscilla ran the household and took care of her younger brothers.

Marcus's first wife Jenetta (or Janetta) had died in 1849. In 1857 son Gordon named a daughter Janetta following Ashkenazi tradition of naming a child after a dead relative, and when Louis Rosenthall married in 1867, he listed Marcus and Jenetta as his parents.

The family stayed in Virginia until the outbreak of the Civil War, when they headed north. By 1862 they were in Marion, Ohio, where Aaron Rosenthall, the last of Marcus's children, was born. Marcus, obviously, had remarried, and his second wife was Henrietta Werner. Aaron and his parents returned to Richmond at the end of the Civil War. That year a G & D Rosenthall store was housed at 183 Broad Street, Richmond, Virginia.

A slightly different version of the Rosenthall family was given by Isaac Rosenthall when he lived in Mount Vernon. He said that the family had moved to New York City in 1853 when he was nine. They lived there two years and then moved to Pittsburgh. Perhaps some of the oldest children stayed in the North when Marcus returned to Richmond with his wife and Aaron.

The Rosenthall brothers established businesses throughout Ohio and Pennsylvania. George and David ran the Excelsior Clothing Bank in Findlay, Ohio, in 1864. Two years later G (Gordon) & D (David) Rosenthall had a store in Pittsburgh. David lived in the Eagle Hotel in Pittsburgh, while Gordon stayed in Richmond.

The 1870 census provided a new picture of Marcus. He was the only Rosenthall still found in Richmond. He was seventy years old, retired from commerce, and living in a boarding house. Parallel to the Richmond census, an Aaron Rosenthall lived in the Jewish Foster Home in Philadelphia. If Marcus were a widower, again, it's possible that he was unable to care for an eight-year-old child and placed Aaron in the Home. It's possible Aaron never reunited with his father.

By 1880 Marcus had moved to New York City and lived with his widowed daughter Rosetta Voloski and her three daughters, Jenetta (another daughter named for the mother), Flora, and Bertha. Marcus died there in 1888, but the Rosenthall business model had been established. Brothers started businesses; at one time they had twelve stores. The siblings visited each other regularly and often moved from store to store. Gordon was a clerk in the Pittsburgh store in 1860 and ten years later ran the Akron branch. Brothers and later nephews traveled east three to four times a year to purchase seasonal clothing. Because the men bought in bulk, their cost of goods was less than that of other buyers and they passed the savings on to their customers. The brothers Rosenthall had contacts throughout several states and knew when a clothier declared bankruptcy or closed a store. Rosenthalls often bought the entire inventory at low prices and then divided the goods among all the stores.

Isaac and Aaron Rosenthall will be the two brothers whose lives impacted Mount Vernon.

# Isaac Rosenthall

## *The Man Behind Rosenthall's Young America Clothing House*

The Rosenthalls were merchants. Father, uncles, brothers, cousins, and brothers-in-law--all were clothiers in Pennsylvania, Virginia, and Ohio. **Isaac (aka Ike) Rosenthall** was born in Richmond, Virginia, in 1844; he was definitely first-generation American.

In 1860 sixteen-year-old Isaac and brother David lived in Pittsburgh with another brother, Gordon. All the men were clerks who probably worked in a Rosenthall clothing store. Ten years later the clan included Gordon, his wife Eliza, their six children (Janetta, Abraham, Julius, Lee, Ida, and Bertha), and brothers David and Isaac. Eliza had live-in help to care for children ranging from nine to thirteen years and for the adult men in the household. All three men referred to themselves with the elegant title of clothier.

The paragraph above seems definite and straightforward, but conflicting information in Isaac's obituary said that he came to Ohio in the fall of 1860. This, however, does not square with census information of 1860 and 1870 which found David and Isaac Rosenthall living in Pittsburgh. (In fact few of the dates in Ike's obituary allow him to open his store in Mount Vernon in 1878 as he in fact did.) The obituary also stated that he worked in Bellefontaine, Wooster, Akron, and finally Altoona.

Sometime in the early 1870s Isaac met Rose Hess of Philadelphia. He must have been considered a good catch because Rose's parents let their twenty-year-old daughter marry Isaac in March of 1874. The marriage license said he was thirty-two, but if he had been born in 1844, he was younger. The ceremony took place at the Rodelph Shalom synagogue in Philadelphia. (Throughout their lives this synagogue played a part in Rosenthall weddings and funerals.)

Isaac and brother David set up the Young America Clothing House in Altoona, Pennsylvania. The store gained a reputation for thrift and

**Above**
Rodeph Shalom Synagogue in Philadelphia where Rosenthalls were married and buried.
*digital.library.temple.edu*

honorable business dealings. When Isaac left to open a store in Mount Vernon in 1878, the *Altoona Sun* and the *Morning Tribune* bemoaned the loss of Isaac, "a good citizen and an upright fair dealing business man. Our loss will be that town's gain for they will secure a liberal citizen . . . and a gentleman in life." Isaac moved his wife and two-year-old daughter Jeanette (named after his dead mother) first to a house on Sugar Street and then to East High Street. In March 1878 the Young America Clothing House (often referred to as YACH)--at Leopold's old stand in the Woodward Block corner of Main and Vine--opened for business. The owners were Isaac and David Rosenthall; Dennis Quaid was the head salesman.

Early newspaper advertisements for YACH mentioned that there were six Rosenthall stores throughout the area, which gave them leverage in purchasing and the ability to "manufacture all our own goods." Throughout the years, Ike's ads announced that there were six, then eight, then ten Rosenthall stores. (Trying to determine which Rosenthall was where, and then his relationship to Isaac, proved to be a rabbit hole I chose not to fall down too far.) Ike and David bought the Canton store of Ed Goldberg and changed its name; half-brother Aaron worked there. In Findlay the Excelsior Clothing Bank was owned by G. and D. Rosenthall. One of their ads began, "The Jews Ahead. THEY CAN'T BE BEAT for quantity, quality, and price." The family's surname identified them immediately as Jewish and the brothers were not shy about using economic stereotypes for their benefit. David ran the Altoona store, then came to Mount Vernon, and finally settled in Canton.

When Abraham Rosenthall (Isaac's nephew, the son of Gordon and Eliza of Pittsburgh) died in 1919 in Kenton, his obituary said he had worked in Akron, Ashland, Wooster, and Findlay before settling in Kenton in 1884. The Rosenthall men moved around and almost seemed to be interchangeable.

In 1879 the brothers bought $60,000 worth of goods at less than half the actual value. The inventory was divided among the six stores and $10,000 worth of goods arrived in Mount Vernon, where Ike sold a basic, good, lined working suit for $3.11 and the "nobbiest suit of the season" for $11.00. By the end of the decade YACH was an established store in Mount Vernon, and Ike was a respected member of the community.

**Above**
An 1879 Rosenthall advertisement. Isaac was ready to take his place in Mount Vernon retail.
*Democratic Banner*

The *Banner* summed it up perfectly. "Mr. I. Rosenthal [his surname was misspelled regularly in the early days--leaving off the final *l*] . . . left Saturday night for the East via Mansfield where he was joined by his brothers from Ashland and Altoona, and a nephew from Bellefontaine and at Johnstown by his two brothers-in-law." (If only the paper had provided some names or even initials for all the men.)

Isaac traveled to New York at last three times a year on buying trips. Rose often accompanied him, because the couple visited family along the way and she stayed with relatives while Ike and a brother or nephew continued on to New York City. If Rose wasn't visiting family in Altoona, Canton, Philadelphia, or Ashland, family visited Mount Vernon. Most often Solomon from Pittsburgh or David from Altoona (both of whom eventually moved and worked in Mount Vernon for a short time) were in town. Another frequent guest was Adolph Nathan of Johnstown, Pennsylvania, who had married Rose's sister Fannie.

Rose's life revolved around her family. Another daughter, Stella, was born in 1879, and it looked as if there would be no more children, but in 1885 a son was born. Ike was all smiles when he arrived at the store that Tuesday in October. Rose had just delivered an eleven-pound baby boy; he was named Henry Montefiore. (Henry's middle name, Montefiore, honored Sir Moses Montefiore, who had died just months before Henry's birth. Montefiore was a British financier and banker, a one-time Sheriff of London, and a philanthropist dedicated to alleviating the suffering of Jews abroad, especially in the Holy Land. The Rosenthalls obviously had heard of his death, and chose to honor him by giving the newborn his last name.) Another son, Marcus, was born in 1889, and the family was now complete. In future years Rose and the children often spent their summers in Pennsylvania with family while Ike ran the business in Mount Vernon.

As the Rosenthall family and business grew, public information was limited to advertisements, announcements, accidents, thefts, and deaths. Every fall Ike announced in the papers that his store would be closed for the Jewish High Holy Days. He closed for a day for Rosh Hashanah and one day for Yom Kippur. He reopened the store at sundown, usually 6:00 p.m.

Ike and David opened a new clothing store in Mansfield in 1884. The brothers were praised as "enterprising merchants who kept abreast of the times." The grand opening found both men smiling broadly, giving "words of welcome," and listening to a band play.

Ike was in downtown Mount Vernon in early December 1884 walking past the Curtis Hotel. Workmen were erecting a "storm booth" in front of the main entrance to protect guests. A cold, gusty

# SPECIAL ANNOUNCEMENT!

—o—

## NEW FIRM. NEW GOODS.

**MR. I. ROSENTHALL** having purchased and assumed entire control of the

## YOUNG AMERICA CLOTHING HOUSE,

is now prepared to furnish buyers of CLOTHING with

## UNPRECEDENTED LOW PRICES.

Having just returned from New York with an immense stock of **Men's and Boys' Clothing, Furnishing Goods, and Hats,** bought from manufacturers for cash, I am enabled to sell at prices that

## Defy Competition.

I can and will Save all Buyers of Clothing from 20 to 25 per cent. It will pay you to come 50 miles to buy your Clothing of the Young America—the Leading Clothing House of Central Ohio.

REMEMBER THE MAN AND THE PLACE,

## YOUNG AMERICA CLOTHING HOUSE,

**I. ROSENTHALL, Sole Proprietor,**

Opera House Block, Corner Main and Vine Streets, Mount Vernon, Ohio.

—‡o‡—

**For the accommodation of my patrons, I have opened a BRANCH STORE at Fredericktown, in the Odd Fellows Building, in charge of Mr. Alex. Keller. Goods sold at the same prices as at the MAIN STORE.**

**Above**
In 1886 Ike bought out his brother David and was the sole owner of the business. Note the announcement of a Fredericktown branch.
*Democratic Banner*

wind tore a portion of the booth off and knocked Ike unconscious for a short time. The painful scalp wound was stitched.

Like all children of the times, the Rosenthall youngsters were sent outside to play. Stella, age eight, often played around the Civil War monument and once fell and gashed her forehead. Dr. Gordon stitched and dressed the cut. Henry fell from the stone steps on the front porch of his home and broke his arm. Marcus fell, gashed his chin, and needed stitches. Dr. Gordon, again, to the rescue.

Hung Lee's Chinese laundry was down the street from the store. William Bright stole a vest and some other goods from Ike and sold them to Lee. Bright was charged with grand larceny, and the goods were returned to YACH.

For over a decade David and his brother Isaac were the co-owners of the Mount Vernon store. In 1886, the brothers amicably dissolved their partnership. Dave moved to Canton, and Ike took sole ownership of the local store. He opened a branch in Fredericktown in the Odd Fellows Building.

May 1889 brought several days of heavy rains to Johnstown, Pennsylvania. On Friday, May 31, the South Fork Dam upstream from Johnstown broke and released tons of water that carried houses, trees, debris, and people into downtown. Ike frantically sent telegrams to family on Saturday and Sunday to discover if his brother-in-law Adolph Nathan, Nathan's wife Fannie, and their children were safe. Finally a telegram arrived from Philadelphia saying that Fannie and the children had been at home when the dam broke and were, indeed, safe. Adolph Nathan, however, had still been at the store in downtown Johnstown and been swept away. His body had not yet been found as the telegrams passed back and forth. Ike left immediately for Somerset, Pennsylvania, to meet Fannie. Nathan's body was eventually found and taken to Philadelphia for burial. Rose was too ill to go to the funeral, but Ike was there for the interment. (Rose's being too ill to go to a funeral was repeated throughout her life. I believe that the illnesses were not physical but a manifestation of her grief.)

After Fannie was widowed, she often visited Mount Vernon, and Rose planned events to include her and her children. She held a birthday party for Henry and his cousin Helen Nathan. She held an "observation party" (whatever that was) and invited Fannie.

Ike, a staunch Democrat, dipped his toe into local politics. He was nominated to run for mayor in 1888. The *Banner* endorsed him as an "active young businessman" and "very qualified." He was nominated with a "loud hurrah" that was countered when G. W. Wolfe, who also wanted the nomination, left the meeting "in disgust." The *Banner* accused the *Republican* of misrepresenting Ike's words and defaming him by saying he consorted with "bummers and deadbeats." Rosenthall pledged to run a "dignified and honorable" campaign but, realistically, was not "oversanguine about his chances of success." His prophecy proved correct; he did not win. The *Banner* teased him when he bought an eighty-acre farm in Butler township and asked if he thought he was now eligible to join the Grangers or the Farmers' Alliance.

The Rosenthall consortium continued to buy inventory from bankrupt Ohio clothiers. When Ike's in-laws went into assignment in Philadelphia, Ike bought the entire inventory for $42,356. He announced in 1892 that over $18,000 worth of merchandise had arrived at his store and that he had to rent the "commodious basement rooms under their large store-room in the Opera House Block" to accommodate all the stock.

In 1893 Rose and Ike took one of the trains that left Mount Vernon daily to go to the Columbian Exposition in Chicago. They probably stayed at the Mount Vernon Hotel, which an enterprising Mount Vernonite had established in the Windy City for locals visiting the fair.

On Monday night, March 22, 1894, around 11 p.m. pedestrians on Main Street (what were they doing out at that hour?) smelled smoke and saw flames coming from the Woodward Building. Merchant Patrolman O'Brian, the policeman responsible for the downtown beat, and Officers Peoples and George alerted the fire department that the upper portion of the Opera House near the third floor entrance to the auditorium was on fire. Hoses were carried up the stairs as smoke poured from the small check room. This direct quote from the *Democratic Banner* says much. "The colored mute 'Dummy' Hurley was among the first to rush up the several flights of stairs . . . As

# FIRE! FIRE! FIRE!

—AT THE—

# Young America Clothing House.

## THESE GOODS MUST BE SOLD AT ONCE!

As we intend to dispose of the entire Stock and refill the store with NEW GOODS. A portion of the Stock was slightly damaged by water and smoke, and these Goods, with others that have been very little damaged, will be sold at such

## PRICES THAT WILL ASTONISH YOU!

## THEY MUST GO!

**And Our Prices Will Make Them Move!**

We have just settled with the Insurance Companies on such a basis that enables us to give you the **GRANDEST BARGAINS** that you have ever secured. We have engaged the services of several clerks to assist us in this great sale.

## REMEMBER,

The first one that comes gets the CHOICEST GOODS. Come early and you will **REAP THE BENEFT OF THE GREAT BARGAINS.**

## I. &. D. ROSENTHALL, Props.,

Opera House Block. MT. VERNON, OHIO.

**Above**

In 1894 David is again listed as a proprietor in the business. This ad ran after fire in the Woodward Building.

*Democratic Banner*

he broke open the door of the check room, the flames and smoke burst forth nearly suffocating him." The fire burned through the floor to the dental office below of W. F. Semple, and Fire Chief Pickard ordered "a second line of hose laid" to douse the flames. Semple's office was destroyed by water and falling plaster. Rosenthall's rooms were directly below the dentist's and water poured through his ceiling, damaging most of his inventory.

The Woodward manager, Harry Green, had locked up the building around 9 p.m. after an oratorio group finished its performance. He stated that there had not been much fire in the stove when he left the building. He offered that "a certain crowd of boys and young fellows" were in the habit of hanging around the Opera House and smoking in the hallways and rooms. Perhaps during the performance, they had wandered into the check room to smoke and had dropped some of their "stumps" (butts). The fire smoldered in the airtight room until a hole burned through to the dentist's office, giving the flames all the necessary oxygen.

Within a week YACH re-opened, and Ike ran a genuine fire sale to sell "the entire stock and refill with NEW GOODS." Ike announced that he had settled with the insurance companies, hired several more clerks, and was ready for "this great sale."

**The Accident**

The school year was over for 1896, and summer vacation had started. Eleven-year-old Henry Rosenthall spent the day at his father's store waiting for an outdoor supper his mother planned in a grove on Jackson's farm off Green Valley Road. Henry and his six-year-old brother Marcus were going to enjoy the outing with their teachers from Fifth Ward School, Stella Pitkin and Jessie Bryant.

Dolly, the Rosenthalls' docile horse, was stabled across the viaduct. She was brought to 114 East Gambier Street and hitched to a surrey packed with blankets, dishes, and food. Rose and Henry sat in the front, and Marcus was wedged in the back between the two teachers. The grove was a favorite site for the Rosenthalls; in fact the family had been there just the evening before. After the picnic, everyone piled back into the buggy, and Rose decided to return home a different way. Instead of going back down Green Valley Road, she would drive north a bit, turn right onto what is now Beckley Road but was then an unnamed wagon road, cross the railroad tracks, and then return on the Fredericktown Road. (Only Upper Fredericktown Road existed in 1896.)

Judson Ball rested on his porch to catch whatever breeze possible that June evening. His house sat about one hundred feet east of the railroad track, and Ball decided to wait until the 7:45 B.&O. "through train" (a train making a limited number of stops) passed his house. A whistling post stood a third of a mile from where he sat and there was no reason to retire for the night before the train blew its whistle and roared past.

Henry Longshore from Newark was the engineer on Train 8, which had left Chicago Junction (Willard, Ohio) at 6:00 p.m. The train was scheduled to arrive in Mount Vernon around 7:45. The conductor, William Frances, was in the baggage car (four cars down from the engine) as the train approached Ball's Crossing.

What happened next is in dispute. The engineer swore that he gave the two long and two short signals at the designated whistling post. The conductor and the brakeman corroborated Longshore's claim. Judson Ball, however, said that the train did not signal that night, or, if it did, he hadn't heard it. Burton Beach lived a quarter of a mile west of Bell and was upstairs with his bedroom window open. He saw the train approach but did not hear the whistle. Hugh Higbee, a local teamster, was visiting William Lemly, whose home was also near the signal post. Lemly sat on a fence while Hugh stood by his colt, which sometimes startled at train whistles. Higbee said he did not hear a signal.

Everyone did hear a series of continuous whistles when the train was about thirty to forty feet from the crossing. Then there were screams and a screech as the train, which was traveling about forty-five miles per hour, stopped. The train had crashed into the Rosenthall surrey.

Ball ran around the corner of his house and found Marcus Rosenthall crying and running towards him. Higbee and Lemly climbed into Lemly's buggy and raced to the scene. The train conductor and passengers, including a doctor, climbed down to help.

# DEATH IN AWFUL FORM!

Comes to a Carriage Load of Excursionists Tuesday Night,

While Attempting to Cross Tracks at Ball's Station.

Struck by Eastbound Vestibuled Limited No. 8, On B. & O.

Miss Stella Pitkin Mangled Almost Beyond Recognition.

Henry Rosenthall Receives Injuries From Which He Dies Later.

Mrs. I. Rosenthall and Miss Jessie Bryant Very Seriously Injured.

Marcus Rosenthall Escapes With a Few Slight Scratches.

Miss Jessie Bryant's Skull Crushed—Condition Critical.

The Sad Affair Cast a Shadow of Gloom Over the Entire City—Full Particulars.

DEAD:

STELLA PITKIN, Aged 23.
HENRY ROSENTHALL, Aged 10.

SERIOUSLY INJURED:

JESSIE BRYANT, Aged 32.
MRS. I. ROSENTHALL, Aged 40.

SLIGHTLY INJURED:

MARCUS ROSENTHALL, Aged 6.

**Left**
Headlines about the fatal 1896 accident.
*Democratic Banner*

They saw carnage. The horse was dead, and the carriage was broken. Lying under it on the west side of the track were Rose, Henry, and Jessie Bryant. Stella Pitkin's mangled body lay along the track.

In reporting the accident, the *Banner* always wrote that Pitkin's body was mangled almost beyond recognition. But the *Republican* provided details. Parts of her body lay below the cattle guard. She had been decapitated and her body cut in two. Her limbs were cut off at the thigh, and body parts were strewn along the track for several hundred feet. A canvas was placed over her remains until J. McCormick, a local undertaker, arrived and found all her remains. (The newspaper reported that its first run of papers sold out quickly, and a second run which still did not meet readers' demands was printed.)

Passengers, trainmen, and neighbors carried Rose, Henry, and Jessie into the Ball house. The train then continued to town with the awful news that a carriage of Mount Vernonites had been struck by the train at Ball's crossing. And there were fatalities. Somehow by questioning the trainmen and passengers, locals realized that it was the Rosenthall party, and the news spread through town.

When Ike heard, he immediately rode to the scene with Dr. John Russell, the railroad's physician. Doctors James Lee, George Bunn, and L. L. Williams, as well as friends and relatives, arrived at the Ball house, which became a makeshift hospital. Mrs. Ball furnished sheets, pillows, blankets, hot water, and anything else she had to succor the injured. Russell and the other physicians were profuse in their praise for her and her people. "No hospital could have been better supplied."

Jessie Bryant had thrown Marcus out of the surrey when she saw the approaching train. He was bruised, cut, exhausted, and asleep on a lounge when his father arrived.

Henry Rosenthall, deathly pale, had a fist-sized hole in his skull and lay on a lounge in the hall. As soon as the physicians examined him, they informed his distraught father that there was no chance the boy would survive. All they could do was give him morphine to lessen the pain. He died within a few hours as his father sat by his side.

Rose Rosenthall never lost consciousness. As she lay under the broken surrey, she begged people to take care of her children and the other women first. When Ball carried her into his house, she told him she had seen the train coming but thought she had time to cross the tracks. Later she would say that she hadn't seen the train until she was on the tracks and believed her only chance was to keep driving forward. Now she lay on an improvised bed on the floor of the Ball's front parlor. Doctors Scott and Colville arrived and tended her. Rose's left leg was broken and her left arm fractured in eight places. The physicians feared they might have to amputate her arm but assured Issac that she would survive. They believed she would be better served in her own house, and around 2 a.m. she was placed in a covered wagon and journeyed to her house where crowds had gathered to hear news. There were conflicting reports as to whether she knew about the fatalities.

Jessie Bryant lay unconscious on a lounge in the back parlor where Marcus slept. After examining her, doctors Russell, Bunn, Williams, and Lee lay her on the dining-room table to care for her. She had a compound skull fracture, and the men feared hemorrhaging. Her condition was critical, and the medical opinion was that death was imminent. The physicians carried her to an upstairs bedroom where she regained consciousness around 3 a.m. She was not paralyzed, but Lee, who became her primary physician, worried about internal injuries. He still expressed grave concerns about her survival when her mother and sisters arrived the next morning to care for her. A few days later the Central Union Telephone Company installed a free phone in the Ball house in case of a medical emergency. By Saturday, Jessie was lucid and hungry; she asked for bread and coffee. She corroborated Marcus's story that she, indeed, had thrown him from the carriage. Dr. Lee did not allow her to say much about the accident because of her weak condition and restless nights.

Funerals were held for the two victims. Henry's body was taken home. No services were held there because of Rose's critical condition. On Thursday evening, his Uncle David from Canton accompanied Henry's remains to Philadelphia, where the train was met by relatives. The sad party escorted the boy to the Jewish cemetery, where funeral services were held and the body interred. (Although both local newspapers said that Henry was buried in Mount Zion cemetery, his name and those of his parents and a sister are listed in the Rodeph Shalom Cemetery book.)

That same Thursday Stella Pitkin's funeral was held in the local Presbyterian church. Flowers decked the pulpit and the vestry. Most of the city's teachers attended as did Stella's Sunday School class. The service was short, and then her family and mourning friends accompanied her coffin to Milfordton (Five Corners today) for burial.

Her name was Edith Estella Pitkin, and she was twenty-four when she died. She was survived by her parents, Mr. and Mrs. Theodore Pitkin of Miller Township, and her seven siblings. She graduated from Mount Vernon High School in 1893 and immediately began teaching. She had been rehired for the coming year and was "preparing herself for seminary work" and was known for "earnest and active church works."

A week later, just as coroner Harry Blair began the inquest into the accident, the newspapers reported that both Rose Rosenthall and Jessie

Bryant were improving and would, barring any untoward problems, recover. Jessie stayed at the Balls' house and received excellent care from Mrs. Ball and Dr. Lee. Rose was at home, confined to her bed and ordered to stay in one position. Her doctors were confident that she would not lose her arm. Both women's conditions were much better than anyone had dared hope. Dr. Lee was highly praised for his work in saving Jessie Bryant.

The inquest lasted just two days; it began on Saturday, June 20, and concluded on Monday, June 22. Testimonies were taken from Judson Ball, the train's conductor, the engineer, the brakeman, Burton Beach, and Hugh Higbee. The coroner's finding was that Henry Rosenthall and Stella Pitkin "came to their death by being run over by the B&O train at Ball's crossing on the evening of June 16." Death records from then on would say that they were "killed by the cars."

What happened next? How did the family grieve, recover, and move on? Ike had his store to go to daily and could take care of the routine details of buying and selling. He certainly received the sympathies of his customers and answered their questions about Rose's health. Rose was at home--bound to her bed. Were there any days when she did not rethink the events of that evening? As she convalesced with round-the-clock care, her Philadelphia nieces Hortense and Stella Nathan arrived to help. By October Ike felt that he could go to Athens, Ohio, and open a new store. At the end of 1896, he purchased the clothing store of Samuel Sulzbacher in Marietta. Eight months after the accident, Rose was well enough to accompany Ike to Philadelphia for a three-week visit as he continued to New York City to buy spring and summer stock.

**Above**
Stella Pitkin, class of 1893, in the senior class picture. She is on the far right, sitting in the second row. She died three years later in the accident.
*Centennial 1958 Forum / Mount Vernon High School Yearbook*

For some reason, the next year saw an upswing in social events for Nettie (age 21) and Stella (age 17). Either they became more active, or the papers mentioned them more often. Stella belonged to the Beethoven Club, where she often gave piano performances. Her repertoire included Tekla's "A Maiden's Prayer," Chopin's "Polonaise," a "Hungarian Intermezzo," Woodman's "Dove Wings," "Mazurka" by Strelezki, and various "Irish tunes" for a Saint Patrick's Day meeting. In 1901 she was elected president of the musical club. She and her mother were also in the Monday Club and Sorosis.

Ike upgraded the facade of his store, and the result was "greatly admired and put a new face on the business." The addition of a new room increased his store to "two nice large rooms connected by an arch and well lighted." The store now sold Hart Schaffner & Marx clothes and gave Brown Trading Stamps with every purchase.

The century turned and early in January Ike, Jeanette, and Marcus almost died in their home. Jeanette awoke around 2 a.m. and smelled gas. She called out to her father. When he entered her bedroom, he found her unconscious. He rushed to an adjoining bathroom, filled a pitcher with water, and threw it on her. She revived, but he then fainted. Jeanette now shouted for her brother, who ran to help, but he, too, fainted as soon as he entered. A servant heard all the noise, rushed in, and opened bedroom windows. She then ran to James Israel's house for help. He came, turned off the gas furnace, and opened all the windows and doors in the house. The children were fine but Ike was still in serious trouble. Dr. Colville arrived, and, although it took some time, Ike regained consciousness. A clogged chimney was the cause of the gas leak.

Rose's parents and a brother died. Marcus grew up and was the Mount Vernon High School *Forum*'s sports editor. And in 1903 Jeanette Rosenthall (also called Nettie) met Louis May, a lumber merchant from Steubenville. The year started with parties and ended with a wedding.

On a cold Wednesday afternoon in February, Rose hosted a "handsome luncheon" at her home. Although called a luncheon, it was a "very beautiful and elaborate eight course" meal. Two long tables were set where Rose and Nettie each presided. (You can always tell which Rosenthall girl is referred to, because, as in a Jane Austen novel, the elder was called Miss fill-in-the-surname and the younger was referred to by her first name.) Yellow and red decorations adorned the tables. No menu exists, but the twenty-three guests are listed. It's a who's who of Mount Vernon's society.

Who were the women? What did their husbands do? Had the men conveyed status upon their wives or had some of the women brought their father's status to the marriage? To answer those questions it was necessary to give the women back their first names so they weren't just Mrs. Husband's First Name. (Re nineteenth-century newspaper protocols--I think that if a woman was a widow, her name was written as Mrs. + Surname. If she wasn't, her name was written as Mrs. + Husband's Initial + Surname. However, in the list below, I'm not sure that is the case. For example, I can find only one Wilber family living in Mount Vernon at this time. Francis A. Wilber was the minister at the Presbyterian Church and his wife's name was Flora. He was still living at the time of the party. So either the Mrs. Wilber listed below is Flora, or perhaps she is Francis's widowed mother who lived with them.)

The following women attended the luncheon:

Mrs. Wilber, related to Francis, minister
Lula Bell Sapp, wife of D. E. Sapp (lawyer)
Kate Harper Russell, wife of John Russell (physician) and daughter of Lecky Harper (newspaper editor)
Tammy Devin, wife of H. C. Devin (attorney)
Isabel, wife of Ben Ames and granddaughter(?) of Dr. Robert Kirk, related to Cooper Family. If these connections are correct, she was as close to Mount Vernon royalty as one could be.
Bertha, wife of Frank Harper (newspaper editor)
Sarah Gilliam, widow of George
Sarah, wife of J. C. Armstrong (businessman)
Mrs. McConnell
Florence Wolverton, wife of Irving (superintendent of the Mount Vernon Bridge Company)
Marian Forbing, wife of Irvin (gas and oil contractor)
Emily Forbing, wife of Guy (lumberman)

Mrs. Avery
Mrs. Berry
Sarah Curtis, wife of Charles Curtis (bookkeeper)
Eva Bunn, wife of E. J. Bunn (paint store owner)
Mary Coup, wife of William Coup (superintendent of the Northwestern Elevator and Mill Company)
Bessie Young, wife of Frank Young (jeweler)
Cecelia Sturges, widow of Harry Allen Sturges
Mrs. Murray Garber
Amelia Cooper, widow of William Frederick Cooper.

The above guest list shows that Isaac and Rose Rosenthall were an accepted part of Mount Vernon's upper crust. Just as telling is that no other Mount Vernon Jewish women--Hannah Wolff, Ricka Hyman, Sophia Hyman, Fannie Weill, Sara Meyers, or even Amelia Rosenthall--were invited.

In April Rose held another eight-course "delightful luncheon" in honor of Mrs. May, Jeanette's future mother-in-law. Flowers decorated the tables, and an "elegant menu was served." (Alas, still no menu.) In addition to many of the women from the previous month's party, guests also included

Abby Semple, wife of William Semple (dentist)
Nannie Bope, wife of Charles Bope (hardware merchant)
Elizabeth Bogardus, wife of William Bogardus (hardware merchant)
Lucy Bird, wife of Charles Bird (another hardware merchant)
Mrs. May Curtis
Jennie Ready, widow of Armstrong
Amelia Rosenthall, Nettie's aunt and wife of Aaron Rosenthall (clothier)

Amelia was, however, the only local Jewish woman invited.

On July 10 Mrs. John Russell of 407 East Gambier Street invited ninety-eight guests to her house for twenty-eight tables of progressive euchre. Stella and Rose Rosenthall were invited.

The wedding was in October and as the date approached more luncheons were held to honor the bride-to-be. (The paper always headlined these events as a "Handsome Luncheon.") Annie, Belinda, and Ruth Bogardus, sisters all, hosted one. The usual women were invited but several new guests made the list:

Helen Alsdorf, wife of Saurin Alsdorf (then a bank teller who would eventually become a bank official)

Amy Frances Williams, wife of B. B. Williams (president of Cooper Bessemer)

Mary Baker, Harriet Goss, and Elizabeth Sperry, unmarried girls.

At the end of the meal, Jeanette was surprised with a "kitchen shower." She was given a decorated basket filled with "pretty and useful articles." I assume all were kitchen utensils.

A second party--this time a card party--was hosted by Mrs. Aaron Stadler and her daughters the week before the wedding. This party honored two brides-to-be--Jeanette Rosenthall and Jane Stamp, daughter of Dr. Jacob Stamp and his wife Alice née Cooper. (I know, I know . . . Alice Cooper.) The Stadler house was decorated with autumn leaves, and "unusually handsome" prizes were piled on a table to be awarded to point-winning players. Jeanette and Jane were each given a large bouquet of carnations.

The card-playing guests included Jeanette's sister, a Steubenville Rosenthall, a Leopold cousin from Philadelphia, and a Nathan cousin from the same city. Local women, in addition to the women mentioned above, now included

Miss Nan Miller
Mrs. Hills of Gambier
Mrs. Dunnick
Mrs. F. R. Jones
Isabel Ames, wife of Ben Ames (stock farmer)
Mrs. Jack Little.

Even though the Stadlers were Jewish, no other Jewish women were invited to this luncheon.

Finally the wedding day arrived--Wednesday, October 14, 1903. Rabbi David Klein of Columbus performed the ceremony at the Rosenthall home on East High Street. Nettie was twenty-eight on her wedding day and Louis was thirty-seven. Stella Rosenthall and a Leopold and a Nathan cousin attended the bride, and Louis May asked his brother Samuel to be best man. Newspapers now had begun describing the bridal gown, and Nettie's was "panne crepe built over chiffon and trimmed with duchess point lace. The long tulle veil was held in place with a wreath of lilies of the valley and the same fragrant flowers composed the shower bouquet." The guests were mostly out-of-town relatives and a few "invited friends of the family." Bertha Rosenthall née May, a widow, came from Steubenville with her son Gordon. (This connection might have been how Stella met Louis. Bertha was a May who had married Julius Rosenthall, Isaac's nephew.) Rosenthalls came from Pittsburgh, Canton, and Kenton while Leopolds traveled from Philadelphia and Altoona.

**Above**
One of the few personal advertisements Rosenthall ran in 1905.
*Daily Banner / Mount Vernon*

After the ceremony, the couple took a wedding trip through the East and then returned to Steubenville to begin their married life. In February 1904 Jeanette, now Mrs. Louis May, visited Mount Vernon for a party her mother and sister hosted in her honor. Since it was around George Washington's birthday, small American flags, red, white, and blue candies, and hatchet-shaped place cards greeted the twenty-seven guests.

Ike's standing in the community continued to grow. He was one of the pallbearers at Dan Emmett's funeral and the only businessman quoted in the *Banner* on the Citizens' Committee's plans for the town's centennial. "I have lived in various cities but find Mt. Vernon one of the best little cities in the U.S."

Stella, unmarried, continued to live at home or spend extended visits

**Above**
Senior class picture of 1895 – Nettie (Jeanette) Rosenthall is in the third row on the left with her head tilted.

*Centennial 1958 Forum / Mount Vernon High School Yearbook*

**Below**
No senior class picture was taken in 1897. From the senior class play, Stella Rosenthall is in the first row, fourth from the left.

*Centennial 1958 Forum / Mount Vernon High School Yearbook*

**Above**
Senior class of 1907 – Marcus Rosenthall is in the last row, second from the right.
*Centennial 1958 Forum / Mount Vernon High School Yearbook*

with her sister in Steubenville. Marcus graduated from high school in 1907, attended college, and then went to law school in Birmingham, Alabama. He met his future wife, Leah Stiefel of Philadelphia, and brought her to Mount Vernon in August 1913 to meet his family. Two months later, Isaac Rosenthall was dead.

Isaac took the train to Steubenville on Tuesday, October 14, to attend the birthday party of his granddaughter Alice, who was three years old. Having business in Columbus, he traveled there and told his family to expect him home on Thursday. He would take a morning train to Newark and then catch the afternoon express home. On October 16 about one o'clock he walked into the Jackson Hotel in Newark near the B.&O. Station and asked a clerk for a glass of water and some peppermint to ease his indigestion and severe stomach pains. After drinking the combination, he left the hotel, walked across the street, reeled, and collapsed. People rushed to help but could tell that he was dead. Rosenthall was easily identified by the papers and letters he carried. An ambulance was called, and Ike's body was taken to a local undertaker. Aaron Rosenthall was at the store in Mount Vernon. He took the call and then notified the rest of the family. Ike's body was brought home, and two days later pallbearers from the five lodges he belonged to carried the coffin to the B.&O. Station for the trip to Philadelphia. Max Meyers and Charles Bird represented the Masons; Charles Iams, the Odd Fellows; Jacob Dubinsky, the Knights of Pythias; David Tuttle, the Elks; and Paul Sawvel, the Eagles. Honorary

**Above**
A 1907 Rosenthall advertisement.
*Daily Banner*

pallbearers James Israel, Frank Moore, Frank Kirby, G. W. Armstrong, Frank Beam, and M. J. Smithhisler followed the mourners. Rose was too ill to make the journey to Philadelphia. The paper stated that "the probability" was that Aaron and Stella would stay with her. Perhaps Marcus arrived in time to accompany his father's body. When the train reached the Broad Street Station in Philadelphia the next day at 11:00, a service was held there and then the body taken to the Rodeph Shalom Cemetery where Isaac was buried beside his son Henry.

Two years before he died, Ike had been in Logan, West Virginia, and, for some unknown reason, he made a will there. He left all his household property, goods, furniture, fixtures, horse, harness, carriage, and real estate to Rose. She inherited $22,000 (about $500,000 today). Nieces Bertha and Flora Volsaki each received $250.00, and half-brother Aaron inherited $1,000. The rest of his estate and property was to be divided equally between his three children unless Stella was unmarried at the time of her father's death. Then she would receive

**Above**
Iconic 1915 photograph of South Main and Vine Street showing Rosenthall's store.
*Knox County Historical Society*

$2,000 more than her siblings.

After Isaac's death, Marcus gave up his law practice, returned to Mount Vernon, and married his fiancée. In February 1914 Rose sold the Young America Clothing House to Marcus. "After an honorable career of 35 years, the business of the Young America Clothing House, conducted by the late I. Rosenthall, terminated Saturday, Feb. 7th." Marcus and his Uncle Aaron, who was secretary/treasurer of the business, took over, reorganized, and changed its name. On February 25 the I. Rosenthall Clothing Company opened.

Rose moved to Atlantic City but never seemed to recover from her husband's death. She was ill for several years until she died from a stroke on January 1, 1916. Her body was taken to Philadelphia, where she was buried beside her husband and son.

Sometime around 1920–21, Marcus and Aaron had a falling-out. Marcus wanted to start the Rosenthall Motor Agency. Aaron wasn't interested; their partnership was dissolved. (See the chapter on Aaron Rosenthall for details.)

Marcus announced a huge reorganizing sale in August 1921. He would continue as president and take on the treasurer's duties. Park Worley became vice president but would also have an "active personal charge of the store." These changes reflected Marcus's plans to start the car dealership and be less involved with the store. Despite the reorganization, architect's plans, and a press release, the car dealership never happened.

In 1928 Marcus and Leah still lived in Mount Vernon, and Marcus was listed as the president/treasurer of the Rosenthall Company. However by the next year, and after a presence in Mount Vernon of fifty-one years, the Rosenthall store and the family were gone. Kilkenny & Rinehart, "A Good Store in a Good Town--Clothing, Hats and Furnishings for Men, for Young Men, and Boys," now occupied the former Rosenthall site. Rosenthall's had been such a presence in Mount Vernon that for many years after, any business that occupied Ike's former rooms in the Woodward Building would reference "at the Rosenthall site" in their newspaper ads.

**Above**
Leather change purse with the rosenthall name.
*Photo by the Author from a Personal Collection*

162

| | | | | |
|---|---|---|---|---|
| Henry M Rosenthall | June | 16. | 1896 | 2 |
| Isaac Rosenthall | Oct | 16. | 1913 | 3 |
| Rose H Rosenthall | Jany | 1 | 1916 | 4 |
| Stella Rosenthall | Sept | 1 | 1937 | |

| | | | | |
|---|---|---|---|---|
| Henry Hess | June | 15. | 1895 | 1 |
| Lippman E. do | Apr | 17 | 1929 | 2 |
| Emilie do. | Jan | 23 | 1938 | 3 |

**Above**
Rodeph Shalom Cemetery records showing interments of Henry, Isaac, Rose, and Stella Rosenthall. The other page shows Rose's Hess relatives.
*Ancestry.com*

# Aaron Rosenthall

## *Isaac's Younger Half-Brother*

**Aaron Rosenthall**, the youngest of fifteen children and Isaac's half brother, was born in Marion, Ohio. His father was Marcus and his mother was Henrietta Werner. He returned to Richmond with his parents after the Civil War and stayed there until his father died. Then he came to Mount Vernon and worked with his half-brother Isaac. That would have made Aaron about thirteen years old when he came to Knox County.

Or possibly he *was* the Aaron Rosenthall who became a ward of the Jewish Foster Home in Philadelphia when his father, because of his age, could no longer care for the boy. After leaving Philadelphia, Aaron probably worked in a Rosenthall store, either in Canton, Findlay, or Altoona, Pennsylvania. When Brother Solomon, who had worked in Mount Vernon for several years, left to go to Pennsylvania (according to the *Banner*) or to Dayton (according to his obituary), Aaron moved to Mount Vernon and replaced his brother as a clerk. Regardless of his origin story, Aaron Rosenthall lived in Mount Vernon for over sixty years.

**Above**
Aaron Rosenthall in his Knights of Pythias regalia.
*Private Collection*

In April 1896 Aaron's wedding announcement appeared in the *Banner.* The bride-to-be was Amelia Rosenbaum of Germantown, Pennsylvania. Her parents, Isaac and Leah, had immigrated from Poland and Prussia respectively. Amelia was first-generation American--born in Detroit in August 1860 or 1864. On June 16, 1879, the Rosenbaum family lived in Philadelphia, and Isaac supported his wife and three daughters Charlotte (age 8), Annie (age 6), and Amelia (age 10) as a tailor. By November of the same year, all three girls lived in the Jewish Foster Home in Philadelphia. The only logical conclusion is that Leah, aged 38, had died, and Isaac could not care for his three motherless daughters. By 1880 Isaac had remarried, had two more daughters, and reunited with Charlotte and Annie. Only Amelia was not living with the family. She disappeared from the public record until 1885, when she taught at the

**Above**
Amelia Rosenbaum Rosenthall.
*Private Collection*

**Above**
Aaron's and Amelia's signatures in their *siddurs*, Hebrew prayer books. Aaron's was printed in Roedelheim, Germany in 1815; Amelia's in Prague in 1841.
*Private Collection*

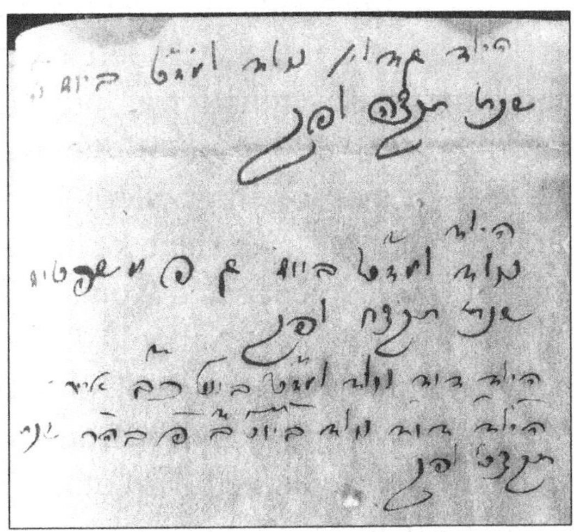

**Above**
As of now, untranslated inscription in cursive Hebrew from Aaron's *siddur*.
*Private Collection*

same foster home where she had once lived.

When the three sisters were at the Foster Home, Aaron Rosenthall was also there. Perhaps Amelia and he knew each other as children and years later met again, fell in love, and married. Or perhaps this Aaron Rosenthall was a totally different Aaron because (believe it or not) there were other Aaron Rosenthalls in the United States at the time.

A second scenario is also possible. Amelia's life didn't change--a family, her mother's death, the Home, perhaps teachers' college, and teaching in Philadelphia where Isaac Rosenthall's wife's family lived. Some of her kin knew both Amelia and Rose's bachelor brother-in-law, Aaron. A meeting and an engagement ensued.

Whatever version you choose, the two married, went on a wedding trip, and were back in Mount Vernon within a few weeks to stay with the Isaac Rosenthalls until they moved to a rental home at 405 Vine Street. On Valentine's Day 1897 Miriam Henrietta, their only child, was born. As long as brother Isaac lived, Aaron worked at YACH--as a clerk, manager, and later secretary/treasurer of the company. The family's life was uneventful. Miriam attended local schools and graduated in 1915. Amelia ran the household and was a founding member of the Mount Vernon Sisterhood, a Jewish women's group.

Minutes of the Sisterhood meetings exist from 1928 to 1934, and Amelia Rosenthall was president all those years. She ran the meetings and did most of the work. She corresponded with the Newark branch of the Sisterhood, wrote letters of congratulations and condolences (Did she take on that responsibility because she was the only college-educated woman in the club?), explained the Jewish holidays at "Sunday School" for Mount Vernon's Jewish children, bought appropriate Chanukah presents for the children, was an active member in Mount Vernon's Federation of Women's Clubs, and, in her spare time, was on the board of the Home for the Aged.

She organized a Purim party for the children in 1928. About twenty-two adults and eight children attended. The Sisterhood paid for two pounds of salami, five pounds of corned beef, and five pounds of "knockers." Jewish families donated the following:

Rose Ross--quarts of potato salad

Sarah Dubinsky--meat
Ben Dubinsky (a widower)--pickles
Rose Kohn--two quarts of potato salad
Clara Hyman--baked beans
Amelia Rosenthall--cookies, coffee, cream, and sugar
Stella Hantman--table cloths and napkins

Around 1920–1921 Aaron and his nephew had a falling-out. In March 1921 Marcus announced plans for a new business--the Rosenthall Motor Agency. An architect drew up blueprints for a four-story garage of reinforced concrete on the northwest corner of the Square on land purchased from the Curtis estate. The first floor would hold an office, a large sales room, and a wash room. The second floor would be storage, and the third floor would be the service department. The top floor would have a dustproof paint shop and an upholstery department. One can imagine that Aaron, the Rosenthall Company treasurer, looked at the estimated costs, voiced some negative opinions about the proposal, and finally decided he wanted no part in the endeavor.

Aaron had been with the Rosenthall Company for forty-five years, and in July 1921 he sold his interests in the company and resigned his position. He formed a partnership with Francis

**Above**
An advertisement in the Mount Vernon High School yearbook for Aaron's store after he separated from his nephew Marcus.
*Forum 1922*

Esely, who had been a vice president at YACH for thirteen years. Rosenthall & Esely opened at 17 W. Vine Street across from the Vine Theater. "Walk half a block and save a dollar," their ads cried. Aaron had a reputation as a "careful and conservative merchant whose advice and suggestions as to qualities and values" were followed by Mount Vernon's citizens.

In 1925 Aaron bought out Esely and continued working until 1935 when his failing health--a stroke--forced him to retire. He sold his business to Lester Smilack, a Russian Jew who was a Toledo clothier. He had heard from a traveling salesman that Aaron's store was for sale and planned to purchase and liquidate the business. But the town, the store, and the store's reputation looked good to Smilack. Locals urged

**Above**
Interior of Aaron's store – Aaron is second from the left behind the counter. His partner Francis Esly is standing beside Aaron.
*Mount Vernon Sesquicentennial paper – Public Library of Mount Vernon and Knox County*

him to keep the store going, and Smilack decided to "carry on in the Aaron Rosenthall tradition with the same shrewd judgment of values."

**Above**
Amelia, Aaron and daughter Miriam on their front steps in Mount Vernon, Ohio.
*Private Collection*

Both Amelia and Aaron became ill around the same time. At the December 18, 1934, meeting of the Sisterhood, Amelia announced her resignation as president because of ill health. The women "regretfully accepted" her announcement, and Florence Shamansky stepped into the position. Around this time Aaron had a stroke which left him partially paralyzed. It was probably Aaron's ill health that caused Amelia to step back from the organization.

Amelia was Aaron's caretaker for five years. She slept on a cot in a double doorway so she could care for her husband throughout the night. Neighbors made sure to call and help her out. About 6 p.m. on Tuesday, September 17, 1940, a neighbor called the house, but no one answered. She realized that Amelia had not raised the blinds all day and called some other neighbors. They entered the house and found Amelia dead on the cot "with a heating pad still turned on." Aaron had been unable to call for help. Dr. Julius Shamansky was called and reported that Amelia had died of "mitral stenosis" the night before. Rabbi Samuel Gupp came from Columbus to officiate the funeral service.

Aaron, obviously, could not stay in the 601 East Vine Street house. His daughter lived in Chicago, and it was necessary for Aaron to move to a rest home in Palatine, Illinois. He survived his wife by just one year, dying on September 16, 1941.

Aaron Rosenthall's legacy continued at Lester's Men's Wear.

# Schanfarber Brothers

## *An Interlude*

The **Schanfarber Brothers,** Jacob, David, and Isaac, ran Schanfarber Brothers Clothiers in Columbus. Between 1900 and 1903 David, who was a widower, moved to Mount Vernon and started a local branch called The Philadelphia in the McDermott Building. Like all the other clothiers, Schanfarber said his suits "looked best, fit best, wore best and cost least." A July 1904 ad sold men's two-piece serge, homespun, and flannel suits for the sale price of $19.95. The company gave Sperry & Hutchinson trading stamps with each purchase.

David was diabetic and became too ill to run the store. A younger brother, William, took over the business, and David returned to Columbus to live with his married daughter, Celia Rosenthal. He died in her house in Bexley on April 9, 1903. He was just forty-three years old.

William continued running The Philadelphia for at least another year. In July 1904 he helped the Congregational Church bring his brother Tobias, who was a rabbi in Chicago, to town to speak at the Sunday morning service on the "Relation Between Judism [*sic*] and Christianity." He came "highly recommended by both Jewish and Christian clergymen." After 1904 no ads for The Philadelphia ran in either Mount Vernon newspaper.

# Dubinsky Family

## *The Russians Are Coming*

In 1880 there were about 250,000 Jews living in America and most were from Germany. Over the next three decades, 2.8 million Jews arrived in the United States from Eastern Europe--Russia, Poland, Austria-Hungary, Romania, Lithuania, Belarus, Latvia, and Ukraine. Fleeing state-sanctioned pogroms (attacks on Jews), repressive laws (special taxes levied only on Jews, quotas on Jewish university students), and severe conscription laws mandating twenty-five years in the Czar's army, young men, families, and entire *shtetls* (small Jewish villages) found a way to come to America. Some traveled farther east to Harbin, China, and sailed to California. But most made their way through Europe to find a ship sailing out of Germany, Holland, or France to the United States. Since the ships were returning to America with empty cargo holds, passage was fairly cheap and always horrible. These immigrants made up the third wave of Jewish migration. Unlike the German Jews of decades earlier, these Jews were poorer, less educated, rural, and more religiously conservative. Many of them settled on the Lower East Side of New York. But others, either because the city was too crowded or because they had relatives in other states, moved west. Many landed in Cleveland. This is what the Dubinsky family--consisting of parents Moses and Bessie, and children **Berman, Isaac, Jacob, and Dora**--did.

According to Moses and Bessie's granddaughter and Berman's daughter Odessa Dubinsky whom I interviewed in 2010, the family's surname was not Dubinsky. It was Naman. Moses Naman was in St. Petersburg on his honeymoon with his already-pregnant wife Bessie. He was kidnapped to take the place of a wealthy young Jew who most certainly did not want to serve in the Czar's army. Money exchanged hands; Moses Naman became Moses Dubinsky and reported for duty in Riga. Because he could read and write, he became a quartermaster in the czar's army. A salesman came one day to sell "broadwoven material" for uniforms. That man was Moses's brother-in-law, who told Moses that his wife was being harassed and accused of prostitution because she had had a child, Isaac. Moses brought her and his son to Riga, where they first lived in barracks and then in a house with Persian rugs on the wall. Two more sons, Berman and Jacob, were born to the couple. All the boys went to *chedar,* Jewish religious school. Eventually Moses, Bessie, and children Isaac, Berman, Jacob, and Dora emigrated and ultimately ended up in Cleveland.

The family arrived in the United States between 1880 and 1882--years of mass migration from Eastern Europe. It's unclear if they all emigrated together or if Berman arrived in America two years before his parents, because the answer to the census question "When did you immigrate?" changed every tenth year. Jacob or perhaps Isaac arrived with Berman in 1882 or two years later. Or Isaac and Berman arrived in 1880 on the *Gellert* out of Hamburg, Germany. Berman, who was around eighteen at the time, would have wanted to avoid the czar's army. Suffice it to say that by 1885 the Dubinsky family lived in Cleveland, and Moses and his sons were peddlers or rag men.

In a large city where most immigrants did not yet speak English, families lived near others who spoke their native tongue. The Dubinskys settled into a home on Jackson Street in a Russian Jewish enclave where everyone spoke Yiddish. A quick survey of their neighbors found that most of the men were cigar makers or junk dealers. The Dubinskys had a "rich" uncle in Cleveland who owned either a brewery or a bar. Although this relative gave Berman a bar job, he wanted nothing to do with this relative, so an aunt bankrolled the Dubinskys as peddlers. They had at least one horse and wagon, and they traveled around Cleveland buying and selling rags, metal, and paper.

At thirteen Berman collected scrap metal from trash piles around the city. He was always too hot or too cold. One winter, some nuns noticed how red and chapped his hands were and how badly he was dressed. They knitted him mittens and a scarf. From then on Berman had a special affection for nuns and would help them whenever he could. He honored that promise when he lived in Mount Vernon. He said Sisters had kept him warm, and he would do the same for them; he always sold coal to the local convent at cost.

Odessa said that her father Berman (aka Ben) was the first of the family to come to Mount Vernon, but her sister Isabel said that Jacob came too. He/they spent his/their first night in town sleeping in his/their peddler's wagon underneath the viaduct.

The Dubinskys definitely were in Knox County in 1900. Census takers in both Cleveland and Mount Vernon listed Moses Dubinsky in their records. He and Bessie lived in Cleveland with son Isaac, his wife Sarah, and their five children. Moses, now called Max, was listed as a junk dealer and Isaac was a jeweler. When Moses was also enumerated in Mount Vernon two months later, he called himself an iron merchant, and he and son Berman lived at 307 South Main Street. Son Jacob was a boarder at 24 West Vine Street in Mount Vernon; he was a scrap iron merchant. Moses returned to Cleveland and eventually Isaac moved to Mount Vernon. All three brothers now lived in Mount Vernon, and thus began the Dubinsky Brothers enterprise--peddlers, junk men, coal purveyors, and respected businessmen.

**Dubinsky Family Tree**

Moses Dubinsky m Bessie Rosenblatt

| | | |
|---|---|---|
| **Isaac** m Sophie Burstein<br>one daughter | **Berman** m Sarah Nathan | **Jacob** m Sarah Bernstein |
| **Isaac** m Sarah Orkin | | |
| Max<br>Florence<br>Rachel<br>Herman/Hyman<br>Rebecca | Miriam<br>Rhea<br>Odessa<br>Isabel | Naomi<br>Myra |

**Dora** Dubinsky m Abraham Kurlander

Max<br>
Joseph<br>
Becky / Beatrice<br>
Louis<br>
Charles<br>
Jacob<br>
Arthur ? ?

# Isaac Dubinsky

*Brother #1*

**Isaac** (also known as Ike) was born in Russia in 1859 or 1860. Later he was more specific and cited Riga, Latvia, as his birthplace. To avoid serving in the czar's army, he and most of his family arrived in the United States between 1880 and 1882. The Dubinskys' immigrant story is typical of most Russian Jews at this time. They were very poor and took whatever jobs they could find once they arrived in the United States. And like generations of immigrant Jews before them, the Dubinsky men became peddlers or rag men. They bought old clothes, paper, used housewares, whatever they could purchase or find, and then resold their wares. By 1888 the family fortunes improved enough for Isaac to marry Sophie Burstein. A daughter was born within a year, but I can't verify that she survived. Certainly the marriage did not. Knowing how the death of a child can tear apart a family, I would guess that the couple probably divorced, because a "Sophia" Dubinsky worked in a Canton hospital in 1930.

An interesting occupational blip occurred in 1882 and 1883. Isaac did not identify himself as a peddler but as a jeweler. His niece Odessa Dubinsky told me that he once made her a pair of gold earrings.

He became a naturalized citizen in 1890, and then he and brother Berman formed Dubinsky Brothers, a scrap iron business in Cleveland. On June 9, 1892, Isaac married Sarah Orkin, a Russian immigrant (probably also from Latvia) who had been

| Family name | Given name or names |
|---|---|
| Dubinsky | Isaac (Isaak) |
| Address | |
| 39 Cross St., Cleveland, Ohio | |
| Certificate no. (or vol. and page) | Title and location of court |
| 8331 | U.S.Dist.Ct.,Cleve.O. |
| Country of birth or allegiance | When born (or age) |
| Russia | Dec. 9, 1860 |
| Date and port of arrival in U. S. | Date of naturalization |
| Oct. 25, 1876 | Oct. 24, 1890 |
| Names and addresses of witnesses | |
| Max Rosenblatt-, 52 Berg St. | |

**Above**
Isaac (Isaak) Dubinsky's naturalization record.
*Ancestry.com*

in the United States for just over a year.

Over the next several years, Isaac once again called himself a junkman or scrap dealer in the Cleveland city directories, but in the 1900 census, he again said he was a jeweler and that he was in his second marriage. His family now consisted of Sarah and five children. Everyone lived with Isaac's parents in Cleveland.

Max--born in 1893 (According to his cousin Odessa Dubinsky, he didn't look like "the others")
Florence--born in 1894
Rachel--born in 1895
Hyman (sometimes called Herman)--born in 1896
Ruth (sometimes called Rebecca)--born in 1899

Three years later the Isaac Dubinsky family lived in Mount Vernon at 306 W. Gambier Street. No longer a jeweler, Isaac was a clerk at Dubinsky Brothers, where the "highest cash (was) paid for scrap iron, rags, old rubbers, and rope." As his sons came of age to work (around age 16) they all found jobs. Max worked at one of the local glass factories, and Isaac continued to vacillate between referring to himself as an iron dealer or junkman or jeweler.

Isaac and his two brothers all married women named Sarah, so the spouses had to be differentiated in some way. Mrs. Isaac Dubinsky was known within the family as Tante Sarah. Jacob's wife was known as Sadie, and Ben's wife kept the name Sarah. Tante Sarah often hosted the Seder, the traditional meal that ushered in the Jewish holiday of Passover. Isaac would drive his wagon to the local boarding houses, pick up all the Jewish traveling salesmen, and bring them home.

Talking about her uncle, Odessa said, "He was the smart one." She often stopped at his home after school for help in algebra. He did all the calculations in his head because he had had no paper when he grew up in Russia and had had to do all the work mentally. Odessa recalled that she, however, had to show all her work to her teachers.

By 1913 other Russian Jews arrived in Mount Vernon, and Isaac and Sarah hosted a Sunday evening reception in their home for the newly married Fannie and Joseph Levison. Other Jewish couples invited were Aaron and Amelia Rosenthall, Harry and Bessie Lurie,

Joel and Henrietta Levy, and Sarah Meyers.

Nineteen twenty was an eventful year for Isaac and his family because they returned to Cleveland. Everyone worked. Most of this first generation of American-born Dubinskys had progressed from junkmen, ragmen, or scrap dealers. Both sons Max and Hyman were electricians. Rachel was a stenographer, and Rebecca, who now was called Ruth, was a typist. Berman Dubinsky's wife died that year, and Ruth returned to Mount Vernon to care for her young cousins. She did not stay too long because she married Jack Rothenberg, a "really nice man," in October 1920. Isaac's oldest son Max changed his surname to DuBoy; he was the only one of his siblings to do so. He married Florence Benson and in 1927 they moved to Mount Vernon, where Max worked in the family business for a few years before returning to Cleveland.

Sarah Dubinsky died August 31, 1924, at the age of fifty-seven. Isaac was now a widower and his eyesight was failing. In 1927 or 1928 he returned to Mount Vernon. At first he lived at 713 E. High Street, but he later moved to the second floor of Dubinsky Brothers at 404 South Main. Odessa said he became blind and moved to Mount Vernon to be near his brothers.

In 1930 Isaac moved to Lorain, Ohio, and lived with his widowed sister Dora, her children, and his ninety-year-old mother. He died on November 9, 1932.

# Ben Dubinsky

## *Brother #2*

In 2010 I ran a classified ad in the *Mount Vernon News* asking for any information about nineteenth-century Jewish families in Mount Vernon. Nancy Edick responded and told me she had contact information for Odessa Dubinsky, who lived in Los Angeles. (The Dubinskys were the first Russian Jewish families in Mount Vernon and referred to the other Jews in town as "the Germans.") I called Odessa, who was ninety-eight at that time, and over the next few years had many talks with her and then with her younger sister Isabel.

The Dubinsky narrative is, therefore, different from the other biographies in this book because theirs includes first-person accounts. Often both sisters retold the same story exactly--probably because it was an oft-repeated tale. A few times older sister Odessa snorted, "How would Isabel know that? She was too young." Several times a recounted story was contradicted by a newspaper account. And certainly family squabbles and fights between the three Dubinsky brothers and their wives colored Odessa's and Isabel's memories.

But here it is--the lives of Berman, Sarah, Miriam, Rhea, Odessa, and Isabel Dubinsky.

**Berman (also known as Ben) Dubinsky** was born around 1865 in what is now Riga, Latvia, but was then part of Russia. (Odessa often referred to her father as a Litvak, a term used by Jews to identify fellow Jews from Latvia, Lithuania, and Estonia.) Immigrating in the early 1880s along with other family members, by 1885 the blue-eyed, blond-haired Ben was in Cleveland where he became a naturalized citizen. He was definitely in Mount Vernon five years later. (See the Dubinsky Family chapter for more about Ben's life in Cleveland.) After years of peddling in Cleveland, in 1900 Berman and his father Moses were in Mount Vernon and living at 307 S. Main. Perhaps they had already started the family scrap business because James

Ramsey, a thirty-seven-year-old day laborer, boarded with them.

By 1901 the Dubinsky Brothers' scrapyard bought and sold scrap at 404 S. Main Street. The junkyard was on the Kokosing River near the railroad tracks. The enterprise consisted of a series of sheds and a scrapyard on the south side of the river downstream from the viaduct. Moses returned to his family in Cleveland, and Ben and Jacob ran the local business. Around this time Ben met and became friends with Dan Emmett.

**Above**
The hatless man in the back might be Ben Dubinsky.
*Private Collection*

On a Thursday in January 1903 Ben was working near one of the sheds when it toppled, and he was caught under a falling roof. He was rescued, but his left leg was badly fractured, and he limped for the rest of his life. The newspaper reported the accident with the headline "Leg Broken: Ben Dubinsky Badly Injured by a Shed Falling Over Him."

Odessa told me her version of the accident. During the 1913 flood, structures at Dubinsky Brothers collapsed. (See photos.) Ben went to the yard to rescue some horses, and the accident occurred then. Over time Odessa obviously conflated the accident and the flood into one story.

By now Ben was about thirty-seven years old and still a bachelor. This situation just could not be allowed. An aunt in Cleveland said she knew just the girl, Sarah Nathan, a Cincinnati native. (Jewish matchmakers knew no boundaries.) Ben traveled to the Queen City to meet her, and that was that. On August 25, 1905, Berman Dubinsky married eighteen-year-old Sarah at her home on Kenyon Avenue. Ben had grown up speaking Yiddish in Russia and spoke English with an accent. Sarah was born either in Illinois or Ohio and had graduated from high school. Despite their ages and their educational differences, this was a love match. Ben brought his bride back to their house on West

# Application for a Marriage License. No. 183

The State of Ohio, Hamilton County, ss.

The undersigned respectfully makes application for a Marriage License, and upon oath deposes and says that his name is Berman Dubinsky, that he is 37 years of age, that his residence is Mt Vernon. Ohio, that his place of birth was Russia, that his occupation is Merchant, that his father's name is Moses Dubinsky, his mother's maiden name was Bessie Rosenblat, that he was not previously married —, and that he has no wife living.

That Sarah Nathan is 21 years of age, that her residence is 636 Kenyon Av Hamilton County, Ohio, her place of birth was Chicago. Ill, her occupation is none, her father's name is Max Nathan, her mother's maiden name was Rebecca Levi, that she was not previously married, and is not a widow or divorced woman, her married name being — —; that she has no husband living. Said parties are not nearer of kin than second cousins, and there is no legal impediment to their marriage, and that neither of said parties is an habitual drunkard, epileptic, or insane, and is not under the influence of any intoxicating liquor or narcotic drug.

It is expected that Rev A. N. Zeff will solemnize the marriage of said parties.

Berman Dubinsky

Sworn to and subscribed before me this 25 day of Aug 1905

Chas L. Malsbary
Judge and ex-officio Clerk of the Probate Court of said County.

By L Williams Deputy Clerk.

Probate Court, Hamilton County, Ohio, Aug 25 1905

Marriage License was this day granted to the above named persons.

Chas L. Malsbary
Judge and ex-officio Clerk of the Probate Court of said County.

By L Williams Deputy Clerk.

**Above**
Berman Dubinsky and Sarah Nathan's marriage license.
*Ancestry.com*

High Street. It was either 407 ½ or 413. (The addresses are taken from city directories, newspaper advertisements, and phone conversations with Odessa. It's possible that address numbers changed for the same dwelling over the years.) Family legend said that a returning Civil War soldier had found his wife and her lover in bed and had killed them both. That tale made the large two-story house, with four store rooms on the bottom level and living spaces above, hard to rent. This is where Ben and brother Jacob, their wives, and their children lived—not always in peaceful coexistence. According to Odessa, her mother once was taking something from the oven when Jacob's wife (also a Sarah but called Sadie to differentiate her from the other two Sarahs) either hit her with a stick or tried to push her into the oven. Whatever the specifics, the family believed that Sadie had tried to kill Sarah, and the two sisters-in-law never again spoke to each other.

Ben liked red so Sarah planted red flowers around their house. She always put some household money aside and invested her savings. She and Ben started a family--all girls. Miriam, a blue-eyed blonde like her father, was born in 1907, followed a year later by Rhea. Odessa was born in 1912, and Isabel in Mercy Hospital around 1920. Ben owned a pasture across the viaduct that held several horses and a Jersey cow. He believed that Jerseys gave the best milk and hired a man to milk her daily. Every summer Sarah took the girls to Cincinnati where her mother lived. Ben visited every weekend, and Sarah and the girls returned to Mount Vernon just before school started.

Ben's day began early, and he would sometimes be at the scrapyard by 4:00 a.m. One spring morning he arrived at the yard and found George Widoe, a "junk and rag buyer," lying on a blanket in front of the office door. Ben could tell that Widoe was dead and called the coroner. The evening before, a doctor had visited Widoe, who lived near the yard. Widoe felt ill, but the physician found nothing wrong with him other than that he had been drinking heavily. The coroner ruled that the cause of death was alcohol related. More destruction and death, unfortunately, would affect Mount Vernon and the Dubinsky family.

The rain started on Easter Sunday 1913 around 9 a.m.; the Easter Parade was a soggy affair. It rained incessantly the rest of that day and all of Monday. Residents did not worry until about 4:30 p.m. on Monday when a second cloudburst dropped even more rain on Mount Vernon. Locals who remembered the 1898 flood became worried. Anyone who was still awake around midnight in the southwestern section of town saw the water reach front doors. Within a half hour many abandoned their homes. At 4 a.m. water broke over the "lower part" of the dike at Riverside Park, and a half hour later, a workman at the waterworks power house in the park blew the whistle to warn residents of a flood. Then the dike broke, and muddy water poured through the streets.

*The Daily Banner* wrote, "From High Street south, substantially the entire West end below the B. and O. tracks was submerged. On West Vine and West Gambier streets the water nearly reached Mulberry street. On West Front and West Water streets there was not a dry spot. The whole was inundated. Ambulances, carriages, moving vans, drays, express wagons and all kinds of conveyances" raced to the west end to move people to safety.

Houses were flooded; cellars filled with water. Railroad tracks were washed out. Harry Mays's sawmill on the west end of Front Street was under four feet of water and many sawed timbers washed away. Trees, grapevines, and shrubs were uprooted. Hogs, chickens, and horses drowned. Fences were torn out, and house foundations damaged. Merchants on South Main below Gambier lost any stock they had stored in their cellars. Thousands of dollars' worth of damage was incurred.

The south wall of the Dubinsky building on South Main was washed away, and a large quantity of baled hay swept into the Kokosing River.

Three months later on a muggy July day, five-year-old Rhea ran a fever and then began vomiting. Soon thereafter a rash appeared. A doctor probably visited the sick child and told her frantic parents that she had cerebral meningitis. Rhea died on July 13, and her small coffin was taken to Cincinnati and buried in a Jewish cemetery there.

The big house on West High Street had four storerooms below the living quarters. Because of overcrowding in the local school, the eighth grade took over the bottom floor of the Dubinsky Building (as it was called in the newspaper) in 1914 and 1915. In February 1919

**Above**
Dubinsky Brother's scrapyard after the 1913 flood.
*Private Collection*

---

Dubinsky advertised that there were rooms to rent in the building, but it took until November of that year for the Mount Vernon Cigar Company to announce plans to move into the building.

Would the family live above a cigar company or were there two West High Street buildings owned or inhabited by Dubinskys? In the 1910 census, Ben and his family live in a rental on West High

Street. Four years later, a West High Street building is called the Dubinsky Building. Would that have happened if the Dubinskys did not own the structure? But Odessa said that the eighth grade classes were in the storerooms below her house. I am sure that in 1920 Ben and his family lived at 413 West High Street because that is where tragedy struck.

**Above**
Rhea Dubinsky's grave. There was no Jewish cemetery in Mount Vernon so Rhea was buried in the Schachnus Jewish cemetery in Cincinnati where Sarah's family lived.
*Findagrave*

World War I was over, and the influenza pandemic was abating. But that didn't mean there weren't still flu victims. How long Sarah Dubinsky was ill is unknown. But on Good Friday, April 2, 1920, at 10:30 a.m., she died at her home at 413 West High Street. She was thirty-five years old; she was buried in Cincinnati near her daughter.

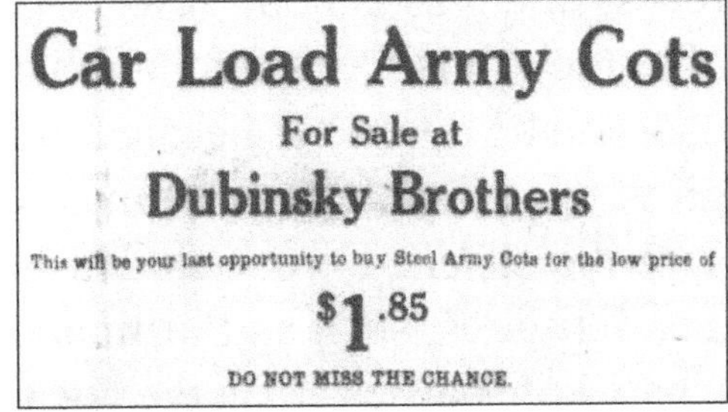


**Above**
Post World War I Dubinsky advertisement.
*Daily Banner / Mount Vernon*

She was survived by a grieving husband, who never remarried because he said he "had had the best," and three daughters. Miriam was thirteen, Odessa was eight, and the baby Isabel was about seven months old. Ben needed household help immediately and advertised for a "good woman for housekeeping, no laundry, good pay and good home at 413 W. High." It was hard to find help because most women wanted office work. This might have been when cousin Ruth, Isaac's daughter, came to help out. Ultimately oldest daughter Miriam took on much of the household duties and child care. As an adult Miriam told Odessa that she felt she had never had a childhood because when other fourteen-year-old girls were playing, she was pushing a baby buggy. Miriam was a gifted pianist and might have attended Case Institute if her mother had lived. Ben bought her a piano, and Odessa believed it was to make up for her having to take on so many adult duties. "She was doing the best she could," Odessa said.

The Dubinskys were as religiously observant as they could be living in Mount Vernon. They kept two sets of dishes, one for everyday use and one for Passover. (A more observant family would have had three sets of dishes--one for meat meals, one for dairy, and one for Passover.) Both Ben and Jake bought their meat from a kosher butcher in Columbus but ultimately believed he was cheating them. Like everyone else in Mount Vernon, they began buying their meat from Pitkins. A meal was in the oven when their sister Dora arrived for a visit. She kept such a strict kosher home in Lorain that hers was the only house where her rabbi would eat. As Jake and Dora talked in the parlor, Ben threw all the non-kosher food out.

Isabel remembered that a neighbor, Issa Cole, was very kind to her after her mother's death. But that didn't make up for Odessa's feeling isolated and alone as the only Jew in school. She sat by herself at recess and was called "Jewey" on the playground. Even eighty years after the event, Odessa remembered the name of Charles Seavolt, who had said he pitied her because she was Jewish. As the motherless girls grew up, other Jewish women, especially Amelia Rosenthall, made sure the sisters were included in any activities, such as Purim and Chanukah parties, that the local Sisterhood planned.

Odessa took dancing lessons, and a year after Sarah's death, she and her cousin Naomi (mistakenly identified as her sister in a newspaper account) performed in a local revue called "The Dance of the Christmas Fairies." "Little Miss Odessa Dubinsky lead the other girls

COAL! COAL! COAL!
DON'T FREEZE! Order
Hocking Valley and Pocahontas
Lump Coal for quick delivery at DUBINSKY BROS.
Phone 154

DUBINSKY BROS.
HIGHEST CASH PRICE PAID FOR
SCRAP IRON, RAGS AND OLD RUBBERS. ALSO ROPE. ASK FOR PRICES.
401 SOUTH MAIN ST. MT. VERNON, OHIO
CITIZENS PHONE 154 BELL PHONE 134

**Above**
Two typical Dubinsky advertisements.
*Daily Banner / Mount Vernon*

with a solo dance." Later in the program she and Naomi "entertained with some Russian dances." Odessa started school when she was five and walked to Fourth Ward school. In the winter she wore long underwear and galoshes. When the local Jewish women started a Sunday religious school that Marcus Rosenthall taught, the Dubinsky sisters attended. When she was older, Odessa walked to Ringwalt's each week to see what new books had arrived. She was a voracious reader and borrowed four to six books weekly for a nickel a day. *The Secret Garden* was her favorite book.

All three girls attended Mount Vernon High School. Miriam took college courses and sang in the girls' glee club. According to her senior year book, she could "appreciate and laugh at a good joke. Independence . . . almost her middle name."

Odessa was brilliant and skipped enough grades to be a twelve-year-old freshman. In some of the photos in yearbooks, she looks like a little girl beside her classmates. Her favorite subject was English because she had good teachers. Her math teachers, however, always seemed to be a few chapters behind the students. From her sophomore year on, she wrote for the newspaper and the yearbook. She wrote the class prophecy for 1928 in the form of a letter to "Ann" from an ocean liner somewhere in the Atlantic. She was also in the math club, debate, a literary magazine called *Cermeth*, boosters' club, athletic club, senior song committee, senior chapel committee, and orchestra. She graduated with 19 ½ credits (the other seniors on her page in the yearbook had an average of 16 credits) and in her spare time she helped plan a pep party, an indoor carnival, the French party, and a class party. Because it had an active youth group, she spent a great deal of time at the Episcopal Church.

After graduating she attended Monticello Seminary, the oldest female seminary in the United States, in Godfrey, Illinois. She was there for two years and then transferred to The Ohio State University, where she majored in economics and graduated in 1932. She returned to Mount Vernon and enrolled in a six-week business class for women held on the B. B. Williams estate.

The Ku Klux Klan was active in Mount Vernon. Once a Klan parade marched past the Dubinsky house on the east side of town. Odessa

MIRIAM DUBINSKY "Jake"

College Course 18½ Credits

"Laugh and the world laughs with you, weep and you weep alone."

Miriam surely can appreciate and laugh at a good joke. Independence is almost her middle name.

Hello Algy (3); Girls Glee Club (2, 3).

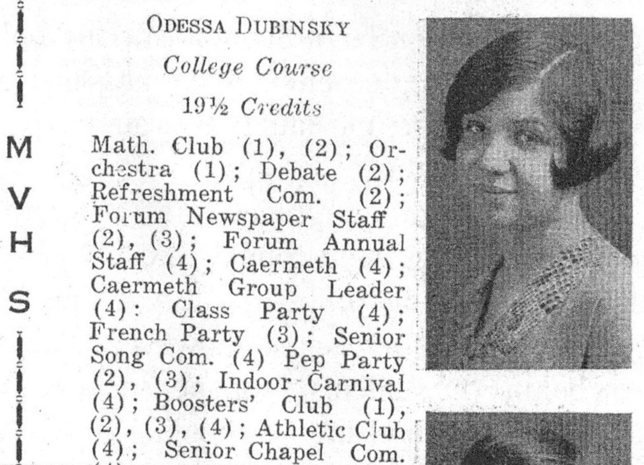

M V H S

ODESSA DUBINSKY

*College Course*

19½ *Credits*

Math. Club (1), (2); Orchestra (1); Debate (2); Refreshment Com. (2); Forum Newspaper Staff (2), (3); Forum Annual Staff (4); Caermeth (4); Caermeth Group Leader (4): Class Party (4); French Party (3); Senior Song Com. (4) Pep Party (2), (3); Indoor Carnival (4); Boosters' Club (1), (2), (3), (4); Athletic Club (4); Senior Chapel Com.

**Above**

Senior class photographs of Miriam, Odessa and Isabel Dubinsky.

*Miriam 1924 Mount Vernon Forum / Odessa 1928 Mount Vernon Forum / Isabel 1937 Mount Vernon Forum*

and her father watched from their front porch as one hooded klansman separated from the group and approached Ben, calling him a "dirty old Jew." Ben replied, "Get away from me, you bum. I recognize you by your shoes, and you probably owe me money."

All three girls were still at home in 1938, Isabel's senior year in high school. Ben had not felt well for several weeks. On Monday, October 10, at 10:45 in the morning, he had a fatal heart attack and died at the age of seventy-two. The sisters were now orphans. And Ben died without a will.

Within days their uncle Jacob came to the house and demanded Sarah's diamond ring. Jake said that Miriam was too young to take care of it. Miriam insisted that she could and would keep the ring.

(Family lore believed that Sadie had sent her husband Jake over.) The young girls had no idea what all their father owned. Jake and nephew Joe took over the scrapyard. The girls stayed in town until Isabel graduated, and then they moved to Cincinnati. They believed that Jake and Joe were cheating them of their inheritance. A lawyer told them that they could go to court but that the suit would use up most of their money. He advised that they should take what Jake offered, which was $130.00 a month. The payments lasted for about a year but stopped around the time Joe took over the business. Odessa always blamed Sadie for the girls not getting any money from Ben's properties. "Sadie was always doing good for other people when they were sick, but she was 'a devil' to Ben's children," Odessa insisted.

Isabel attended Ohio State for at least two years starting in 1938. In 1942 all the girls still lived in Cincinnati. Isabel was a commercial artist, and Odessa was a typist in the State Unemployment Office. Prior to her father's death, Odessa had been at the top of the civil service list to work as an economist for the state. But when her father died, she relinquished her place on the list and moved with her sisters.

**Above**
Sarah Dubinsky's grave near her daughter Rhea.
*Findagrave*

Miriam was probably the first to move to California. In 1948 she lived in Los Angeles, where she died in 1993 at the age of 86.

Odessa, who hated Ohio winters and what she referred to as "crazy Knox" County, eventually moved to California. She never married because she didn't like the way men treated their wives and she "wanted to be in control of herself." She worked as state economist (one of only three women at the time) for California and was active in Democratic politics. She attended all the inaugural balls in Washington for Lyndon Johnson. Odessa died October 12, 2017, at the age of 105. The last time I spoke to her, she said she was ready.

Isabel married Charles Stoner Kayser in Cincinnati on August 3, 1942. At the end of the war, they moved to Los Angeles. Charles died in 1995, and Isabel eventually moved to Chicago to be near her children. She died there in 2012 at the age of 87.

The Dubinskys were just the first of the Russian Jewish families who found work and homes in Mount Vernon. But, as with the German Jewish families who had lived and worked here, parents died, children moved away, and their names were forgotten.

**Above**

Berman (Ben) Dubinsky's grave in Cincinnati.

*Findagrave*

# Jacob Dubinsky

*Brother #3*

**Jacob**, the third Dubinsky brother, lived in Mount Vernon for over sixty years. Like his siblings, he was born in Riga, immigrated to the United States, lived in Cleveland with his immediate family, and by 1900 was in Mount Vernon living in John Hoot's boarding house at 24 West Vine Street and working at the scrapyard.

Jake traveled a great deal for Dubinsky Brothers. In the years 1901–1903 he was in Centerburg, Cleveland, Buffalo, and Coshocton buying scrap metal and machinery from defunct plants for the junkyard, which was located near the railroad tracks on South Main Street. Because scrap often arrived by rail and lay unprotected in the yard, theft was always a temptation. Once Jake saw two young boys stealing lead pipe and ran into the office to call the police. When Chief Dermondy arrived, the boys were gone and all the police had was a description.

Like his brothers, Jacob remained a bachelor well into adulthood. He was in his mid-thirties when he married Sarah (usually called

Application No. 36958 Filed and Marriage License Issued Jan. 9 1904

| | |
|---|---|
| Name Jacob Dubinsky | Name Sadie Bernstein |
| Age 34 Residence Mt. Vernon O. | Age 22 Residence 456 Orange St. |
| Place of Birth Russia | Place of Birth Canada |
| Occupation Merchant | Occupation Stenographer |
| Father's Name Moses Dubinsky | Father's Name Max Bernstein |
| Mother's Maiden Name Betsey Rosenblatt | Mother's Maiden Name Rachael Maratzky |
| Number of times previously married None | Number of times previously married None |
| Applicant Jacob Dubinsky | Married Name |
| Marriage to be solemnized by Rev. Gittelsohn Orange St. | License issued by Frank Zizelman Dep'y Clk. |
| Consent of Filed 190 | Consent of Filed 190 |

...RETURN...

The State of Ohio, CUYAHOGA COUNTY, ss.

I Certify, That on the 10 day of Jan. 1904 Mr. Jacob Dubinsky and Miss Sadie Bernstein were by me legally joined in marriage.

Rev. B. Gittelsohn

**Above**
Jacob Dubinsky and Sadie Bernstein's marriage license in Cleveland.
*Ancestry.com*

Sadie) Bernstein in Cleveland in 1904. She had been born in Canada to Polish immigrants and was a twenty-one-year-old stenographer when she married. A year later the couple took a "honeymoon" trip to spend a week on "the Lakes" around Detroit. According to her niece Odessa, Sadie often visited Detroit.

Sometime around 1908 or 1909 Sadie returned to Detroit and adopted a baby girl whom they named Naomi Ruth. The family of three shared the house on West High with Ben's family where, again according to Odessa, the two wives scarcely spoke to each other. But Naomi seemed to have had a normal life. She took piano lessons, and when she was eight performed a solo at Fourth Ward School. She continued with her music throughout high school, but for some reason had to repeat her junior year. Nevertheless, she was in the first violin section of the orchestra for at least three years.

**Above**
Naomi Dubinsky's baby picture.
*Centennial 1958 Forum / Mount Vernon High School Yearbook*

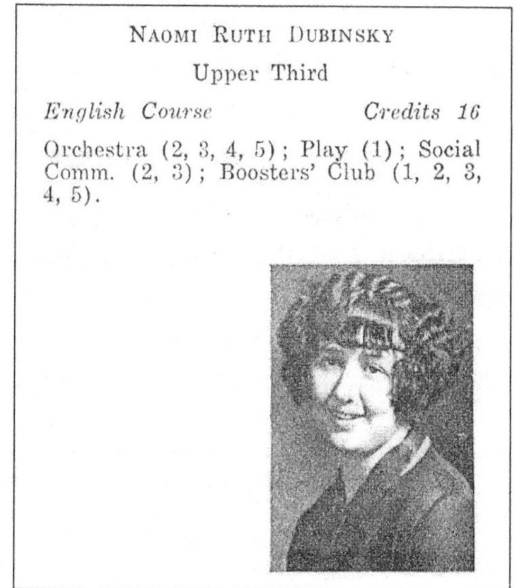

NAOMI RUTH DUBINSKY
Upper Third
*English Course* *Credits 16*
Orchestra (2, 3, 4, 5); Play (1); Social Comm. (2, 3); Boosters' Club (1, 2, 3, 4, 5).

**Above**
Senior class photograph of Naomi Dubinsky.
*Mount Vernon Forum Yearbook 1927*

In 1912 Jacob was involved in the kind of public legal battle between two Jewish businessmen which would have had the other Mount Vernon Jews questioning, "But is this good for Jews?" Joseph Levison owned clothing/furnishing stores in both Mount Vernon and Buckeye City. David Cohen managed the second store, and Levison accused him of embezzling $300. A warrant was issued, and Cohen was arrested and spent eighteen hours in a Columbus jail. The charges were published in Columbus and local newspapers, but the case was dismissed for insufficient evidence. Levison immediately swore out a second embezzlement accusation but reduced the amount to $190. After another hearing, Cohen was bound over to the grand jury under a $500 bond which Jacob Dubinsky paid. To make things messier, Cohen retaliated with charges against Levison alleging that his credit and reputation had been damaged; he wanted $5,000 in compensation. Like so many stories, both cases then disappeared from the newspapers. (The only document on file in the records department in Mount Vernon is the Cohen vs Levison petition but with no resolution.)

Jacob ran for city council to represent the Second Ward. In the November 1911 election, he was defeated by a socialist, Charles Whittington. In April 1912, Whittington resigned, and Jacob was nominated to succeed him. He was elected by acclimation and served on Council until 1916. Interestingly, Dubinsky's name was not on the November 1915 ballot. Perhaps he simply decided not to run again. However, Marcus Rosenthall did run for City Council at that time. He was soundly defeated, but--and this is pure speculation--the men might have thought that two Jewish men couldn't be elected and Jacob allowed the younger man to have his chance.

Jake was a Republican but voted for Democrat Al Smith in 1928 because he believed that the first Catholic presidential candidate ever would not receive many votes. He was correct. Herbert Hoover won a landslide victory that year.

In 1920 the family lived at 413 West High and consisted of Jacob, Sadie, and ten-year-old Naomi. A decade later they were at 300 East High, and the family now was made up of Jacob, Sadie, and five-year-old Myra. In January 1930 Naomi had married Dan Yamshon in Detroit. What happened to Naomi remains a bit of a mystery. A Dan Yamshon died in 1938 in Cleveland Heights; the couple had only been married for eight years. (I believe that Naomi remarried and is the Naomi Dubinsky Toch who died in 1993.)

So who was daughter Myra? Odessa said she was a "change of life" baby. The 1930 census said that she had been born five years earlier in Michigan. Did Sadie deliver a child in Michigan or was

MYRA LEE DUBINSKY

**Above**
Senior class photograph of Myra Dubinsky.
*1940 Mount Vernon Forum Yearbook*

Myra, like Naomi, adopted in Detroit? Jacob and Sadie had no more children. But between brothers Ben and Isaac, sister Dora, and all their children, there was family aplenty to love, argue with, and help.

In 1928 there finally is a glimpse into the life of Jewish women in Mount Vernon. Six women started the Mount Vernon Branch of the Newark Sisterhood, a philanthropic organization. Charter members were Amelia Rosenthall (Aaron), Clara Hyman (Max), Stella Hantman (Sam), sisters-in-law Sadie Ross (Herman) and Rose Ross (Maurice), and Sadie Dubinsky.

Monthly meetings were held in the women's homes. Each meeting began with a prayer, the *Sh'ma* ("Hear O Israel, the Lord our God, the Lord is One"), before the minutes and any reports were read. One of the organization's main purposes was outreach to Jewish patients at the local Ohio State Sanatorium for tuberculosis. In the early twentieth century, the state built special TB hospitals to combat an epidemic. One such hospital was in Mount Vernon--where the Developmental Center later stood. The women often visited patients, taking fruit and other "delicacies" and once a chicken (alive? roasted?). At Rosh Hashanah, the patients received apples; at Passover, matzah. One woman asked for a sweater and received one for Chanukah. Anywhere between two and six Jewish patients were at the sanatorium over a span of eight years and were visited monthly by one of the women. Sadie Dubinsky usually volunteered to visit patients. She reported that patient Sara Kaufman was "improving and happy to receive the basket of fruit . . . at Passover."

Another goal of the group was to plan Chanukah and Purim parties for the local Jewish children. Unfortunately, the parties were usually canceled due to some "problem." In 1932 a Chanukah party was held at the Dubinsky house, where the children "took their respective parts [in a play? receiving presents?] in a very pleasing manner." Were they really pleased to receive Star of David pins?

In 1933 the group agreed that someone should write articles about the Jewish holidays for the local newspapers. In addition to the charter members 1934 saw the largest membership yet--sisters-in-law Florence and Ethel Shamansky, Helen Zelkowitz, Anne Epstein, Lina Zwick, Ethel Sussman, Mrs. David Rabishow, and Mrs. J. Landesman joined. Most of the new women had come with their husbands who were Shellmar executives. The women tried to bring a rabbi from Hebrew Union College in Cincinnati for the High Holy Days in 1935 but were told "no rabbi could be sent." What the women did with the $150 they had raised to pay the rabbi is unknown, because the secretary's notes after 1934 have been lost.

Jacob Dubinsky belonged to several fraternal groups. He was a life member of the Elks and a Knight of Pythias. Sadie was part of the women's groups associated with the lodges; she belonged to Ladies of the Elks and the Pythian Sisters.

Jacob played more of a civic role in Mount Vernon than his two brothers. One reason was that he lived in town for over sixty years. He served on City Council for four years, which put his name in the paper weekly. An unusual event occurred in 1904. At that time deer, a lion, a bear, and some birds were housed at Hiawatha Park but now were to be transported to a zoo in Columbus. Jacob secured new cages for the move, but as the bear's cage was lifted to a wagon which would haul it to a waiting flatcar at the park gate, the animal tore off part of the cage top. Its claws whirled in the air as men worked frantically to keep the bear in captivity. The bear was finally contained, and no one accused Jacob of buying shoddy cages.

When brother Ben died in 1938, the Dubinsky Brothers truly broke apart. Ben's children always believed that Sadie was responsible for their not inheriting Ben's estate. As one contemporary told me, "Sadie inherited all the assets." Jacob and his nephew Joseph Kurlander, son of Dora Dubinsky Kurlander, took over the scrapyard. Jacob retired, and Joseph became the sole proprietor.

Around 1949 Jacob became ill, and after he had suffered for two years he and Sadie moved to Detroit, where he went into a nursing home. He died several months later in 1951. (I believe that Sadie is the Sadie née Bernstein Dubinsky who died in Los Angeles in May 1957.)

The Dubinsky Brothers arrived in Mount Vernon with a wagon, a horse, and some scrap metal. They became entrepreneurs and played an integral part in Mount Vernon's economy. (Local resident Dude Conway remembered trying to sell something from his mother's house for scrap, but the Dubinskys told him to return it home; his mother needed it.) They helped the city as much as they could. They married and had families. They made sure that their children were better educated than they were. And, as in Jewish families in most small towns, the children moved away.

# Dora Dubinsky and Abraham Kurlander

*The Distaff Dubinsky*

Twenty-one-year-old **Abraham Kurlander** left Germany around 1880 and settled in Cleveland, where he married seventeen-year-old **Dora Dubinsky**. (Yes, Dora was a Dubinsky and sister to Ben, Isaac, and Jacob.)

Because most of the 1890 United States census was destroyed by fire, the Kurlanders disappear from the record until 1900 when Abraham, now a clothier, Dora, and their five children live in Lorain, Ohio. The oldest son Max (b. 1884) was fifteen, and Joseph (b. 1887), who will play an important part in the future of Mount Vernon, was thirteen. The only girl, Beckie (or Bictus or Beatrice), was eleven. Louis (b. 1890) was nine, and the youngest child, Charles, was five. Two years later both Max and Joseph clerked in the family store, A. Kurlander and Son. Some time between 1902 and 1909 Max and Joseph started Kurlander & Company in Mount Vernon at 101 West High Street. Calling their business "The Popular Price Store," the two brothers sold men's clothing, men's and women's shoes, and "gents' furnishings." At this time their uncles Ben and Jacob Dubinsky were still in town, and the young men had family support here.

Almost as soon as the boys started their business, however, their father Abraham died suddenly in Lorain. Max had to return home and take charge of the stores there, so he sold the local business. Once all the spring and summer goods were sold below cost, Uncle Jacob sold all the "store fixtures, cash register, etc." Max returned to Lorain, where he and his mother Dora managed the dry goods store and provided for Beckie, Louis, Charles, and another child, seven-year-old Jacob. It is uncertain whether Joseph returned to Lorain. In 1910, a year after Abraham's death, there was no mention that Joseph

Kurlander lived in Lorain. His cousin Odessa Dubinsky said that her father felt sorry for his nephew Joseph and "took him under his wing." Although not found in the 1910 census, Joseph probably now lived in Mount Vernon and worked with his uncles in the Dubinsky scrapyard.

Sometime before 1913 Joseph changed his surname from Kurlander to Landers. By 1913, when he married Malvine Rich of Cleveland, Joseph Kurlander had become Joe Landers and was an iron dealer in Mount Vernon. After the Jewish wedding officiated by Rabbi Jacob Klein, Mr. and Mrs. Joseph Landers took up residence on North Main Street in Utica, Ohio. A year later their first child, Arline, was born, and in 1920 their second and last child, Richard.

When Ben Dubinsky died intestate in 1938, Jacob Dubinsky and nephew Joe Landers took over the Dubinsky scrapyard. Ultimately Joe became the sole owner. Odessa Dubinsky always believed that the Landers' wealth, which benefitted his children and ultimately Mount Vernon, was built upon her father's legacy.

Joe died in 1963 and Malvine followed four years later. Their children Arline and Richard were their heirs.

KURLANDER & CO.,
THE
Popular Price Store,
High and Mulberry,
Clothing, Furnishings and
Shoes.

**Above**
Kurlander advertisement in the Mount Vernon High School Forum.

**Above**
After his father's sudden death, Max Kurlander closed his Mount Vernon store and ran this advertisement for a month.
*Mount Vernon News*

# Conclusion

They came for the American Dream. They came for freedom, safety, and opportunities they could only imagine in their mother country. They eschewed large cities where they would have found religious support--a synagogue or temple, a Jewish burial society, a Jewish cemetery, and a kosher butcher. They braved what for them was a religious wilderness and settled in Mount Vernon, where they made personal and economic decisions about how to practice their religion publicly and privately.

Jewish store owners closed their businesses to observe the High Holy Days but were open on Saturday, the Jewish Sabbath. There was no Jewish burial society to prepare a body for burial in a Jewish cemetery. Without a society and a cemetery, the dead were buried in Cleveland, Cincinnati, Columbus, Wheeling, or Philadelphia.

It wasn't until 1883 that there was any movement toward creating a Jewish cemetery in Mount Vernon. A Jewish burial society *might* have been organized or at least discussed in 1883 because a "Jewish society" approached City Councilman Cole, who then told Council that the society was "negotiating for the purchase of a strip of land East of the present cemetery to establish a burial ground." Nothing, however, came of this, and most Jews continued to be buried out of town. Not until 2010 was the Jewish Cemetery Society of Knox County established and a cemetery consecrated.

No place of worship was ever established. Services for the High Holy Days were sometimes held in rooms in fraternal organization buildings and led by one of the Jewish men. In 1939 the Mount Vernon Hebrew Congregation was organized, with Jacob Dubinsky elected president of the synagogue. Services were held on the upper floor of Lester Smilack's store at 16 S. Main Street.

Jews are expected to rejoice with the bride and groom on their wedding day, to visit the sick, and to comfort the bereaved. From lists of wedding guests, minutes from the Sisterhood, and newspaper accounts, we know that Mount Vernon's Jews followed those three traditions. Jews were expected to "relieve a neighbor of his burden," and local Jews often helped pay fines and bonds of their co-religionists. They witnessed each others' wills and attested to their character for naturalization.

A baby boy is to be circumcised eight days after birth. As local newspapers reported, this--the oldest of religious rites--was performed in Mount Vernon.

Jews are expected to eat matzo on Pesach (Passover), and Aaron Stadler's taking matzo to the *Democratic Banner*'s office proved that the unleavened bread was eaten during Passover week.

Jews are to recite the *Shema* prayer daily; Sisterhood meetings started with the prayer.

Throughout the late nineteenth and early twentieth centuries, Jewish men and women attempted to explain their beliefs and traditions to the public through the newspapers. Rabbis from large cities often came to town and gave public lectures which the papers covered.

Although the following did not originate with the local Jewish population, it did bring Judaism to the locals' attention. In 1862 General Ulysses S. Grant tried to control the black market on cotton by expelling all Jews from Tennessee, Mississippi, and Kentucky. He said that "mostly Jews and other unprincipled traders" were responsible for the smuggling. When Jews from Paducah, Kentucky, brought Grant's Order 11 to President Lincoln's attention, he revoked the order immediately. Six years later when Grant ran for president, Democratic newspapers like the *Banner* ran articles reminding "the Hebrew vote" that Grant had "cruelly insulted their religion and their nationality" and that to vote for Grant "would be to turn renegade against the faith of their fathers and invite insult to themselves." Considering how small the Jewish vote was in Mount Vernon, especially because only men could vote, one wonders why the paper made such a public announcement. Were the Jewish families respected enough that this reminder of Grant's perfidy might sway some locals to vote for the Democratic nominee?

Privately there are few clues as to what happened within Jewish homes. Pesach was celebrated and guests invited to the Seder. It was probably too difficult to follow all the dietary laws. As the Dubinsky narrative said, getting kosher meat (meaning that the animal had been killed in accordance with Jewish law) was almost impossible. Within their homes, did they eat ham and shellfish? We don't know. Did they light candles on Friday night to welcome the Sabbath? There are no answers. Certainly most wanted their children married by a rabbi. What is evident is that they cared for their families and relatives and that children honored their mothers and fathers.

What is also evident is that the Jewish families were accepted into Mount Vernon. The community, however, wasn't always sure about the Jewish stranger. Yes, the newspapers would often identify ethnicity and race in their stories. A headline from 1896 stated, "Mount Vernon a Hot Place--Thinks a Jewish Traveling Man After a Short Stay," and the lede was, "A traveling salesman of Jewish extraction, giving the name of E. Teschner, got into quite a 'mussup' in this city, last Thursday afternoon." He and a companion tried to rent bicycles from Ed Sapp's repair shop on South Main. Even though Sapp said he had none to rent, there were some on the sidewalk in front of his store. Had Sapp not wanted to rent to these men, and if so, why? Or was there some other reason for saying no? The men "borrowed" the bikes anyway and took a short ride. When they returned, one of the tires was punctured, and Sapp wanted payment. The men refused, and Sapp filed a "writ of attachment" which the constable took to the St. James Hotel, where he seized Teschner's baggage. When an arrest warrant was issued, Teschner paid the costs for the attachment and the warrant and $5.00 for the tires.

One can only assume that privately people held anti-Semitic statements and that they believed certain stereotypes. And certainly as the Ku Klux Klan became more prominent and popular in Knox County, Jews, Catholics, African Americans, and foreigners became targets of Klan bigotry and hatred.

For Mount Vernon's nineteenth-century Jews, however, throughout their sojourn here, the businessmen and their wives were Our Worthy Townsmen.

# Acknowledgments

Many people have helped and listened to me over the past years as I researched Jewish families in Mount Vernon.

Thanks to my daughter, Rachel Strongin, for starting me on my quest with her query, "When was the last Jewish wedding in town?" I'm sure she didn't think that this would occupy me for years. But I thank her wholeheartedly for wanting to know and encouraging me to find answers. I love you, Rachel.

Lorle Porter's single remark about finding newspaper accounts of a Jewish wedding in town when she researched her book *Politics and Peril* was just the tantalizing hint I needed. Thank goodness for her phenomenal memory because she gave me Adolph Wolff's name, and I was on my way.

The reference librarians at the Public Library of Mount Vernon and Knox County helped me find the early records I needed, re-taught me how to use the microfilm reader, and listened to some of my stories. Thank you, Mary McGavick, Cassie Peters, and the late, great Janet Wacker who often sent me copies of newspaper clippings that she thought I could use.

Thank you, Jim Gibson and all the docents at the Knox County Historical Society who were always there to open the museum and allow me to look through volumes of historical newspapers. They were quite tolerant of my whoops of joy when I found an article which explained some arcane familial relationship or what "death by car" meant when there were no automobiles.

The bound newspaper volumes at the Society were a blessing. However the Civil War years were missing. Thanks to the Mount Vernon News for allowing their microfilm of those papers to be copied and then digitized. Thank you Ariel Foundation and the Community Foundation of Mount Vernon and Knox County for the grant which allowed that to happen.

The local Jewish community helped keep me going as they asked questions about when the research would be finished.

Denise Ferenbaugh is a jewel. Housed in the basement of the Service Center, she is the keeper of historical records. Denise helped me find wills, birth certificates, death certificates, marriage licenses, civil and criminal court reports, and inventories of shopkeepers who went into assignment or died. The contemporaneous records are archived and Denise walked into the back room and returned with wonderful documents. Denise, thank you so very much.

Thank you to all my friends who listened to my stories probably when they really wanted to be doing something else. Kami Diehl was always patient with me when I wanted to share. Maxwell Leaning has been the go-to guy for all things computer-ish. He scanned the images for the book and was very patient with my luddite questions. Linda Smith, you are the best of friends. Thanks for being interested in my work. And Marilyn Nagy, my early-morning walking partner, is the embodiment of a friend. We walked miles in all kinds of weather, and Marilyn allowed me to share any new stories I had discovered. She asked good questions which helped me clarify what I had written. See you at seven, Marilyn, on the path.

Carrie Kepple Jadud is a most careful copy editor. She found more errors in my stories (and I don't mean typos) than I care to admit. Her stylistic changes always made my writing better. I think this is where I say that any errors and mistakes in the book are entirely my fault because Carrie can only do so much. Thank you, Carrie.

Thank you Aaron Keirns for designing the book I had imagined.

I want to thank my sisters Rebecca and Joanne. They listened to stories and even more stories. They are my best friends and always, always there when I need support.

My husband Burt has visited Jewish cemeteries with me, listened to my stories and read the narratives, tolerated bins of research shoved under the dining-room table and lined up against a wall, and been patient and loving throughout the years.

# The Minyan

The very first task I set for myself was to generate a list of Jewish families who had lived in Mount Vernon. I called this list a minyan which is a quorum of ten people (men or women depending on the branch of Judaism) needed to recite certain prayers during a service. Below is a list of the Mount Vernon minyan.

If you know anything about any of these families or if you know any names to add to the list, please contact me at the email below: **lkhanson@columbus.rr.com**

Abrahams, Phil
Adler, Moses, Louis, and David
Atlas, Ralph
Block, Moses
Bronner, Bernard
Dubinsky, Jacob, Isaac, and Berman
Epstein, Jacob and Nathan
Epstein, Sam
Erlanger, Leo
Erlanger, Lothar
Frankel, Leo
Friedman, H.
Galena, Michael
Goodfriend, Louis
Gomer, Richard
Gurwick, Irving
Hantman, Samuel
Hassel, Aaron
Haymann, Leopold
Henley, Isaac
Hornstein, Jack
Hyman, Max, Louis, and Isadore
Kahn, David
Kohn, Louis
Komito, Louis
Kurlander, Abraham
Landesman, J.
Latner, C.
Leopold, Marx
Levison, Joe
Levy, Joel and Henry
Liebenthal, Moses
Lowenthal, David
Lurie, Harry
Marks, Bernard
Meyers, Max
Morris, S.
Munk, Leopold
Oppenheim, S.
Pincus, Herman
Rabinshaw, David
Rosenthal, Aaron
Rosenthal, Ike
Rosenthall, H.
Ross, Herman
Ross, Maurice
Schanfarber, David and William
Schwartz, Eugene
Shamansky, Isaac
Shamansky, Julius
Smilack,Lester
Stadler, Aaron
Susmann, Ben
Verson, Ben
Weill, Sam
Wolff, Adolph
Zelkowitz, Charles
Zwick, Oscar

Made in the USA
Columbia, SC
05 March 2020

88781457R00137